AIRBORNE

Edwin P. Hoyt

AIRBORNE

THE HISTORY OF AMERICAN PARACHUTE FORCES

C. 1

STEIN AND DAY/*Publishers*/New York

Photographs of unit insignia are reprinted with permission from *U.S. Military Shoulder Patches of the United States Armed Forces* by Jack Britton and George Washington, Jr., Copyright © 1978 by Jack Britton. M.C.N. Press, P.O. Box 7582, Tulsa, Oklahoma 74105

All other photos are reprinted courtesy of the U.S. Army.

Maps 1 through 7 and 9 are reprinted from *Rendezvous with Destiny*, by Leonard Rapport and Arthur Northwood, with the permission of the 101st Airborne Division Association.

First published in 1979
Designed by David Miller
Printed in the United States of America
Stein and Day/*Publishers*/Scarborough House
Briarcliff Manor, N.Y. 10510

Library of Congress Cataloging in Publication Data

Hoyt, Edwin Palmer.
    Airborne: the history of the American parachute forces.

    Bibliography: p. 221
    Includes index.
    1. United States. Army—Parachute troops—
History. I. Title.
UD483.H69   356'.166'0973   78-24524
ISBN 0-8128-2573-X

Contents

LIST OF ILLUSTRATIONS

Shoulder Patch Insignia *follows page 47*
Photograph section *follows page 137*

AIRBORNE

Airborne

1

One day in the fall of 1918 in France, Brigadier General Billy Mitchell asked his boss, U.S. Army Expeditionary Force commander, General John J. Pershing, to assign him a division of troops to be trained to use parachutes. What for? Why, to attack the Germans from the rear.

Pershing was used to ideas coming from his young air commander—ideas that might have seemed mad had anyone else offered them.

Until Brigadier General William Mitchell of the United States Air Service came to France in 1917, air power had been sharply limited. The trench-oriented European military leaders regarded aircraft as useful for observation of enemy troop movements and for limited bombing. The desperate engagements of fighter pilots in the first three years of the war were undertaken primarily to protect observation planes on one's own side, and to destroy them on the other. As for the romantic legend that grew up around flyers, in the beginning it was regarded by the general staffs as a discipline problem, and aviators were treated as necessary nuisances.

Mitchell changed all that. His brilliant strategic ideas for the use of air power captured Pershing's imagination. Mitchell was allowed to train an American air corps in France and assemble the largest air armada in history to support American and British operations. One day he put 1,500 aircraft into the sky. He extended the use of bombardment and convinced Pershing of its ultimate effectiveness as a strategic as well as tactical weapon.

Mitchell's parachute troops of World War I would be armed

primarily with automatic weapons and machine guns. By this time the Allies had developed the Handley-Page bomber and the Caproni. (The Italians were very good airplane builders.) These aircraft could carry 10 to 15 armed, parachuted soldiers and drop them well behind enemy lines.

Pershing and his staff examined the plan and saw how airborne troops could surprise the enemy and provide an island in enemy territory toward which a force could drive overland. The results ought to be confusion and diverted efforts of the enemy and rapid consolidation of one's own forces. Pershing approved. Mitchell was to have his troops and his program in 1919.

All plans came to an end with the Armistice of November 11, 1918. The airborne idea had to wait. But it was not forgotten by Billy Mitchell or his air staff, which included Major Lewis H. Brereton. As Mitchell's operations officer, Brereton would have been entrusted with carrying out the plan.

Mitchell went back to the regular army of peacetime, where the airborne concept soon bogged down in army tradition. Mitchell did conduct a successful mass airdrop at Kelly Field, Texas, but the military authorities in Washington were not impressed, and after Mitchell's quarrel with the general staff—which led to his court-martial and military disgrace—the army sank back to the old ways: Plan for the next war with the weapons of the last. In America the airborne idea went begging for attention.

In the military sense, the Russians and the Germans were beneficiaries of World War I. The Czarist military machine was destroyed by the revolution and the Bolsheviks, because they had no traditions, did not hesitate to undertake new military programs.

The Germans were forced to new ideas and tactics by the strictures of the Treaty of Versailles. The genius of this German effort was Hermann Goering, German World War I ace and squadron commander who watched with anguish as the Allies took away and destroyed his air force at the end of the war. He promised Adolf Hitler a new air force, and as soon as the Nazis seized power he set about building it, although the Germans were allowed no air forces. So they began to consider the glider to train pilots, who then could go on rapidly to learn the intricacies of powered flight. Using gliders purposefully, they eventually developed troop-carrying gliders that could land behind enemy lines. They also established parachute troop units. By the late 1920s the Nazi youth dominated the international glider field and German glider design led the world. In the 1930s the Germans began building large gliders to carry men into combat—first 9, then 20, then 200 equipped troops in a single giant 242A.

The Russians led the field in developing parachute techniques for infantry warfare. During Red Army maneuvers in 1930, a lieutenant and 8 men jumped from a cargo plane and accomplished "their mission." By 1935 the Russians had organized an Air Landing Corps and transported an entire division by air from Moscow to Vladivostok. The world was warned when the Red Army produced a propaganda film on the subject.

This film caught the watchful German eye. So did maneuvers in Kiev, in 1936, that showed how far airborne warfare had progressed: The Russian troops parachuted into action two battalions with 16 light field guns and 150 machine guns.

By the late 1930s American military students were aware of these developments in airborne operations, and problems of airborne warfare were part of the teaching program of the Command and General Staff School at Fort Leavenworth, Kansas. Lewis Brereton, who remained in the U.S. Air Service, had not forgotten what Billy Mitchell taught him. But in Washington, airborne operations were considered fluff. No serious attention was paid to the organization of an airborne striking force or to glider development.

In 1939 the Germans showed the world how outmoded were the war concepts of 1918. The dive-bomber and the armored column suddenly appeared as vital elements of attack. The Germans also used paratroops to capture airfields in Poland in these first days of the war. The Nazis moved into Poland on September 1, 1939. Nineteen days later the last major Polish army unit surrendered. Then came a long period of apparent stalemate in which an enormous French army and a smaller British one remained entrenched on the eastern frontiers of France, facing the Germans. Neither side seemed willing to make the first move, and so boring was the "war" that newspapers christened it The Phoney War. But the aura of stalemate was illusory. Hitler was busy just then, occupying Czechoslovakia, Poland, Denmark, and Norway. Early in May 1940 he was ready to move against the Netherlands, Belgium, and France.

The German attack plan was a modification of the Schlieffen Plan, which they had used in World War I. The Germans would lure the French and British into Belgium and northeast France, and then the German armies would drive to the sea and cut the enemy off. On May 10 German paratroops landed in the Netherlands and captured the bridges that were vital to Dutch defense around Rotterdam and The Hague. The Dutch defenders were virtually immobilized. The Germans also landed paratroops to capture various airfields, which enabled the Germans to resupply their forces by air. By the end of the first day the Dutch air force was destroyed and the army crippled.

In the defense of Belgium, a line had been drawn along the Meusé river between Namur and Liége and the Albert Canal from Liege to Antwerp. The key to defense of this line was a series of fortresses, "impregnable" bastions built up between the two wars. Fort Eben Emael was the central fortress and the most powerful of them. On May 10 the German Luftwaffe sent 10 gliders against Fort Eben Emael, carrying 78 airborne troops. Armed with modern explosives, they landed atop Fort Eben Emael, and cracked it open almost as easily as a housewife opens a sardine can. At the same time 30 gliders carrying 350 men were landed around the three vital Meuse river bridges. The airborne troops captured the bridges, and the Wehrmacht (German Army) then had passage across the river. Later, the Belgians managed to attack and destroy one of these bridges, but two were enough for the Germans. Belgium's army was rolled up like a straw mat in the face of Nazi power.

Eben Emael convinced the American general staff that the glider was more than a plaything; when a force of 500 German parachute troops captured the Albert Canal in Belgium, intact, they began to think seriously about the parachute. Then came Corinth, in Greece, where gliders were used to seize the strategic canal. And in May 1941 German paratroopers and glider troops sailed in on Crete and, in a very short time, overpowered the defenders. Crete was the absolute proof of the efficacy of airborne operations.

The Crete experiment was costly to the Germans because the

British controlled the sea. Although the Luftwaffe held the air, the airborne troops could not be resupplied as they ought to have been. Hitler, misunderstanding the lesson of Crete, decided airborne operations were too costly and abandoned them. Few of Hitler's decisions were more fateful for the conduct of the war. In the final days, when "Fortress Europe" was besieged, German airborne troops might have created havoc among the advancing armies. Luckily, after Crete, the initiative in airborne operations moved to the western Allies.

Learning
the Drill

The Eben Emael operation made believers of the Americans. When it was followed by Corinth and Crete, and the Germans overran Europe, the proof seemed to be complete. The U.S. Army Ground Forces began paying attention to the techniques of airborne operations.

In the beginning the generals in Washington believed all that was necessary was to train ordinary infantry troops in the techniques of dropping by parachute. The paratroopers would operate against key points in small groups but would remain part of a standard infantry division. The idea, sound enough on paper, was to give greater flexibility to infantry tactics.

In April 1940 the War Department approved plans for a test platoon of airborne infantry. There was much controversy among the armed services as to which command should have control. The infantry said these troops were nothing more than infantrymen delivered by air. The army air corps said they were air grenadiers, who would be the marines of the air corps. The War Department said they were soldiers who would function temporarily under the U.S. Army Infantry Board.

In July the facilities were established, and First Lieutenant William T. Ryder of the 29th Infantry volunteered to command the platoon. Lieutenant James A. Bassett was chosen assistant platoon leader. The tradition of the airborne—every man a volunteer—was established then. The 48 men were selected from a final pool of 200. The criteria were good health and general toughness.

The platoon moved into tents near Lawson Field in the Fort

Benning area and used an abandoned hangar for parachute packing and lectures.

Lieutenant Colonel William C. Lee, on the staff of the chief of
infantry, had the sensible idea that the men could learn much
from drop experience. Some facilities were available—the parachute drop towers left over from the New York City World's Fair
of 1939. These were owned by the Safe Parachute Company and,
after the fair, had been relocated on their grounds in Hightstown,
New Jersey. So the "airborne" experience began there, on the
250-foot towers. The troops learned that they could trust their
parachutes, and they acquired experience in the sensations of
landing. The army was impressed and bought four towers to erect
at Fort Benning. Three are still used there.

The first jump was made by members of the platoon from a
Douglas B-18 bomber on August 16, 1940. Lieutenant Ryder led
his men. The first enlisted man out was Private William N. King,
who had won the honor in a lottery. Two weeks later the platoon
made a mass jump.

The success of the training program led to organization of the
501st Parachute Battalion, commanded by Major William M.
Miley.

From this unit came the paratrooper's war cry. One day a
Private Eberhard of the 501st was arguing with a friend, who said
he was so scared when he jumped that he couldn't open his
mouth. Private Eberhard said he would show his buddy—and
when he jumped he shouted "GERONIMO!"

It became the battle cry of American paratroopers and has
been ever since.

The paratroopers then were equipped as infantrymen, with
flat bowl-shaped helmets of World War I, puttees, and ordinary
infantry clothing. They trained at Fort Benning in jump techniques, with an actual first jump from 1,500 feet. Out of those
beginnings virtually the only equipment that remained in use for
paratroops a few months later was the type of aircraft from which
they jumped. The Douglas C-47—the workhorse of the military—
began and continued as the basic jump aircraft all during the war.

By April 1941 a parachute school was operating at Fort Benning. The force was growing.

In September Company A of the 501st was sent to Fort Kobbe

in the Canal Zone to guard the installations against possible German surprise attack. These were days when Nazi submarines were ranging the waters of the Caribbean, and Washington was seriously concerned about surprise at the Canal.

On Pearl Harbor day Company A became the first parachute unit to assume a combat status, taking over outpost duty at Venada Beach and manning antiaircraft positions on Huwand Field.

In the formative period, unit names became thoroughly confused, an indication of the rapid change in airborne organization. Company A was attached to the new 550th Infantry Airborne Battalion, activated at Fort Kobbe. In a matter of months the men joined the 503rd Parachute Infantry Regiment aboard a transport and soon found themselves in Australia. Before 1942 had ended the name of the unit was changed to Company E, 503rd Parachute Infantry. The troops would remain in Australia for many months before going into combat.

The chief administrative officer in the field was Lieutenant Colonel William C. Lee, "father of U.S. Airborne forces," who ran the training show at Fort Benning and, later, at Fort Bragg. He would become first commander of the Airborne Command, and then of the 101st Airborne Division.

But in the spring of 1942 there were no plans for airborne divisions, although the airborne men knew that what they called vertical envelopment was a problem too complex to be left to ordinary infantry divisions. In these early months the tactical units kept forming: 502nd Parachute Battalion, 503rd, 504th, 501st, 505th, 506th, 507th, 508th, 511th, and down the line, twenty-seven battalions in all.

As the generals worried about organization and strategy, on a lower level the troops moved. That spring of 1942, as the men of Company A sweated in the jungles of Panama and made ready for the South Pacific, the 2nd Battalion of the 503rd Parachute Infantry Regiment headed for England. Major Edson D. Raff was battalion commander, and his orders were to proceed to Ilfracombe, a seaport on the Bristol channel of Devon in southwest England. There he was to place the unit under command of Major General F.A.M. Browning, D.S.O., for training by the British airborne forces.

At the same time Colonel Lee went to Britain to study the organization of the more experienced British forces. He returned home after several months, convinced that the most effective use of airborne troops must be within the division framework.

The old idea of dressing up regular infantry tactics continued to dominate staff thinking in Washington. Even as the airborne divisions were authorized—two of them, both to be created from the 82nd Infantry Division—the idea that "airborne" meant only a method of transport into battle continued. Colonel Lee recommended adoption of the British system of combining parachute and glider troops. Each division was to have one parachute and two glider infantry regiments, plus engineers, artillery, and other forces specially trained for the operations they were expected to conduct.

By August 15 the two airborne divisions were created—the 82nd Airborne, under Brigadier General Matthew B. Ridgway, and the 101st, under Brigadier General William C. Lee. Both were assigned to the Third Army. All too soon Lee was out of it, forced from combat status by a heart condition.

The complexity of organization and training during these hectic months of the first year of the war is hard to grasp nearly four decades later. Air forces, ground forces—the entire American military establishment—had to undergo enormous expansion and change of method to meet the challenges of two quite separate wars, in Europe and in the Pacific. New or improved weapons and tactics came almost every day, outmoding much of what had been learned before.

Meanwhile the war could not wait. By the summer of 1942 Hitler threatened so severely in the Mediterranean that Britain's hold seemed tenuous. On the Russian front the Germans seemed ready to overrun Stalin's forces, and from Moscow came recrimination and demand for the creation of a second front to divert German strength from the East.

The decision was made at Allied command level to invade North Africa. It was to be a British-American operation, headed, for political as well as military reasons, by the American commander, General Dwight D. Eisenhower. The Americans were to commit themselves to the European ground war here.

The 2nd Battalion of the 503rd would undertake the first American airborne combat mission.

In the East the Russians were clamoring for a second front. What they wanted was an immediate British-American assault on

France, but that was impossible. Hitler had made a fortress of the European coast along the North Sea and English Channel, and it would be a year and a half before the Americans could produce and ship enough war matériel to assure the success of an invasion. The Russians did not care about success or failure; they wanted the German pressure against their armies released. To pacify the Russians and to get American "feet wet" in the European war, the Combined Chiefs of Staff of the United States and Britain decided that the Americans would invade North Africa to assist General Montgomery's Eighth Army, which was fighting German General Rommel's Afrika Korps. The invasion would be made in French North Africa, where the Allies hoped to secure cooperation of at least some of the French military forces. But they did not know precisely what attitude the French would take. In those spring and summer months of 1942, as Eisenhower and his staff prepared for their first action, they saw that paratroops could be valuable in the action. Taking a leaf from the German book of successes in Poland, Belgium, and Crete, they considered use of paratroops to capture vital airfields. It would not be a large-scale operation; the American paratroops were not yet tested. Indeed, it really would be a test of the airborne ability to produce results.

The where and how remained uncertain all summer and fall as the troops conducted drop exercises in Devonshire and learned what their British comrades could teach them. It was not even certain at Eisenhower's headquarters that the paratroops would engage in the initial phase. But in October 1942 Eisenhower finally decided to test the paratroops in the North African landings of November.

General Browning, a disarmingly dapper figure, put the Americans through their paces that summer. They went to Ireland and jumped into a North Irish peat bog for practice. They slogged miles over Devonshire's hills and valleys to get into combat trim. Mrs. Franklin D. Roosevelt visited them. They had camp shows and trips to London on leave. But in November the orders came.

The training period was over. Lieutenant Colonel Raff was to lead the men into battle.

They packed their gear on Saturday night, November 7, and trucks deposited the men at two airdromes used by the 60th Troop Carrier Command. There the men of 2nd Battalion climbed into thirty-nine C-47s, and Raff pored over his orders.

Like so much about the North African invasion, the orders were equivocal. No one knew whether or not the French of North Africa would fight their former allies, the British, and the new contingent of Americans. The French government at Vichy, of course, was committed to the Rome-Berlin axis, but did that mean the generals in the field would do as the puppet government ordered? It was known that the vast majority of French officers and soldiers hated their forced role as part of the Axis. The difficulty lay in the concept of duty, and to try to resolve it Major General Mark Clark went by submarine to meet with Admiral Darlan and the highest French officials.

At the level of the 2nd Battalion, nothing of the political difficulty was known: All Raff knew was that they might ride the planes down into the fields of the Tafaraoui and La Senia airports, near Oran, or they might jump and fight for the fields. They had to be prepared, physically and morally, for either course.

Either way they were to assure Allied control of the fields. If it came to a fight they were to destroy enemy fighters on the fields at the airdromes, seize the control towers and facilities, and cut communications to the West.

The flight from England took 12 hours, and as the planes reached the drop zone the pilots saw they were low on fuel. But they knew—the word had been flashed from Gibraltar—that they faced a peaceful landing.

As the formation began coming in, the long flight and the conditions of the flight had made it certain this drop would be ragged. For many of the pilots this was the first night formation flight; and none had trained with the airborne troops. Several of the navigators had been assigned to the operation just hours before the planes took off.

The trouble had begun as they approached the Spanish coast. The formation ran into fog and began to break up. By dawn half the pilots were hopelessly lost and there was no formation. Not more than six planes had stuck together in any grouping.

Operations and intelligence had tried to do their best. A warship was stationed 25 miles off the Algerian coast to give homing signals to the approaching C-47s. The operator was working the wrong frequency, so most of the pilots missed them. Allied agents flashed signals, but the pilots missed or misunderstood them.

As day broke, only half a dozen planes were on course. But in the light, most of the others managed to find their way toward the objective.

The first flight came in, and Raff wondered about those words from Gibraltar. As they moved above the field they saw the white smoke of antiaircraft fire. The field was under aerial bombardment. The C-47s made a pass and Raff saw ground troops pinned down by an armored column. This certainly did not appear to be a peaceful reception. He decided that he and his men would jump. They prepared to drop on the Sebkra, a dry lake bed 30 miles west of Tafaraoui. The troopers stood up in the planes, static lines attached to the anchor cables, and each man checked the parachutes of the man next to him.

Fourteen okay. Thirteen okay . . . six okay . . . two okay . . . one okay. Raff was ready to go.

They jumped, and the white parachutes opened. After them came the antitank guns, machine guns, ammunition, and communications equipment they would need. Raff had a bad landing and broke a rib, but the accident was not serious enough to stop him. They moved on.

Soon they discovered the armored column that had bothered Raff was American.

The objective was Tafaraoui, some 35 miles across the dry lake. They were wearing heavy winter underwear and full field equipment. It was not long before the heat began to bother them, and the woolen underwear began to go.

They were attacked by half a dozen French fighter planes but suffered no casualties. Still, it was a difficult situation. The command was badly scattered and Raff did not know where most of his men were. In fact, three planes had landed in Spanish Morocco, and all aboard were interned. One landed at Gibraltar, one southeast of Oran, and two in French Morocco.

Raff assembled some 300 of his paratroopers in the Sebkra the next morning, and they surveyed their situation. Three C-47s were available to them, with enough gas to make the Tafaraoui objective. These were loaded, and Captain Berry was put in charge of the landings. Raff would lead the others overland to the objective.

As the three transports approached Tafaraoui Field, they were jumped by four French De Woitine fighters and shot down. Three parachutists and two airmen were killed, and fifteen parachutists were wounded. The airborne had suffered their first casualties of the war. As the survivors watched, six British Spitfires swooped in on the French fighters and shot them down, one by one.

When Lieutenant Colonel Raff and his men reached Taf-araoui, they discovered that the airfield had already been oc-cupied by an American armored column. They took over defense of the airfield, but there was no further action. The next day Algiers was occupied and Casablanca and Oran were falling. The men who had landed by error in French Morocco were treated as "visiting" Americans by the French and given a huge banquet. They rejoined the unit two days later, no worse for wear.

Raff assessed the operation. It had been at best a limited success—more valuable for training than anything else, as it turned out, for the contribution of the airborne had been almost nil. For that the unit had suffered 5 men killed, 16 wounded, and 88 missing.

So there really was a war on. And the airborne men who had participated had an idea of how much there was for all concerned to learn.

On to Sicily

Lieutenant Colonel Raff had little time for recapitulation. In the week after the drop at Tafaraoui, the military situation continued to be confused, and therefore the paratroopers were to play an unknown role again. On November 13, II Army Corps called Raff into action on almost no notice. The objective was to be an airport near Tebessa on the Tunisian frontier. Intelligence had learned that this airfield contained a vital portion of the French gasoline reserves.

Raff waited for information. Nothing came. There had been no reconnaissance, no terrain study, no photographs. Even the orders issued by Colonel Hewitt of II Corps were incomplete: Capture the airfield and deny it to the enemy. What was the airfield? Who were the enemy? These were questions left unanswered.

On the eve of the mission, intelligence came up with a new estimate: The more important field was at Youks les Bains, not Tebessa. The paratroopers would take that objective.

Lieutenant Colonel Raff assembled his men at Maison Blanche airport, near Algiers. By 11:00 A.M. on November 12 he had 150 men and enough equipment, gathered from a dozen places, to make a drop. Two days later another 150 of his men showed up. The British paratroopers were already in action against the town of Bone. Their supply corps, under Brigadier Flavell, helped supply Raff—particularly with wicker baskets, which, as the Americans learned, took much of the shock and saved equipment damage on hard landings.

On this occasion the paratroopers were to have company that promised them publicity. Jack Thompson, war correspondent for *The Chicago Tribune*, would come on the drop.

By the afternoon of November 14, the unit was assembled and had all the equipment that could be found. Raff also had 25,000 francs for negotiation with Arabs and, perhaps, Frenchmen. He was ready to go.

The orders said take off at dawn. The briefing of the pilots took only minutes; about all the mission leader could tell his pilots and navigators was "Follow me." But this time, at least they would have an escort of six fighters to keep the French away.

The takeoff was delayed until 8:00 A.M. Then 33 C-47s left the field, heading for Youks les Bains. Still neither Raff nor anyone else knew what they would find.

Two and a half hours later the planes reached Youks les Bains. There on the field was a French battalion, dug into trenches, with machine guns sweeping the field. French armored cars were deployed on the roads. At the signal, the C-47s moved in and the sergeants opened the rear doors of the transports. The planes came directly over the field and the parachutists began tumbling out.

As they came down, Raff half expected to be greeted by a hail of fire. But there was no firing. The French were ducking into trenches.

On the ground in the middle of the field the Americans would have been in serious trouble had the French begun shooting. But after the drop all was silent. Under a flag of truce Raff moved forward and met the colonel commanding the Third Zouave Battalion. They negotiated a surrender that really was not a surrender but gave the Americans control of the airport.

And why had the French sought cover so quickly? Not because they were afraid of the paratroopers—not the Third Zouaves. But so many of the parachutes on the equipment tumbling down failed to open that the French soldiers were afraid of being squashed.

Youks les Bains was captured. Raff's battalion had suffered 15 casualties, all men injured in the drop. And still, after two combat drops, the American parachutists' ability to take an objective was untested.

As it all turned out, the 2nd Battalion had been very lucky not to have to add fighting to its other troubles.

But II Corps and General Eisenhower were not badly impressed by the performance of the airborne men. Lieutenant Colonel Raff was promoted to full colonel. For the moment there was no mission for the troops, so they patrolled the Youks les Bains area and were pulled into action in other places. The Germans were building strength in Tunis, and were using paratroopers and glider troops. One German unit, dropped west of Tebessa, missed its objective and was rounded up by Allied forces.

Glider troops were occasionally landed behind Allied lines on special destructive missions. That same sort of mission would be the employment of the 503rd on the 2nd Battalion's third mission in North Africa.

In the interim, Colonel Raff had been writing reports. Supply was an enormous problem. One reason so many of the equipment chutes had failed was that the men had repacked them themselves after the first drop. There was no depot for resupply or parachute packing or repair. Many of the chutes of the first drop had been abandoned and became parts of Arab tents. The coordination between airmen and parachutists was fragmentary, and the ground commanders' understanding of parachute techniques was infinitesimal.

In this next mission the same difficulties arose. It was too soon to expect changes in the supply system. Again the paratroopers had insufficient briefing, maps, and intelligence about their objective. They were ordered to blow up a railroad bridge six miles north of El Djem, in Tunisia, to try to stop the German advance. This meant a distinct infiltration behind enemy lines, but German and Italian, not French, this time. The team would consist of one officer, two French soldiers who spoke Arabic, six demolition men, and twenty-one riflemen. Colonel Raff could not go on this mission; it was his job to command the battalion; this was a job for a lieutenant.

Just before midnight on December 26, three C-47s took off from Thelepte and headed for El Djem. In the night the pilots became disoriented and missed the drop zone. The lieutenant and his men found the rail line and decided they were a mile north of their objective. Actually they were a mile south of it. They moved south, away from the bridge, and when they did not find it they stopped in an orchard and slept.

In the morning, as they scouted the line, they discovered several German patrols searching—obviously for them. The lieutenant in charge took his men to the rail line, and then the French soldiers realized that they were miles south of their objective, with Germans all around, alert to their presence. The officer put the men to work destroying rails in the area, for what small good that would do. He was growing nervous.

The patrols seemed to become more frequent. The lieutenant gave up all hope of blowing the bridge and began heading back, 70 miles to the Allied lines. The Germans found the destruction and began to track them. By 3:00 in the afternoon the paratroopers were surrounded. The lieutenant ordered them to break up into small groups, infiltrate through the German patrols, and make their way back. It was a fatal decision. Of the whole force only the lieutenant, the two French guides, and three other parachutists appeared a month later.

One of these was Private Underhill, a rifleman. Private Underhill had been sent with two demolition men, for he had a Garand rifle, 60 rounds of ammunition, and 4 grenades. The demolition men carried only Colt .45 automatic pistols. Heading west, they trudged through the heat and sand, Underhill taking the point. Suddenly he dropped and motioned the others down. On a hill before them was a machine gun. Underhill worked his way up to observe. He saw an Italian scout platoon. One of the Italians spotted movement, and the machine gun fired. Private Underhill motioned his companions back to cover and held the enemy off until they escaped. Later in the day he joined up.

The demolition men decided the going was too hard and the danger too great. They wanted to surrender. Underhill refused. The others insisted. So they went their separate ways. The demolition men put up their hands and walked into the Italian lines. Underhill picked up his rifle, made his way around the Italian force, and lobbed a grenade into an Italian truck, killing or wounding two soldiers. Then he took off.

Private Underhill slogged his way west, mostly by night, holing up and hiding from Axis patrols. He subsisted on the K rations in his drop pack and on eggs he managed to buy from Arabs, who gave him water and information about the enemy's position. Eventually he made his way to the Allied lines at Foudouk.

So the third American air drop had been an almost unqualified failure. Inadequate intelligence, unsure planning, precipitate assignment, and unfinished training had left officer and men unprepared for the task they were given. Under the circumstances, there was almost no chance that they could have succeeded. But the adventure of Private Underhill showed the caliber of men who had opted to fight from the sky. What was necessary was to give them the tools and training for the task.

Sicily

4

When the North African campaign ended in the spring of 1943, the Americans and the British faced the same problem they had the year before. What were they to do next? At a "summit" meeting in Casablanca President Roosevelt and Prime Minister Churchill pondered the question. One thing was certain: In spite of Stalin's urgent demands, the western Allies could not launch the major offensive against Germany for another year. Yet the United States had thousands of troops in Africa and England, and it was wasteful and dangerous to Allied morale to fail to employ them. Churchill wanted to strike at the "soft underbelly" of Europe, which meant in the Balkans. The Americans did not like that approach. General George Marshall, the American army chief of staff, did not want to strike anywhere until the Allies were ready for the major blow. But the political considerations were as important as the military ones, and so a compromise was reached. They would invade Sicily. If the invasion went badly, they would have tied up many German troops anyhow, and the commanders would have learned from the operation some lessons that would be valuable in the major invasion, which all agreed would be from England across to the mainland. If the Sicily invasion went well, they might move against Italy, which was known to be unhappy with its role in the war. The Italians had taken enormous casualties in the desert war in Africa, and public opinion was turning against the Germans. All these matters were considerations in the plan that was devised in Algeria in May 1943, by American and British leaders.

One of the major difficulties for parachutists, once they

reached the ground, was disengagement from their chutes. The T-5 parachute harness, from the vantage point of the troops, was a pain, sometimes a danger. Some of the injuries to Colonel Raff's men, as well as most of the injuries in training, could be attributed to the difficulties with the release device. In a high wind, a man might be dragged over the worst sort of terrain before he could disengage.

Combat brought the answer. The Germans were far ahead in this department, as Colonel Raff learned one day when he examined a captured German parachute harness with a quick-release device. He sent it back to Airborne Command with a recommendation for immediate action. The German release mechanism was something like one made by the Irving Parachute Company, and the Irving company was asked to incorporate the German design. The result was the T-7 parachute assembly, which would be ready for operational use in the spring of 1944.

But this was the winter of 1942–43, and the war was not going to wait for Airborne Command to catch up. The paratroopers would have to make do with the T-5 in the next few operations.

The North African invasion had been designed as a preliminary to attack on the Axis at home, and the weakest part of that axis was Italy. The decision to attack Sicily was made for several reasons: to seize the 30 German landing fields that jeopardized supply into the Mediterranean; to hit at the weakest partner; to fight in a confined area as the Allies tested the strategy of a combined British-American command.

The decision was made at Allied headquarters to use paratroops to spearhead the invasion. But in the American force there was only enough airlift capacity to carry a reinforced regimental combat team. General Ridgway selected Colonel James M. Gavin's 505th Parachute Infantry and gave him the 456th Parachute Artillery Battalion, the 3rd Battalion of the 504th Parachute Infantry, and B Company of the 307th Airborne Engineers. Assignment: Parachute into Sicily on the night of July 9.

They would be under the command of General George S. Patton, Jr., and were to link up after the landing with General Terry Allen's 1st Infantry Division. The job of the airborne was to shock the enemy, seize key points, and hold them until reinforced.

In the spring British Intelligence had begun its attempts to mislead the enemy about invasion plans. They rigged up a dead body with fake papers purporting to indicate a coming Allied invasion of Greece and dropped the corpse off the Spanish shore. The elaborate ruse succeeded, and the Germans moved their key forces east. But the Hermann Goering Panzer Division was in Sicily, the 15th Panzer Grenadier Division was in Sicily, and Field Marshal Kesselring had promised the Italians two more German divisions. One would hardly say that Sicily was a soft spot.

The invasion plan called for Field Marshal Bernard Montgomery's Eighth Army to attack on the southeast side of Sicily, with the American Seventh Army in support on Montgomery's left. The attacks were to be simultaneous; Montgomery would drive north to Syracuse and the Americans would drive east to Licata, taking the airfields in the area. The major assault, of course, was amphibious; the task of the airborne was to seize key points to block enemy movement of reinforcements. British 1st Airborne Brigade, for example, was to seize a key bridge south of Syracuse. These troops would go in by glider.

The 505th's assignment was to drop behind Gela, on the southwestern shore of the island. All the 505th would parachute in.

From the beginning there was the confusion that might have been expected in this combined operation. On the field in Tunisia, ready to take off, Colonel Gavin was given a message: The wind would be blowing at 35 miles an hour over the drop zone, west to east. Gavin gulped. In training, operations were suspended when the wind reached 15 miles. But there would be no suspension this night. The timing of the operation had been one of the difficult problems in planning. The navy demanded darkness for its approach with the seaborne troops. The airborne demanded moonlight for a night drop. The compromise was reached by setting the invasion on this date, in the second quarter of the moon, when there would be moonlight early at night and pitch darkness after midnight, when the moon set.

This time the training had been intensive for the airborne troops and the Troop Carrier Command fliers who would take them. Paratroops and pilots had aerial photographs. They had practiced drops. They had made a night reconnaissance over the objective.

At dusk the airborne operation began. To carry the 505th and its support troops, the 52nd roop Carrier Wing brought 226 C-47s to the fields to pick up 3,400 paratroopers.

The plan called for a flight east to Malta, then north to the coast of Sicily, west to the Gela area, north to the drop zone. All troops were ordered to drop; the planes must return empty.

The high winds played hob with the whole airborne operation. Seventy of the British gliders came down in the sea. Only 12 landed anywhere near the zone, and although a handful of valiant British troops seized their bridge, they were not reinforced and had to withdraw. Luckily, soldiers from the beachhead came up in time to seize the bridge before the Germans could bring up demolition forces.

The American airborne unit ran into the same winds. The orders had set altitude at 500 feet, to avoid enemy radar. There was no escaping the ground winds, then. The pilots missed the Malta checkpoint, and the straggling began. As they approached the coast of Sicily, none of the known landmarks appeared. Bombing had stirred up smoke and dust. But the orders were that every man and every bit of equipment was to be dropped in Sicily, and they were, all the way from Cap Moto to Licata, a spread of 60 miles.

It had been the plan for the 505th to drop in front of the U.S. 1st Division. One-eighth of the force did. Seven-eighths dropped all around the U.S. 45th Division, the Canadians, and the British. Troopers of 3rd Battalion and Regimental Headquarters learned that quickly enough. The Americans had been given the sign "George" and the countersign "Marshall." After the drop, when the men had released themselves from their chutes and were assembling, they found themselves close to other troops.

"George!" shouted a paratrooper.

The response was a fusillade of fire. Not until one trooper managed to corner a Briton and explain without getting his head shot off did they learn the British countersign and join their Allies on the front.

The 2nd Battalion dropped near Cap Scaramania, far east of the assigned zone. Some of the men came down in an area stuffed with Italian pillboxes. Systematically, they set about reducing the pillboxes with rifle fire and grenades.

A group led by Major Mark Alexander moved against San

Croce Camerina. They captured that town and then the town of Vittoria.

The troops of 1st Battalion, commanded by Lieutenant Colonel Art Gorham, were to drop at the Piano Lupo, which was 172 meters high and dominated approaches to the Ponte Olive airfield. The pilots of the C-47s were at first as thoroughly lost as any others, but they managed to find checkpoints and headed for the drop zone. The paratroopers dropped into the midst of antiaircraft fire and machine-gun fire from the airfield and its outskirts.

Captain Edwin M. Sayre of A company assembled 15 men and began assault on a pillbox position at 3:00 A.M. The fire was severe, and the Americans backed off until another 50 men came up at around 5:30 A.M. Then, in the light, they moved in, with rifles, carbines, grenades, and bazookas. Forty-five minutes later they had captured the Italian garrison. This attack had gone like clockwork.

Just after the garrison was taken, Lieutenant Colonel Gorham came up with another 30 men, just before a German armored column from the Hermann Goering Armored Division appeared on the road. Coming from Niscemi, the column was led by an advance patrol of two motorcycles and a Volkswagen command car. The paratroopers let the patrol come until it passed the American perimeter, then opened fire. The three vehicles were knocked out and all the Germans captured or killed.

When the firing began, the German armor stopped about 3,000 yards from the American positions on the hill. The German commander sent his infantry—some 200 men—out ahead, moving across open ground that led to the hills where the Americans were concealed. Gorham ordered his men to hold fire. The Germans advanced to a point 100 yards in front—then Gorham gave the order, and the automatic weapons and the rifles opened up. The German infantry was pinned down on the open ground, and many were killed. Some were captured.

The armored column moved up to help, but the American bazookas knocked out two tanks and damaged two more. At that, the German commander ordered a withdrawal.

Lieutenant Colonel Gorham's objective was Piano Lupo, on the high ground off to the left. He moved up, using prisoners to bring the wounded, and prepared a defensive position. He sent

Captain Sayre with a detachment to attack a road fork, an important defensive position surrounded by Italian pillboxes. He persuaded the Italians they were surrounded by a large force. They
surrendered, Gorham's men occupied the pillboxes and fought off
an attack by four German tanks. In mid-morning troops of the
16th Infantry showed up, and took over. Sayre joined the 16th
Infantry for the moment. When he reached a radio point, he sent
word to General Ridgway that all the 505th's missions had been
accomplished.

It was true, a handful of the troops of the 505th had reached
the proper area and had done the job.

They had learned a good deal about German armor and the
German capabilities. They had also captured a weapon quite new
to them, a version of the German *Panzerfaust,* a far more powerful
and effective rocket than anything the Americans had in their
arsenal. The *Panzerfausts* would serve well in the future, to destroy German tanks. So the 505th came out of the first few hours of
Sicilian operations with a most satisfactory record.

Drop
to Disaster

5

Colonel Gavin and the headquarters group were as badly lost as
any others. Their pilot found himself flying almost into naval
gunfire, but because of it he was able to find the corridor between
British and American fleets. They dropped—they had no idea
where—and soon were engaged in a firefight in an olive orchard.
They moved out, found a ditch to hole up in, and waited for the
whole day to pass. There were six of them, with a tommy gun, a
pistol, an M-1 and two jammed carbines. Moving out at nightfall,
they encountered a small group from the 505th Parachute Infantry and then finally reached the lines of the 45th Division. Gavin
made contact with the 3rd Battalion of the 505th, which had
assembled 250 men at the edge of Vittoria. Together they moved
west toward Gela, stopping at a point called Biazza Ridge. Here
they encountered a strong unit of the Hermann Goering Parachute Division and took a large number of casualties; but they
managed to hold Biazza Ridge against tanks. One artillery squad
with a 75 mm. pack howitzer, engaged a tank and persuaded it to
back away behind a building. With reinforcements from Headquarters Company, and half a dozen Sherman tanks, Gavin
launched a counterattack, drove the Germans from their positions, and captured the first Tiger tank the paratroopers had ever
seen. They had hit it several times with bazooka fire, but when
they examined the tank, they found that the armor was four and a
half inches thick and that their rockets had penetrated only an
inch or so of it. The tank mounted heavy machine guns, light
machine guns, and an 88 mm. gun that was larger than any
weapon the Americans had outside field artillery units. That was
something to think about.

Back in Tunisia, Allied high command had planned on a second air drop in a matter of hours to support the American paratroop forces. On return of the troop carrier planes debriefings showed they had lost 6 percent of the force and first indications were that all troops were approximately in the drop zone, except 2nd Battalion. What headquarters wanted to know was: How many planes would be available for the second airlift? The answer was 153.

So the plan was to continue, even though delayed by the confusion. The original plan had called for drop of the 504th Regimental Combat Team on the night of D day—and here it was a day late. This factor would become important, because the naval commanders off the southeastern shore were not warned of the change.

The ground commanders of Seventh Army had been told to expect friendly flights of troop carrier planes for six nights after the invasion. They either forgot the plan, or assumed that it had been cancelled in view of the failure of the high command to reinforce the paratroopers the first night of battle.

General Ridgway had tried several times to get promises from the naval forces that they would not fire on his planes. Instead he received evasive answers. The American and British naval commanders had assured him that if the planes followed the prescribed course, they would be safe.

When the 144 transports carrying 2,000 men of the 504th Regimental Combat Team appeared over the battle area, it seemed that the men at sea and on the ground knew what was coming. The first flight of C-47s reached its drop zone. The men jumped and the equipment was dropped. But the second flight was greeted by a hail of fire from ships and the ground. Allied guns were turned on everything in the air. Just minutes before, the troops and ships had been bombed by German planes. The Germans got off almost scot-free, but the low flying, slow C-47s were sitting ducks, and they made their situation worse by turning on their lights for recognition.

In a few minutes 23 C-47s were shot down, some of them carrying their parachutists, and 37 planes were damaged. Some paratroopers, dangling in their harnesses, were killed by fire from below. Several planes turned back without dropping their men. Several groups of men were attacked as they hit the ground and tried to disengage from the unwieldy T-5 harnesses. Paratroopers were scattered all over the area, from Gela to the east coast. One C-47 landed back in Tunisia with a thousand bullet and shrapnel holes in the wings, tail, and fuselage. When the casualties were assessed, the 504th losses were 81 men killed, 132 men wounded, and 16 men missing. Fifty-second Troop Carrier Wing had 7 killed, 30 wounded, and 53 missing.

Ridgway was furious and frantic. After all the warning he had delivered, for his men to be killed by friendly fire was a dreadful shock. Just after midnight, when the first planes came limping in to the airfields to report the mix-up, Ridgway sent a message to General Patton recommending (one did not order a superior officer) that unless fire of all troops ashore against all aircraft was stopped, further troop movement by air be cancelled indefinitely. This restriction was accepted.

During the rest of the campaign for Sicily, the airborne troops fought as infantry. The 82nd's part in it really ended on July 22, when the 505th captured Trapani and Colonel Gavin accepted the surrender of the Italian admiral in command.

As for the rest, Gavin later stated the case: "The battle for Sicily pitted Patton and his newborn U.S. Seventh Army against Montgomery and his veteran British Eighth Army." It was a rivalry that would last.

The 82nd was out of it. General Ridgway was called to Patton's headquarters to discuss a parachute landing on the north coast. Gavin was there. He looked over the terrain maps and saw that the troops would be dropped and operate in a narrow valley in mountain country, to cut off the Germans. Gavin had some experience in "cutting off" Tiger tanks with bazookas, and he did not relish the idea of trying to fight German armor in confined quarters. Patton was advised against it, agreed, and instead launched two successful amphibious assaults.

When Messina fell on August 16, the troops of the 82nd Airborne were moved back to North Africa to prepare for the invasion of Italy. While they had been marking time in Sicily, Colonel Gavin had persuaded some nuns in a convent to embroider special insignia for the bazooka men. The Tiger tanks had really impressed Gavin, and the bazooka was the only effective weapon against them that he had.

In North Africa and Sicily the airborne forces had gained

valuable, if bitter, experience. It seemed more than a matter of months since Lieutenant Colonel Raff and the 503rd had made that first drop near Tafaraoui, and in retrospect the paratroopers could shudder at how little they had known and how lucky they had been. The bad luck and mix-up of the 504th drop caused General Ridgway to organize training units to improve assault techniques. One outcome of this was the establishment of path-finder groups, consisting of experienced pilots and troops, who would drop ahead of the main body, with electronic homing equipment, to lead the others in. They would have lights to mark out the drop zones.

As the units trained, their future was under discussion at higher headquarters. From General Eisenhower on down, no one was happy with the disaster of the night of July 11. The scattering of Gavin's force two nights earlier convinced some senior officers that use of a parachute division as such was out of the question. Army Ground Forces command began talking about abandonment of the airborne division concept. Someone suggested that they convert the 101st, the 17th, and the 82nd Airborne Divisions into light divisions, capable of many sorts of special action. Paratroop units would be organized in special battalions.

General Eisenhower lent his weight to that argument. Having seen how the 505th scattered in its night drop, he came to the conclusion that no divisional commander could maintain control of such forces.

Standing very nearly alone were the airborne men themselves, led by Major General Joseph M. Swing, commander of Airborne Command.

But Eisenhower insisted that, for the moment, they would use airborne troops in combat teams and not as a division. General Ridgway's hope that the entire 82nd would go into action in the coming Italian campaign was frustrated. At that point very little was known of the German view of the airborne landings. Had the American commanders known of the reactions of General Con-rath, of the Hermann Goering Division, and Marshal Kesselring, commander of German forces in Italy, they might have changed their minds. The very confusion of the 505th's drop had indicated to the enemy that hordes of paratroopers were falling from the sky. This overestimation of strength was a major factor in the

German failure to get the Hermann Goering Division moving in time to seriously threaten the Seventh Army invasion.

Since that shock factor was underestimated in North Africa and London, the airborne troops were to be employed in Italy, but in a limited fashion.

One reason that the Allies in Western Europe were unable to launch the mighty invasion of the continent any sooner than the spring of 1944 was that the United States was also conducting a major war in the Pacific. Both Admiral Nimitz in the Central Pacific and General Douglas MacArthur in Australia called for men, ships, planes, tanks, and all the other instruments of war that would be needed to guarantee success of an amphibious operation in Europe.

Until the battle of Midway, the Combined Chiefs of Staff tended to put the requests of the Pacific commanders behind those of the European theater. Midway was an American victory by a narrow margin. An outmanned and in many ways outclassed American fleet under Admiral Raymond Spruance defeated the Japanese Combined Fleet and stopped the invasion of that island. Further, the defeat left another invasion force, in the American-owned Aleutian Islands, without support. The Japanese had considered stepping off from the Aleutians to the North American continent. But to do so, they would have to send an enormous invasion fleet, and the outcome of the Midway battle put an end to that dream.

The lesson learned by the Americans, however, was that they could not hope to stop the Japanese unless they had more war matériel, and it came in a hurry. Any argument that might have developed between London and Washington was ended when the Japanese sent a landing force to strengthen a small garrison they had established at Tulagi, in the Solomon Islands, and in New Guinea. They wanted the Solomons and New Guinea as naval and air bases to cut communications between the United States and Australia, and perhaps even to launch an invasion of Australia. Port Moresby, on the southwest shore of the Palua peninsula of New Guinea, is only 300 miles from the northern tip of Australia so the danger was immediately felt in Canberra. General Mac-Arthur had no trouble in convincing the Australians that it was sensible to move. They agreed that the Japanese must be stopped and driven out of New Guinea. Already, Admiral Nimitz and Admiral King had decided that the Japanese invasion of the Solomons must be stopped, no matter what the cost.

On August 7, 1942, the Americans invaded the Solomons. The struggle there continued until January 1943. At that same time, General MacArthur's American and Australian troops moved against the Japanese who had occupied Buna on the northeast shore of the Papua peninsula, opposite Port Moresby. At the end of January 1943, the Japanese were defeated at Buna. They still held parts of New Guinea, however, and MacArthur felt it important that they be neutralized before he took his next big step: to capture all the Japanese bases in New Britain and the other South Pacific Islands.

Absolution in Markham Valley

After a complicated beginning, which involved shuffling of several units of paratroopers, the 503rd Parachute Infantry Regiment was assembled on the Australian plain 15 miles from Cairns in Queensland. For some of the troopers it had been a hectic trip. The men of Company A and of the 2nd Battalion of the 503rd were aboard the Dutch ship *Poulau Laut*, which zigzagged its way across the Pacific, alone. After 42 days aboard ship (for Company A), *Poulau Laut* was finally brought into Cairns, and the men went to the place where they would build their camp. Colonel Kinsler, the regimental commander, laid it all out for them.

They built at Gordonvale, a mile outside the community. By January 25 they were ready for a practice jump at Kiri. The field was hard, and a 15-mile wind was blowing. Twelve of the men were casualties, with broken bones and sprains. At least part of the difficulty was attributable to the T-5 harness.

A month later the 503rd went on three-day infantry maneuvers in the pouring rain of the wet season. The Mulgrave river was flooding and had become a torrent. It was not at all as marked on the maps. Fording the river, Private John Kobeska was drowned—the first man of the 503rd to die in the war theater.

In March 1943 the training became more grueling. Company A men would never forget one exercise called the Happy Valley March. On March 18 they set off from camp to a point two miles out of Babinda. The terrain was rugged—a hill to climb, a valley to slide down, another hill, a rushing stream to ford, and another hill. On the second day they were to be resupplied by air. At their noon halt they watched as the planes dropped their dinner—high in the trees. The chutes hung there, swinging, tantalizing, out of reach. Company A moved out. There was no dinner on March 18.

Marching in the darkness, the men stumbled over rocks and roots. The medics moved up and down the line treating blisters, sprains, and cuts. Finally, at 2:00 A.M., the weary company pulled into the bivouac area. The camp that night rang with the praise of the medics, in particular Technician, Fourth Grade, Ted White and Private, First Class, Shuffat.

All this activity was preparation for the regiment's initiation into jungle warfare. Captain Haedicke took a reconnaissance trip to New Guinea in April, and Staff Sergeant Bartram in May. Units of the Japanese 20th Infantry were holding an airstrip at Nadzab. With the coming joint American-Australian operations against New Guinea, it would be important that the strip be first neutralized and then made available to the Allied forces. That would be the 503rd's objective.

By mid-spring of 1943 the paratroopers' skills had increased remarkably. They jumped on May 31 and again in mid-July, this time with full field equipment. The field where they landed, near Mount Garnet, was littered with loose rock and scattered with small trees, dangerous to parachuters. But on this drop there were surprisingly few injuries. The paratroopers were toughening up.

In August the 503rd was moved forward to a camp 17 miles south of Port Moresby. On September 3 General Douglas MacArthur visited the camp and inspected the troops. General Vasey made a speech about the coming operations in MacArthur's long island-hopping haul back to the Philippines.

Next day, at 2:00 P.M., the alert came. Six hours later the regimental orders reached the company level, and at 3:00 A.M. on September 5 breakfast was served. An hour and a half later the troops were in trucks and on their way to Ward's Airdrome. They arrived at 7:00 A.M. The weather was overcast, the clouds so low that operations were delayed until 8:30. Then the men were loaded into transports, and the planes took off for the Markham Valley. The drop zone was a mile and a half west of the airstrip. A broad expanse of tall Kunei grass, flanked by thick forest, stood between the troops and their objective. The going was slow. In Company A, Technician, Fifth Grade, E.R. Nelson, Private, First Class, Touminen, and Private, First Class, Flood were injured in the jump; and Staff Sergeant Betz disappeared.

The 503rd was reinforced by an Australian parachute artillery battalion. The three battalions arrived over the drop zone at 10:00 A.M. and dropped in a cloverleaf pattern. The drop, finished in two and a half minutes, was entirely successful.

Everything worked well, even the preparations. A flight of A-20s had laid smoke screens to shield the drop operation. B-25s had bombed and strafed the landing area minutes before. A squadron of B-17s came along afterward to drop supply and equipment "packages," each package carrying 12 bundles of equipment and weapons and each bundle attached to a parachute.

Nearby, P-38s flew cover and more bombers attacked known positions of the Japanese to keep them from moving as the paratroopers established themselves.

In Company D, Private Elmore was hurt in the jump. Altogether in the first phase, the 503rd lost 3 men killed and 20 injured.

In five hours of march the battalions had reached their objectives, meeting virtually no resistance, and had dug in, putting out booby traps for the enemy. They were joined by an Australian Pioneer battalion, which had set out overland, and work began on the airstrip to adapt it for Allied planes. Two days later, elements of the Australian Seventh Division began coming in by air.

The Japanese resisted. In one fight on the night of September 6, when Company A was dug in along the edge of the airstrip, Technician, Fourth Grade, Tsigonis was shot in the leg. A Japanese infantryman got close enough to hurl a grenade, which killed Private Rivas. They buried Rivas near the regimental aid station, and Tsigonis got a Purple Heart.

On September 7 brush fires set the previous day to clear the strip perimeter for observation swept through the jump field and destroyed most of the parachutes and drop bundles of the 1st Battalion.

On September 10 Lieutenant Millican of Company E ran afoul of one of the company's own booby traps outside the perimeter and was killed by the grenade.

That was the end of the action for the Americans. The Seventh Australian Division carried on the fighting against the Japanese. They caught them in a squeeze at Lae and moved into the Markham Valley. But the airborne troops had done precisely what they were supposed to do, and with very little loss in men and matériel.

It was by far the most successful single operation yet attempted by paratroopers. Given the confusion that still existed about the effectiveness of the airborne units at Sicily, the Nadzab drop was the best argument General Swing could have to convince higher authority that the paratroops were valuable.

The success of the Sicilian invasion made certain the next step, which was to while away more time and create more diversion against the Germans by attacking Italy. The Allied victory in Sicily had another effect: It brought about the downfall of Mussolini. He had erred badly in choosing his allies, and the cost to the Italian people had been enormous. Two hundred thousand Italian troops had been killed or captured in North Africa. Another 200,000 were fighting in Russia. Another 160,000 were killed or captured in Sicily. Nearly 600,000 men were fighting or occupying the Balkans for their German partners. The Italian people had lost over a million sons and brothers, then, and they were thoroughly sick of the entire war. Further, they did not like the Germans, with their overbearing ways, and so when Mussolini fell, the government established by Marshal Pietro Badoglio immediately sought peace with the Allies. It was achieved on September 3, 1943, the day that the Allies crossed the Straits of Messina and landed in Calabria.

Everyone knew the Germans would sacrifice every Italian life, every Italian town, and every Italian asset in the defense of their empire. What was needed, if the Germans were to be forestalled, was swift action of the sort that the airborne troops had shown they could deliver. So once again, the airborne divisions were under consideration for a major role in the war. But the Allied commanders moved too slowly, as it turned out. . . .

The 82nd Airborne in Italy

At the top levels of command the dice seemed loaded against the airborne divisions. General Eisenhower did not believe in them, and so wrote General Marshall. How Eisenhower got that attitude was a mystery to General Ridgway and the other airborne men who had been involved in Sicily; Eisenhower had not been within 300 miles of the airborne effort. The only senior general officer to have had any personal contact with the 505th team was General Patton, and he was enthusiastic about the performance of the paratroopers. General Bradley also had seen some of the effects of their efforts, particularly the fight at Biazza, where Colonel Gavin's men had crippled a number of German Tiger tanks that later broke down on the roads.

When the planning of the invasion of Italy was in progress, General Ridgway tried hard to secure a part of the initial action. The best chance seemed to be a drop of a combat team along the Volturno river, 20 miles northwest of Naples, to destroy enemy capability of reinforcing the area around the beachheads. On August 18 General Ridgway apparently had the green light. He selected Colonel Gavin as task force commander. But almost as soon as the detailed planning began, the navy reported that sandbars at the mouth of the Volturno precluded an amphibious assault, which would have to be staged to support the airborne troops and assure their effectiveness. The plan was scrapped.

Just 13 days before D day, General Ridgway was called to headquarters of the 15th Army Group to discuss a new mission for the division. It was to be the seizure of Rome!

The operation was planned for the night of September 8. The

airborne troops would drop and link up with Italian forces operating in the Rome area. By this time Italian Marshal Pietro Badoglio had brought most of the Italian forces to the Allied cause. The Rome show would be almost entirely an 82nd Airborne Division affair, from drop, resupply, and reinforcement, to a landing at the mouth of the Tiber river by 82nd troops. They would capture the airfields around Rome and then the city itself.

The operation got to within hours of the drop. On the afternoon of September 8 the men readied their equipment, and the unit plans were all signed and sealed. The pathfinder planes were loaded on the field at Agrigento, Sicily, and engines were running. Then came the orders from General Ridgway.

"Mission canceled."

In last minute meetings the Italian high command had decided that it would be too risky to all concerned to carry out the operation. The Germans were reinforcing the area. The Italian troops had virtually no gasoline for their mechanized vehicles and very little ammunition. The Germans could be expected to react with great force to the operation, so the chances were too slender for success.

The 82nd was not to be used in the invasion of Italy proper, it seemed.

Lieutenant General Mark Clark began the invasion of Italy on September 8, at Salerno Bay. The 36th Infantry Division drove rapidly inland to the hills. North of them the British 46th and 56th Divisions landed and after a few hours the Allies were congratulating themselves. But General Heinrich von Vietinghoff, commander of the 16th Panzer Division, discovered a 10-mile gap between the 36th and the nearest British unit. He attacked the 36th along its left flank and this division began to collapse. The positions taken so easily were now overrun, and the Germans reported to higher command that they would proceed to throw the Americans back into the sea. General Clark was concerned enough that day to send liaison officers to the navy to plan for evacuation.

By September 12 Clark was really worried, and the Germans were jubilant. Their panzer forces were pressing hard. This was no time for generals to argue airborne doctrine, although General Ridgway had been sending messages to 15th Army Group, hoping to promote a place in the war for his troops. Just before midnight on September 11, General Clark began to call for help. No matter what he had believed before, he wanted a drop on Avellino, a German supply center, to block roads through the mountain passes down to Salerno and cut off the Germans.

On September 12 Clark asked for the drop. On September 13 the crisis was unmistakable. Early in the afternoon a fighter plane landed at Licata Airfield in Sicily, and a tired pilot climbed out with a personal message for General Ridgway. He would not give it to anyone else. Ridgway was in the air, but Colonel Gavin radioed the plane, and he came back.

The message was General Clark's personal call for immediate help. The Germans threatened so severely that Clark wanted a Regimental Combat team dropped inside the beachhead south of the Sele river to reinforce the bedraggled and battered troops and, next night, another Regimental Combat team to drop. Clark guaranteed that the planes and men would not be attacked as they had been at Sicily. He would have guaranteed anything he could deliver: The general was desperate for airborne reinforcement.

In a matter of minutes Ridgway was working out the details. Eight hours later the troops were in the C-47s and moving down the runways. The 504th Regimental Combat Team—the same unit that had been decimated by "friendly fire" at Sicily—was going into action. Colonel Reuben Tucker would again lead his men, and those of Company C of the 307th Airborne Engineers. Ridgway made one absolute demand: The antiaircraft guns in the Salerno area were not to fire at *anything* from 9:00 P.M. September 13 until subsequent notice. Ridgway sent staff officers to the beachhead to check.

The drop was to be made near Paestum, and to this point the 82nd had sent pathfinders ahead. There was no foul-up; the drop zone was to be marked by a flaming T made of gasoline-soaked sand, and it was. The planes came in, the parachute troops moved down the corridors of the C-47s and jumped from 800 feet. Most landed within 200 yards of the drop zone; none was farther than a mile away. The second wave was not so accurate. It came in several hours late, the weather had changed, the flak was heavier, and the companies were scattered. A third wave again hit the target. The men rolled out of their parachutes, picked up their weapons, and got ready to move. Fifteen hours after Mark Clark's frantic message, 1,300 reinforcements were on the ground, and by dawn the regiment was in the line, ready to attack.

That same night the 509th Parachute Infantry's 2nd Battalion landed at Avellino. This was the same unit, renamed, that had made the original jumps in North Africa. Colonel Raff was still the commanding officer.

This attack was by far the most risky undertaken by the paratroopers. Its planning indicated the desperate nature of the mission: The unit commanders had only two hours' map briefing. There was no general battalion briefing, time was too short. The men boarded planes of the 64th Troop Carrier Group, and the flight began.

In the approaches to the drop zone, the planes became separated and some of the pilots were confused. The 640 paratroopers were spread over a hundred miles of mountain territory behind enemy lines. Colonel Raff and his headquarters unit landed in the middle of a German panzer park and were immediately engaged in a firefight. He was wounded and captured. Other small units began operations. The paratroopers carried five days' rations and were considered so expendable that they did not have communications with Fifth Army. They moved around the mountains in small groups, mining roads, ambushing small forces of the enemy, and shooting messengers. The purpose for which they had been sent was generally accomplished. German communications were interrupted in some places. A large number of German troops were assigned to track the parachutists—pinning down far more Germans than the battalion's strength. Eventually, 510 of the 2nd Battalion got back to Allied lines.

That same night the 504th was assigned to seize the town of Altavilla, which was located under a hill 400 meters above sea level. With two battalions Colonel Tucker took the position, overrunning the Germans, and leaving batches of them behind. At dawn the reinforced Germans counterattacked. The 504th held. It was the second time Americans had taken the town and its two hills, important as artillery observation posts. The Germans had driven the 36th Division from these heights. Now they tried to drive out the paratroopers, but they failed. Tucker held for 48 hours, and then, when ordered by General Ridgway to withdraw, refused and asked for his other battalion. He got it.

On the second night, the 505th Regimental Combat Team dropped behind the American lines, to further augment the assault force. With that force, the Americans began to move ahead, and the pressure was withdrawn from Tucker's team at Altavilla. The Germans were driven back and the Salerno beachhead was secured, after four days of touch and go.

As a result of Salerno a corps commander was relieved and sent home. The paratroopers were much more appreciated than before, but they did not particularly like the method in which they had been used to reinforce invading troops. The classic airborne concept called for vertical infiltration: The men would land behind the enemy and disrupt his communications and his efforts to fight. But in this case the paratroopers had been used in another capacity, as firemen. If they had not been available, probably the Salerno invasion would have been stopped in its tracks. Even if it was for the "wrong" reason, the 82nd won a reputation as an organization that could handle the toughest assignments anyone could hand out.

6th Abn. Div.*

9th Abn. Div.*

11th Abn. Div.

13th Abn. Div.

17th Abn. Div.

18th Abn. Div.*

21st Abn. Div.*

82nd Abn. Div.

101st Abn. Div.

108th Abn. Div.*

135th Abn. Div.*

11th Air Assault Div.

Airborne Cmd.

1st Allied Abn. Army

2nd Abn. Inf. Bd.

187th RCT

187th RCT

508th RCT

Co. A, 65th Inf.

* This unit was never organized, but a patch was approved for it.

187th Paraglider Inf. Regt.   **187th Abn. Inf. Regt.**   **188th Abn. Inf. Regt.**   **188th Abn. Inf. Regt.**   **325th Abn. Inf. Regt.**

327th Abn. Inf. Regt.   **501st Abn. Inf. Regt.**   **502nd Abn. Inf. Regt.**   **502nd Abn. Inf. Regt.**

503rd Abn. Inf. Regt.   **503rd Abn. Inf. Regt.**   **504th Abn. Inf. Regt.**   **504th Abn. Inf. Regt.**   **505th Abn. Inf. Regt.**

505th Abn. Inf. Regt.   **506th Abn. Inf. Regt.**   **507th Abn. Inf. Regt.**   **508th Abn. Inf. Regt.**

508th Abn. Inf. Regt.

509th Abn. Inf. Regt.

511th Abn. Inf. Regt.

513th Abn. Inf. Regt.

515th Abn. Inf. Regt.

517th Abn. Inf. Regt.

541st Abn. Inf. Regt.

Special Forces

542nd Abn. Inf. Bn.

550th Abn. Inf. Bn.

551st Abn. Inf. Regt.

Troop Carrier Cmd.

Abn. Troop Carrier

173rd Abn. Inf. Bde.

457th Abn. F.A. Bn.

462nd Abn. F.A. Bn.

674th Abn. F.A. Bn.

127th Abn. Engr. Bn.

307th Abn. Engr. Bn.

596th Abn. Engr. Bn.

82nd Abn. Div.
Cmd. & Control

82nd Abn. Div.
Spt. Cmd.

82nd Abn. Div. Sig. Bn.

82nd Abn. Div.
Recondo.

101st Abn. Div.
Recondo.

Abn. Pathfinder

Abn. Parachute Rigger

U.S. Army Parachute Team

Ready
For France

Most armies treated their shock troops with kid gloves, at least when the armies were in an offensive phase of operations. But the 82nd Airborne was very quickly committed to a sort of military-police operation in Naples, clearing the city and supervising repair of damaged facilities needed for the Allies. Later, the 505th was treated as regular infantry and sent up along the Volturno to fight the Germans. The 504th had the same task and was assigned to very rugged mountain terrain until after Christmas. Then that unit was sent to the rear and rested to fight at Anzio. Its men did fight, but not as paratroopers. The high command had still not accepted the airborne units as more than trick outfits. (In the Pacific, the marines disbanded their Raider battalions for the same reason.) The top brass did not understand how to employ "special" troops, and they suspected anything they did not understand.

Probably General Marshall was more important than anyone else in saving the airborne concept from the ash can, where the traditional infantry officers would have liked to throw it.

Marshall, as chief of staff back in Washington, wanted to use the airborne divisions for deep envelopment of the enemy. They would land far behind the German lines in France and disrupt the enemy's defensive plan. Marshall favored this idea, particularly because of the enormous cost in matériel and the difficulty of staging a major amphibious landing. At the time, in 1943, he was not sure he could put together the forces necessary for a frontal assault.

General Eisenhower was not a man of great imagination, and he was a traditionalist. Eisenhower was not convinced of the possibilities of success of airborne invasion—nor were the other leading generals of the Allied field forces. The matter was debated for months, but in February 1944 Eisenhower and his staff finally decided that the airborne troops would be used as adjuncts to the primary sea assault. They never did get the idea that perhaps it could be more efficient the other way around.

In Washington, General Arnold of the Army Air Force and General Marshall made one last effort to persuade the field commander, but it made no difference. One factor was uppermost in the minds of the general staff in London: It was not positive that airborne units could organize and withstand a determined enemy attack by armor. The deciding factor was probably the Tiger tank, with its 88 mm. guns. The Allies had no comparable weapon, or even a counterweapon; the American bazooka charge would penetrate only a quarter of the thickness of the Tiger's four-inch armor plate. The most effective antitank weapons the Americans possessed in the early stages of the war were the *Panzerfausts* captured from the Germans in Africa and Sicily. The British were far ahead of the United States here. British troops were equipped with a larger bazooka. They had plastic explosive, which could knock out a Tiger tank. They also had a 57 mm. antitank gun (as compared to the American 37 mm. gun, whose charges bounded off Tigers, like tennis balls off the side of a barn).

The men who had fought the Germans with inferior weapons agreed with General Eisenhower that airborne troops were badly prepared to meet armor in the winter of 1944. The 505th's Gavin, promoted to brigadier general and assistant division commander of the 82nd, had a positive solution to that problem, however. He wrote: "Give us anything that will stop the German Tiger Tank, as a counterattack by them is the first thing that will hit us after we jump."

The high command could not give them the weapons. That settled the argument. The airborne would remain in support.

It did not help any part of the invasion effort that American and British military commanders were nearly always at one another's throats. General Gavin was sent to London late in 1943 to help with the planning for the Normandy invasion. Just before he left he was warned by General Ridgway to beware of General Browning, commander of the British airborne forces, who would certainly try to get all airborne operations under his command. This sort of infighting continued right up to the end of May, when Air Chief Marshal Sir Trafford Leigh-Mallory tried to persuade Eisenhower that the American airborne divisions would be slaughtered, and that the operation should be canceled and all the air transport turned over to the British.

While the generals were arguing, the men were training. The 101st Airborne Division arrived in England in the fall. It would consist of three Parachute Infantry Regiments, the 501st, 502nd, and 506th, and two Glider Infantry Regiments, the 328th and 401st.

Before year's end the 82nd Airborne Division moved up from Italy to Belfast. It had lost the 504th regiment, which was committed to fight in Italy. It gained the 507th and 508th Parachute Infantry Regiments.

In February 1944 the elements began to come together. The Army Air Force created IX Troop Carrier Command, made up of three wings and, theoretically, nearly 1,200 transport planes. In fact, however, it was hard to find enough aircraft to make practice drops. For the most part the 82nd had the services of the 52nd Wing, and the 101st used the 53rd Wing, when the planes were available.

The lessons of Africa, Sicily, and Italy guided the troops in training: Each division organized pathfinder teams, which would drop half an hour before the others. They would set up homing devices for the parachute troops and the gliders.

At the end of April General Brereton, commander of the Ninth Air Force, staged a major exercise, Exercise Eagle, to test the effectiveness of the plan. The verdict: ragged but right. As the divisions and lesser units pored over maps, the Germans responded to the potential airborne threat by strengthening their defenses, and the 82nd's drop plan was changed—just five days before the invasion.

The 101st was to land southeast of Ste. Mère Eglise, then destroy important bridges near Carentan and take the crossing over the Douve river at Pont L'abbe and at Beuzeville-la Bastille, blocking German reinforcement into the east half of the Cotentin peninsula. The 82nd was to land, on both sides of the Merderet river, where it could block off the western half of the peninsula, take Ste. Mère Eglise, and establish bridgeheads on the two roads over the Merderet that could be used for German reinforcement. Both divisions were assigned to VII Corps, whose mission was to land at Utah Beach, at the base of the Cotentin peninsula, and drive to capture Cherbourg, which would give the Allies a major port for further operations.

For the Germans' part, they were preparing for just what the Allies planned: a major sea assault, preceded by airborne landings back of the beaches. The German preparations were thorough and continued up until a few hours before the assault. One reason the 82nd's drop zone was changed was the intelligence learned of heavy German troop movements in certain parts of the area, and of the building of effective antiparatroop defenses on hills first planned for drops. A particularly effective device was *Rommelspargel* ("Rommel's asparagus," named for Hitler's most effective field commander). It was made of poles 8 feet long, stuck in the ground about a hundred feet apart. The poles were connected with wires, a device intended to stop Allied glider landings. For defense against paratroopers the poles were booby-trapped with land mines and gun emplacements were connected by trenches, with fields of fire overlapping to cover the whole potential drop zone.

The paratroopers would go in first, then the gliders. General Ridgway would lead his 82nd men. Brigadier General Maxwell D. Taylor, recently artillery commander of the 82nd, had been chosen to head the 101st, after General Lee had a heart attack and was sent home.

All the men and planes were as ready as they would ever be on the night of June 4. They were supposed to take off that night and land in the hours of darkness on June 5. But the ominous weather at sea caused General Eisenhower to postpone the operation for 24 hours.

When darkness fell on the night of June 5, the pathfinders began to move. All was in motion. In a matter of hours the airborne troops would be committed to the greatest Allied attempt of the war. General Eisenhower was counting on them to pave the way for the success of his seaborne assault.

Finally, in the winter of 1943–44, the Allies knew they would be ready in the spring to launch the long-delayed "second front" for which the Russians had been asking. As everyone knew, if the

Americans and the British were to carry out this brave endeavor they must be prepared to launch an amphibious operation that would, by comparison, make the battles for the Central Pacific islands look like local gang fights. The Germans, after all, had 59 divisions of troops stationed in France. Generals Eisenhower and Montgomery agreed that the landings must be on a front so broad that no matter where the Germans turned they could not drive off the attackers. That meant employment of at least five divisions of troops on the first day, with all the backup support and supply they must have within twenty-four hours. In the winter, the air attacks against French communications were increased. It did not take the Germans long to figure out why this was so, but they still did not know when and where the invasion was coming. The German strategy was to withhold the commitment of its major army forces so they could be concentrated on the invaders in a short time and overwhelm them. But the Germans were badly hampered in their estimates. The Allies had achieved air superiority, which meant the Luftwaffe photo planes, which had ranged all over England in the early months of the war, could not fly around England anymore. So the Germans could have some ideas about troop buildup, but not much specific information about localities and concentration of shipping, which would be the key. Field Marshal Rommel, who had earned so grand a reputation in Africa, was sent to France to stop the invasion. He was certain it must be done within the first 48 hours after the landings, but with Allied air superiority, he also knew that the Germans could not use the roads in the daytime, for they would be decimated by Allied fighters and bombers. The Allies did not help him much, either. The British planted dummy gliders all over the airfields of southeast England—the only part of the country the Germans could get near enough by air to photograph. So the countryside of Kent was made to look like the staging ground for an enormous air invasion of the continent, when actually, the major amphibious assault was preparing on the other side of England. The Germans fortified the Pas de Calais area. The Allies planned to invade Normandy.

In spite of the feeling in Eisenhower's headquarters that airborne troops were still trick outfits, it was apparent early in the spring that an airborne effort must really have teeth, if it was to serve its most useful purpose: to prevent the enemy from massing its power against the beaches where the amphibious assault would be made. To be sure, there would be great value in the opening of the hinterland to the landing forces, if the airborne soldiers could manage it. But if they failed almost entirely, their effort would still be enormously valuable. This view, of course, was the most cynical possible and seldom enunciated, but it was true none the less. If the airborne troops could reach and deliver half the objectives assigned to them, the Allied effort would be that much closer to success.

Invasion
at Normandy

Normandy was to be the first battle for American glider forces, although the theory and practice had been tested by the Germans and the British for five years. The glider program was a sort of "ugly duckling" of Airborne Command. Many glider pilots wished they were airplane pilots; the glider troops were assigned, whereas the paratroopers were all volunteers. The glidermen never achieved the high morale of the paratroopers, and this was a constant problem.

One reason for it was the failure of the generals to create the same sort of public relations atmosphere that they had for paratroopers. Another was inherent in the service: Glider troops were at the mercy of the towing aircraft's pilots and then their own. Paratroopers at least had the sense of commanding their destinies from that moment when the bottom of the plane fell from beneath their feet. Paratroopers were better paid (it was months before the army granted glider enlisted men $50 extra flight pay, officers $100 extra, per month). Nor was there any unity between pilots and glider troops. Many glider pilots came to Normandy with no knowledge of infantry weapons or tactics. What use would they be once they hit the ground?

All these factors troubled Airborne Command, but none of them was effectively resolved by the time the assault on Normandy began.

There had been enough indications of what was needed since the formation of the first glider infantry battalion, the 88th Glider Infantry Battalion, in October 1941. American glider pilots had been in Tunisia in 1943, and five of these pilots had volunteered to serve with British glider units. They were needed: The British would conduct the glider operations in Sicily, but they were short of Horsa gliders. They had received a shipment of Waco gliders, but the British pilots had never flown them. Finally, 28 American pilots were involved in the training program, and they volunteered and flew in the Sicily landings as copilots. Some gliders landed in the sea. Many were wrecked. And the pilots learned one fact beyond a shadow of a doubt: If they were to survive, glider pilots ought to be trained and equipped to be fighters on the ground as well as in the air.

But by the time the Normandy invasion came, this intelligence had still not permeated operations.

The assault plans called for six glider missions from the 101st and 82nd Airborne Divisions. The 101st was to land in the east, around Hiesville. The 82nd would land in the west, around Les Forges. The Americans had come to England with their Waco CG-4A gliders, which carried a payload of 3,750 pounds. That meant 15 men or a jeep. In training they had tended toward the British Horsa gliders, which carried 6,900 pounds; but just before D day, when the glider forces had been counting on using mostly Horsas, they were informed that there were not enough of them, and the Wacos would be used.

Worst of all, the glidermen had expected to land in the early hours of dawn. They were informed that their landings would be at night. When that word came out, the troop carrier and airborne commanders met with General Montgomery and complained. He heard them out and then stood up.

"We'll have to suffer it," he said. The plans could not be changed. The landings would be night landings.

Gloomily the glider commanders left the meeting for their bases. Lieutenant Colonel Mike Murphy, the senior American glider pilot in the European Theater of Operations, predicted that the change in plan would mean a 50 percent loss of men and equipment in crash landings.

For weeks the glidermen had been studying their plans. They had films of the run in to the target zone, mosaics of the landing zones, and plenty of maps. They did complain that the aerial photographs seemed to have been taken from such high altitude that they did not give much information about the terrain of the landing zones. What might be the obstacles? They did not see the *Rommelspargel.* Nor did they—or the paratroopers—see that the Germans had flooded the marsh country in which they would land and that some of what appeared to be grass-covered fields were little more than shallow lakes beneath the green. Also, when the higher commands spoke of hedgerows, the Americans thought of hedges and trees of the sort seen on many an American farm, to mark property lines and provide windbreaks. The hedgerows of Normandy, they were to discover, were the French *bocages,* tall barriers packed with earth and trees and stumps, which were as impenetrable as stone walls.

For days the mechanics on the fields had been painting invasion markings on the American gliders to distinguish them from whatever the enemy might happen to throw into the area. Each wing and fuselage was painted with three white stripes and two black ones.

Then came June 4, and the weather forecast for winds of 22 miles an hour, and heavy low clouds that dropped virtually into the hills and the high surf—and the plan was delayed. But on the night of June 5, just as the paratroopers took off in their C-47s, the mechanics began to move the gliders into position on the airborne airfields. They were placed nose to tail, to await the return of the troop carrier planes. There were not anywhere nearly enough aircraft available for the gliders to have their independent air force, so the workhorse C-47s would do double duty.

The ground crews checked the lashings of the jeeps and other equipment that would be flown into Normandy on the first glider landings. At only two airfields, west of Reading, were there planes waiting for the gliders. These would carry 102 Waco gliders loaded with antitank guns, jeeps, and other equipment that would be needed by the airborne troops, particularly if they were to encounter German armor. The most powerful weapon was the British 57 mm. antitank gun.

On the other fields the glider pilots and infantrymen waited nervously for the return of their towing aircraft. Then came the sound of engines from out of the darkness, and lights in the air from the south. But there was something very wrong. The planes should have been flying in neat formation; they were not; they were scattered and straggling, and as the later planes came in they were in no sort of formation but splashed all over the sky at various altitudes.

As the first planes came in over the fields, they circled and the crews shot off red flares: There were wounded aboard. The call went out for ambulances and medics. As the planes came closer, the men on the ground could see that several of them had blue exhaust flame coming from only one engine.

Then the first planes were down, and vehicles rushed to them as they taxied and stopped in the aprons. The pilots were hurried to the operations huts for debriefing, and they began to tell the story.

Advance
Party

The pathfinders went first. The planes took off and headed over fields and forests and villages of England, quiet in the summer night. They crossed the English Channel, where the troop carrier pilots were supposed to stabilize at 600 feet, the jump altitude, which would also give them some protection against enemy radar detection. The total distance from Portland Bill to the drop zones was just a little over a hundred miles, including a dogleg turn the plans demanded, but the flight seemed to take forever.

The islands off the French coast—Guernsey, Sark, Jersey— appeared, and so did the white puffs of German antiaircraft fire. But the planners had estimated the ranges of the German guns, and the C-47s droned by, the flak falling far short.

Soon they reached the French coast and could see the roads and fields below. It was as quiet and summerlike as England had been. No guns fired. No vehicles raced along the roads. A village showed beneath a wing, and then a town.

Suddenly, the first C-47 ran into a cloud bank. The plane behind disappeared. Each C-47 was alone. Some pilots tried to climb above the clouds, some tried to drop below them, some tried to retain formation.

Then the German antiaircraft guns on the west coast of Normandy began to fire. The heavies sent up big puffs that burst around the planes. The light guns sent up tracers that lanced redly through the night. One plane took a direct hit and broke up. The men in the plane behind could see the figures dropping down in the darkness. Would they be able to open their chutes? And where were they about to land?

58 ·

Major General Ridgway was standing in the open door of his plane, watching the formations, when they all disappeared in the clouds. Brigadier General Gavin was following his prescribed tactic: He ordered the men to hook up to their chutes the moment they passed over the French coastline. If Gavin's plane was hit, his men would have a fighting chance to get out.

The pathfinders ahead were scattered, and many of the units did not reach their drop zone positions. The system of directing the following planes did not work out so well. The other planes continued to bore in, scattering, and the pilots navigated as best they could in the foggy, cloudy weather. A few pilots circled and headed back for England, their troops still aboard. Most went on, but the formations were ragged, then scattered, and sometimes there were no formations at all.

The troops of the 101st began dropping in a wide circle southeast of Ste. Mère Eglise. The time was 1:30 A.M. The neat, orderly procedure of the plan was blasted before the men ever hit the ground. Unit commanders found themselves cut off from their troops. They gathered the men they could find and began to move toward the assigned objectives. They did not know it just then, but one of their biggest immediate problems would be caused by this poor airdrop and plain bad luck. Of the twelve 75 mm. pack howitzers of the 377th Parachute Field Artillery Battalion, only one was saved and put into action. Eleven, and most of their crews, went into marshes created by German flooding of the low ground and were lost. That was the sort of problem faced by the division: Fifteen hundred paratroopers would land outside the basic drop area, and most of these were killed or captured without contributing directly to the divisional mission.

General Taylor dropped into a pasture, and after he had struggled out of his parachute harness, he found himself alone except for a circle of curious cows. He pulled out his pistol and began to move, looking for his 14,000 men. Twenty minutes later, at the corner of a hedgerow, he encountered a rifleman from the 501st and was so pleased that he hugged him.

Other 501st men began to appear. Soon Taylor found his artillery commander, Brigadier General Anthony McAuliffe, with a group of artillerymen. They all began to move east to the Ste. Marie-du-Mont–Vierville road.

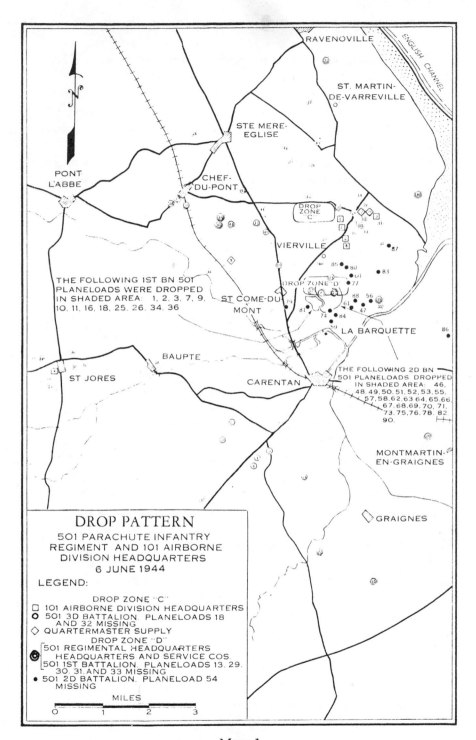

RAVENOVILLE

ST. MARTIN-DE-VARREVILLE

ENGLISH CHANNEL

STE MERE-EGLISE

PONT L'ABBE

CHEF-DU-PONT

DROP ZONE "C"

VIERVILLE

THE FOLLOWING 1ST BN 501 PLANELOADS WERE DROPPED IN SHADED AREA: 1, 2, 3, 7, 9, 10, 11, 16, 18, 25, 26, 34, 36

DROP ZONE "D"

ST COME-DU-MONT

LA BARQUETTE

BAUPTE

ST JORES

CARENTAN

THE FOLLOWING 2D BN 501 PLANELOADS DROPPED IN SHADED AREA: 46, 48, 49, 50, 51, 52, 53, 55, 57, 58, 62, 63, 64, 65, 66, 67, 68, 69, 70, 71, 73, 75, 76, 78, 82, 90.

MONTMARTIN-EN-GRAIGNES

GRAIGNES

DROP PATTERN
501 PARACHUTE INFANTRY REGIMENT AND 101 AIRBORNE DIVISION HEADQUARTERS
6 JUNE 1944

LEGEND:

DROP ZONE "C"
☐ 101 AIRBORNE DIVISION HEADQUARTERS
⊙ 501 3D BATTALION. PLANELOADS 18 AND 32 MISSING.
◇ QUARTERMASTER SUPPLY
DROP ZONE "D"
◉ 501 REGIMENTAL HEADQUARTERS HEADQUARTERS AND SERVICE COS.
501 1ST BATTALION. PLANELOADS 13, 29, 30, 31, AND 33 MISSING.
• 501 2D BATTALION. PLANELOAD 54 MISSING.

MILES
0   1   2   3

MAP 1

The Germans were surprised. Major Larry Legere of the divisional G-3 section, and Captain Thomas White, Taylor's aide, found themselves on a road and were approached by a group of Germans.

"What are you doing here?" demanded a German officer in French.

"I come from visiting my cousins," said Legere, in French— and then he pulled the pin of a grenade and tossed it into their midst.

That local surprise of the first encounter made the battle appear to be far easier than it actually was. General Taylor led his men against Ste. Marie-du-Mont, and they arrived just in time to prevent the shooting of two paratroopers by Germans who called them spies. Legere, who had emerged unscathed from the first encounter, was wounded in the action at the edge of town.

The broad scattering of the troopers meant trouble. The 506th was all over—three planes had missed the drop zone by 20 miles. Colonel Robert F. Sink, the commander, could assemble only 50 men of two battalions to move on Pouppeville, one of their assigned objectives. The 2nd Battalion commander, Lieutenant Colonel Robert Strayer, found himself leading a force consisting of men from his own battalion, from 3rd Battalion, and from the 82nd Division's 508th Parachute Infantry Regiment. Soon he had 300 men and they captured a causeway that was needed to bring troops from the beaches.

Lieutenant Colonel Robert Cole of 3rd Battalion landed on the edge of Ste. Mère Eglise, an objective of the 82nd Airborne, so he led his men toward St. Martin de Varreville, one of his 502nd Regiment's goals. By nightfall he had collected 250 men and had made contact with troops of the U.S. 4th Division coming from the Normandy beachhead.

The 1st Battalion of the 502nd had the task of mopping up a position called WXYZ, the barracks of the German artillery garrison established at St. Martin de Varreville. Staff Sergeant Harrison Summers of Company B rounded up a group of men from various units and led them to the houses. Sergeant Summers did not know a single one of the men, and he decided it would be easier to start the assault himself than to trust in unknown quantities. He walked up to the first house and kicked in the door. Inside, the room was

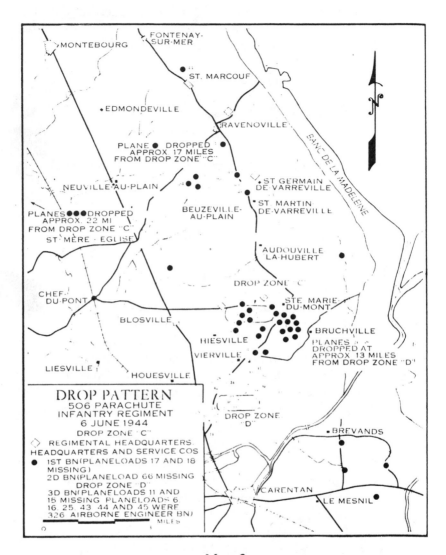

MAP 2

full of Germans firing through ports. As they looked up, he fired his tommy gun, dropping four. The others escaped to the third house. Summers's men took the second house, and Private William A. Burt set up a machine gun to fire on the third house. He kept the Germans there down, while Sergeant Summers and Lieutenant

Elmer Brandenberger of Company C ran for the door. Lieutenant Brandenberger was hit by a grenade. Summers smashed the door and entered, firing. There were six Germans in the room when he entered, and six bodies when he left. Summers started for the fourth house and was joined by a captain from the 82nd Division, but a sniper recognized the captain's insignia and shot him before he had run 20 yards. Private John F. Camien, Jr., joined Summers, and they moved from house to house. Camien had a carbine, so they switched weapons at each house, one covering with the carbine while the other rushed in to sweep with the tommy gun. In five houses they killed 30 Germans. They took no prisoners.

Beyond that last house was the unit mess hall. Summers rushed the door, covered by Camien. Inside were 15 men. He shot them all down at their tables.

Past the mess hall was a two-story barracks. Summers led his paratroopers against the barracks, but the attack resulted in four dead and four wounded troopers. Private Burt saw a haystack next to the building and fired tracers into it to rout any Germans hiding there. The haystack blazed, and the fire spread to an ammunition shed next to the barracks. As the ammunition began to pop, Germans came pouring out of the shed, heading for the barracks. The Americans shot 30 of them.

Staff Sergeant Roy Nickrent arrived with a bazooka and put seven rounds into the barracks. The last one started a fire in the upper floor. A hundred Germans came running out—into the guns of the paratroopers and also those of men of the 4th Division, whose troops were just coming up from the west. That was the end of the WXYZ action. At 4:00 P.M. on D day Sergeant Summers and his men sat down and had a smoke.

Other 101st troops took the positions that secured the beach exits, so the 4th Division, landing on Utah beach, had an easy time. But along the Douve river, where five crossings had been assigned to the division, the going was much more difficult. The 501st was to capture a lock at La Barquette. Colonel Howard Johnson, the regimental commander, took charge of that operation—and ran into a fight that gave the place the name Hell's Corners. The Germans had troops near the lock, but they let the Americans establish a column on the road and then attacked with rifle, machine gun, and mortar fire, supported by 88 mm. guns.

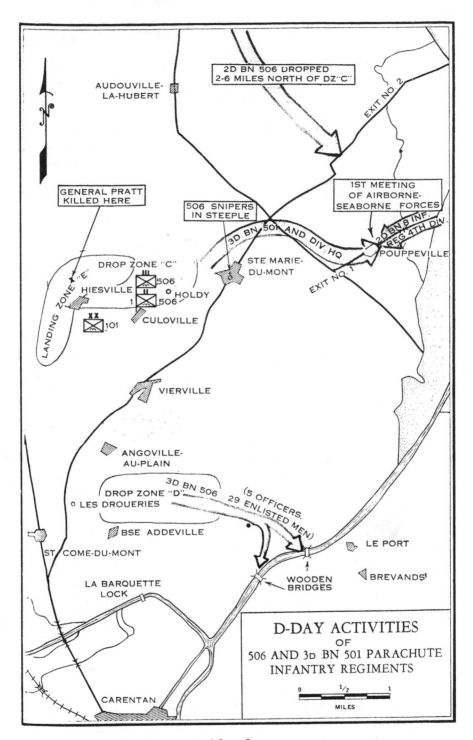

AUDOUVILLE-
LA-HUBERT

2D BN 506 DROPPED
2-6 MILES NORTH OF DZ"C"

EXIT NO. 2

GENERAL PRATT
KILLED HERE

1ST MEETING
OF AIRBORNE-
SEABORNE FORCES

506 SNIPERS
IN STEEPLE

3D BN 501 AND DIV. HQ

2D BN 8 INF.
REG 4TH DIV.

POUPPEVILLE

DROP ZONE "C"

STE MARIE-
DU-MONT

506

LANDING ZONE "E"

HIESVILLE

HOLDY

EXIT NO. 1

506

101

CULOVILLE

VIERVILLE

ANGOVILLE-
AU-PLAIN

DROP ZONE "D"

3D BN 506

(5 OFFICERS,
29 ENLISTED MEN)

LES DROUERIES

BSE ADDEVILLE

LE PORT

ST COME-DU-MONT

BREVANDS'

LA BARQUETTE
LOCK

WOODEN
BRIDGES

D-DAY ACTIVITIES
OF
506 AND 3D BN 501 PARACHUTE
INFANTRY REGIMENTS

0   1/2   1

MILES

CARENTAN

MAP 3

Johnson's men had nothing with which to combat the 88s and mortars. But among the men was Lieutenant Farrell of First Army, who had been trained to call up naval gunfire; and Farrell made contact with the U.S. cruiser *Quincy*, off the coast. *Quincy* began shelling the German positions with its eight-inch guns. The Germans backed off, and the Americans held the locks.

Elsewhere on the Carentan peninsula, the 2nd Battalion of the 501st, on the road to St. Come du Mont, ran into trouble at Les Droueries. After a three-hour fight, the paratroopers took and held the first group of houses in that little town.

The 3rd Battalion of the 506th had the worst time of all. Other paratroopers had dropped into swamp, lost equipment, and gotten lost themselves, but the 3rd Battalion ran into an enemy that was waiting for them. The Germans had decided Drop Zone D was a prime airborne target and had ringed it with machine guns and mortars. They soaked a farmhouse with gas and oil, and as the planes came over, they ignited it so that it became an enormous flare, lighting the whole countryside. Parachutists were shot as they drifted down and as they struggled to free themselves on the ground. Among the first killed were the battalion's commander, Lieutenant Colonel Robert Wolverton, and his executive officer, Major George Grant. By the time the battalion got organized and moving, it consisted of 5 officers and 29 men.

They moved against the two wooden bridges across the Douve and were joined by another 20 men. Before D day ended, they had captured these points in the face of heavy German resistance.

The 1st Battalion of the 502nd was to push to the northern Douve bridges. Just after drop the first elements ran into Germans at Foucarville. Still, they took the town. One group, led by Lieutenant Morton Smit, mistook the town of Haut Fornel for their target of Beuzeville, and there they ran into Germans. Smit and one of his men were caught grabbing loot in a barracks, fought two truckloads of the enemy, drew back into a building for protection, were routed by grenades, and spent an hour in a hog wallow before being rescued by the others.

By parachute and glider the 326th Airborne Medical Company came in and, in short order, set up a hospital in the Château Colombières near Hiesville. Three noncoms of the 101st Airborne Signal Company brought in a large radio and established first contact with England.

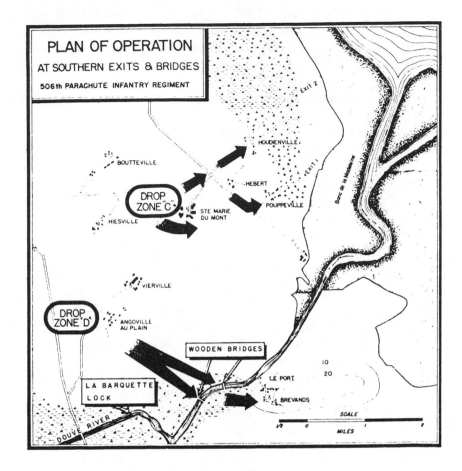

PLAN OF OPERATION
AT SOUTHERN EXITS & BRIDGES
506th PARACHUTE INFANTRY REGIMENT

MAP 4

By evening General Taylor and General MacAuliffe arrived at Colonel Sink's 506th command post at Culoville, where Taylor learned that the highway and railroad bridges on the Douve highway had not been blown as planned. He assigned that task for the next day.

The 82nd Airborne Division began dropping near the Merderet river. General Ridgway and his staff landed safely. So did General Gavin, in the area of the 507th and 508th. All found

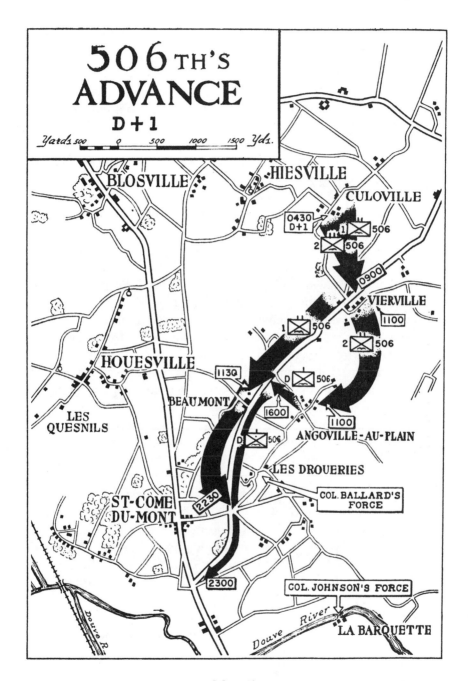

MAP 5

themselves or much of their equipment in water. They had hit in the marshy fields flooded by the Germans.

The 507th's Company D was first plane in the serial (flight formation). As they approached the Merderet, Lieutenant Lewis L. Harris led the jumpers. There was some small-arms fire, but not much, and he landed in a grain field. He could hear bullets overhead but did not have the feeling they were aimed at him.

Lieutenant Harris had difficulty with his chute release but disengaged and began to move. Almost immediately he encountered a figure. He gave the sign and received the countersign. It was the company commander, Captain Clarence Tolle.

"Get that damned thing off your helmet!" shouted Captain Tolle.

Harris felt upward. He was still wearing the luminous cord he had attached to guide his troops to him. He tore it off.

Other men began dropping nearby. First Sergeant Barney Hopkins landed amid a group of buildings 300 yards west of Amfreville. Almost immediately someone began firing at him. His chute was hung up in a tree, but he managed to free himself and move away from the buildings.

Harris and Tolle conferred. Neither knew precisely where he was, and both felt they were carrying too much weight. Each man carried an M-1 rifle or a carbine, loaded, and 156 rounds of ammunition, a pistol with three clips, and a trench knife. They also had entrenching shovels, water canteens, first-aid packets, grenades, K rations, and raincoats. Officers and noncoms also carried despatch cases filled with maps.

The two officers dropped their packs beside a hedgerow, grabbed the maps and left the despatch cases. Tolle had lost his weapon. That was not unusual. Too many nervous pilots failed to slow to drop speed of 126.5 miles per hour. Some had dropped their men at 172.5 miles per hour, which often meant equipment was torn from their bodies. General Gavin, for example, lost a wristwatch that night.

Harris gave Tolle his pistol, and they started forward, or what they thought was forward. In a few minutes they ran into their commander, Colonel Millett, and the three of them tried to figure out where they were. First, they decided, they had best try to collect their men. They headed through an apple orchard, across a hedgerow. As they stepped out of the trees a Schmeisser automatic pistol opened up on them. They ducked right back into the orchard.

They moved around the hedge, trying to outflank the Germans. They came to a communications wire, and Tolle cut it. They went quietly another twenty feet. Then came a shout: "Roland!"

It was the German recognition signal.

They lay on the ground, silent. The shout came again.

"Flash!" shouted Colonel Millett. (The U.S. recognition signal.)

"Flash!" he shouted again.

The Schmeisser opened up.

The fire came above Harris's head. He responded with the carbine. It jammed on the first shot. He fumbled, and then cleared it and got away five more shots.

The hedgerows were silent again. They waited five minutes and nothing happened, so they moved along the side of the hedge and away from the position, looking for their own men. They crossed several fields and came to a small gulley. Millett got out his map and tried to orient himself. He found nothing that corresponded to the map.

It seemed that they had been going for hours, but it was still pitch dark. Having run into one German patrol, they decided to wait for daylight before trying to round up the men. As dawn broke, they saw a German patrol moving along the top of the hedgerow toward them. Lieutenant Harris drew a bead on the lead scout, but before he could fire, the German disappeared. Soon firing began on two sides of them, and they retired back along the gulley.

This was no way to win a war, Colonel Millett decided. They would ambush the Germans. They moved to the side of the draw and waited. But the patrol never showed up. About an hour later they heard firing on the right. Tolle went over to investigate. He found Sergeant Hopkins and 30 men were firing at a German patrol. Soon others came up and joined the force. They saw Amfreville ahead and headed there. As they came into the outskirts, snipers started shooting at them from the buildings. This was a shock. They had expected to find the battalion command post already established.

Sergeant Hopkins and Captain Tolle took the point. As they rounded a corner, they saw a group of Germans in the road ahead of them. They began firing, and the Germans returned the fire, then drew back. Tolle sent Hopkins with a squad to move around the right flank and cut off the enemy. He took one automatic rifleman and three riflemen around the buildings to the right. They flushed four Germans—captured one and shot three.

Hopkins led his group into the buildings, room by room. They found three wounded Americans, left behind by another group that had been involved in a firefight here, and brought these men out. Just then, Hopkins heard Captain Tolle calling him. He headed back to see what the captain wanted. As he got 15 yards down the road he heard a burst of machine-gun fire. When he reached Tolle, he found him in the hands of the medics, who were loading him into a German truck they were using as an ambulance. Tolle was dead, shot through the heart.

Hopkins decided Tolle had spotted the German machine gun and had wanted him to come around and flank it. He returned to the patrol and led them to the building where the machine gun was located. They began firing on the windows and located the gun. A rifle grenade silenced the gun, and the Germans came out, shooting. Some surrendered. Some were killed.

Lieutenant Harris had taken the main body of men down the road. Hopkins and his squad joined them. They came to a self-propelled German 105 mm. gun, abandoned.

Hopkins tried to start the tractor, but it balked. The word came that Colonel Millett had decided to withdraw from Amfreville, so Hopkins tossed a grenade into the gun, wrecking it, and followed the main body.

They had moved half a mile west of the village after Colonel Millett had felt the strength of German fire indicated a force larger than his 30 men could handle. The radioman tried to raise friendly forces, without success. An hour and a half later a German patrol came probing along the road, and the men drove it back with heavy fire. But they were on the defensive. They moved to a better defense position and dug in. For the next two days and nights they stayed put. The Germans came out in such force that Colonel Millett let them pass by, with a 40 mm. antitank gun. They came along the road within 20 yards of the American position, but they did not discover Millett's men.

On the second morning, Major Benjamin Pearson of 2nd Battalion, 507th, came in with another 30 men. They had dropped near the river, outside the drop zone. When they tried to move to the drop zone to reassemble, they were driven off by German fire.

On this second day Millett's men captured a passing German convoy of seven trucks and a motorcycle, and took some prisoners. They had intermittent communication with division, but not enough to help much. Millett was still on his own. The regiment's mission was to capture Amfreville, so Millett decided to stay put and wait for enough men to join him so he could do so. Eventually, he figured, others would show up, and in the meantime he had a good defensive position that harried the enemy if they tried to move along the road.

At the moment Millett's men were sitting pretty. The German convoy had contained enough food and water to last for a week, and two cases of Hennessey brandy. They also had extra weapons—German. One of the trucks had been an ordnance truck.

Late on the second day there were about 100 men in the position. On the third day, Captain Allen Taylor showed up with 250 men, who had been waiting at the drop zone. They had learned of Millett's position from division.

That day they captured a German soldier who said he was part of the advance guard of a German regiment moving out of Amfreville to the north to join the main battle. Later more elements of the German force showed up, and a desultory firefight began. It lasted most of the day, at long range. Millett had the definite impression the Germans were not trying to engage but were covering for another body. The most trouble came from the German mortars, but no men were lost to mortar fire. Two were killed by rifle fire and one by a machine gun.

That night radio contact finally became firm. Division ordered Colonel Millett to move out and join Colonel Timmes. On D+3 at 12:30 A.M. they moved out. On the road they ran into German bicycle patrols, and in the fighting the column split, and then fragmented, as the Germans in the hedgerows opened fire against them. Colonel Millett's little group was captured. The column was stopped before it got to Colonel Timmes' position by the same heavy enemy fire that had kept Timmes pinned down. Next morning the remainder of Millett's force came upon a château, which was a German command post. They assaulted the position and cleaned it out except for one building, which they bypassed when enemy fire ceased. They moved along to the edge of the flooded area, where they joined Lieutenant Colonel Harrison of the 508th. He told them the 507th was attacking across the causeway down the road and sent them along. They moved into the swamp, fighting mud and grass but no Germans, and spent the night with the 505th near Neuville au Plain. Next day, when they rejoined the major elements of the regiment, the group consisted of 155 Americans, and 26 prisoners. When they had moved out of the position near Amfreville there had been 400 men and officers. Some of those missing had joined other units after getting lost in the night. Many had been captured or killed in the fight around the château. Some straggled in next day. But the first phase was over for company D of the 507th Parachute Infantry.

The
Main Battle

In a way, the factors that brought such pain and confusion to the airborne troops had a positive side. Later assessment of the Normandy battle showed that the fragmentation of the airborne landings had created as much confusion among the Germans as it had among the Americans. Everywhere the German defenders of the region turned, it seemed, they were beset by fire from the invaders. The result was a weakening of the German defenses all along the line.

In the 82nd sector, Staff Sergeant Raymond J. Hummel of the 508th Regiment was isolated with 36 men near Picauville. In four days they killed 40 Germans and destroyed a tank, with a loss of 6 men.

Lieutenant General Guillot, of Headquarters Company of the 508th's 1st Battalion, landed north of the river Douve, which he thought was the Merderet. While Colonel Millett's group suffered from a lack of weapons at the beginning, Guillot had the opposite problem. In his drop area he found six men—and four machine guns and three bazookas. So few men could not use these weapons, so they hid them under trees and moved out. Guillot stopped at the first French farmhouse to ask his position. The door was slammed in his face. At the second he learned that they were on the edge of Beuzeville. Soon they encountered another 30 men and 2 officers; then more men came in, some from 101st Division's drops. Lieutenant Edgar Abbott was sent to recover the hidden weapons, and with these they moved up and joined another group, led by Captain Jonathan Adams, who took command. On the main road from Ste. Sauveur de Bicombe, they suddenly ran into a

German position, and the first volley killed three Americans and wounded one.

They drew back, and Guillot and a sergeant moved into an apple orchard. They came to a farmhouse and went in to check it. It was empty, but a few minutes later a group of Germans entered the house by another door. Guillot and the sergeant worked their way up to the attic and hid. They heard the clattering of dishes below. Finally that night they heard snoring. If they were ever going to get out alive, this was the time. The two men crept down into the kitchen, Guillot leading with his tommy gun ready. But he did not fire. He squinted around the room. Two men were sleeping on the floor. He took out his trench knife, and moved to one, and cut his throat, and then cut the other's throat. As the Germans died, he sprang out the door, followed by the sergeant. Soon they found Adams's force. Germans were all around them, but they were in touch with the regimental command post by radio. They told regiment they would try to reach their assigned position at Hill 30. But they were pinned down in the farm field all night.

Captain Adams sent out patrols to break through and take plasma to Colonel Shanley's men, who were stuck on Hill 30. They had plenty of plasma because they had picked up a medical team, led by two doctors, Captain E.L. Axelrod and Captain John Thornquist. Three men, Lieutenant Murray, Corporal Fred Green, and Private Frank Circelli set out at 9:30 A.M. with plasma for Colonel Shanley. They moved 500 yards and then ran into a German ambush. Murray was killed. Circelli was wounded in four places but staggered back to tell Captain Adams what had happened. Green hid in the field and stayed put. For 11 days he was behind the German lines.

The Germans kept sending patrols against the Adams force, and the Americans kept fighting them off. The radio went dead, but on D+3 they had been told they would be relieved next day. No one came. A French family was still living in the farm buildings. On D+4 the farmer's wife came to the Americans and told them the Germans had left, taking her husband to be shot for helping "the enemy," and they could have everything she had. She gave them milk, chickens, rabbits, and a cow to kill.

They were just beginning to enjoy life when, on D + 5, they were rescued.

When the gliders came in, they ran into trouble. The first glider, named *The Fighting Falcon,* was piloted by Lieutenant Colonel Michael Murphy. In the copilot's seat was Brigadier General Donald Pratt, assistant division commander of the 101st Airborne. Pratt had wanted to parachute in, but General Taylor had assigned him to bring the second echelon of 101st troops, who would move across the channel by ship. Then, because of the poor morale of the glider troops, higher command had decided that a general officer should lead the way. General Pratt was chosen. The idea of flying in a glider—"a sitting duck"—appealed to him so little that he had arranged to have armor plate fitted under his copilot's seat.

As the gliders came in over the coast, the German antiaircraft fire began. The planes lurched and twisted on the approach from the east to the landing zone. Soon, as the lights set up by the pathfinders at Hiesville appeared in the fields below, the ropes were released. The gliders began to come down, many of them outside the zone, some released at too high a speed by frightened tow-plane pilots. Colonel Murphy's *No. 1,* with the Screaming Eagle insignia of the 101st on its side, lived up to its name; it came screaming in at over 100 miles an hour, overshot the field, and smashed into a hedgerow. The glider was destroyed. Murphy was thrown out, both legs broken. General Pratt's head was smashed by the steel tubing in the top of the cockpit, and he died immediately.

Other gliders came into the stake-and-wire traps. Wings broke off, many gliders smashed, some 57 mm. guns broke up, some men were killed. Radio equipment was lost, including the big SCR 499 radio for the 101st Division command post, which was supposed to keep army headquarters informed of the division's progress. The SCR 499 was aboard a glider whose tow rope parted just four miles from the airbase at Aldermaston. The equipment was picked up and loaded aboard another glider for a later landing, but during the critical early hours of invasion the 101st was out of touch with higher command.

Approaching the landing zones, pilots became disoriented, and

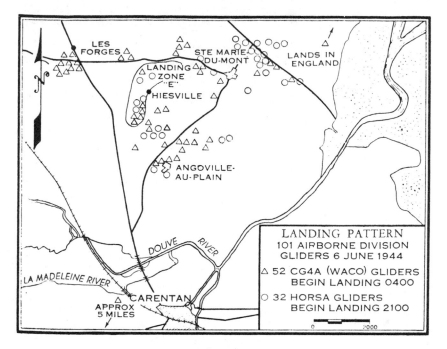

LES
FORGES
STE MARIE-
DU-MONT
LANDS IN
ENGLAND
LANDING
ZONE
"E"
HIESVILLE
ANGOVILLE-
AU-PLAIN
DOUVE RIVER
LA MADELEINE RIVER
CARENTAN
APPROX
5 MILES

LANDING PATTERN
101 AIRBORNE DIVISION
GLIDERS 6 JUNE 1944

△ 52 CG4A (WACO) GLIDERS
BEGIN LANDING 0400

○ 32 HORSA GLIDERS
BEGIN LANDING 2100

0   2000

MAP 6

and gliders began to scatter. The high altitude photos had not indicated that the hedges on the film were really rows of trees 40 feet high. The trees began to take off glider wings.

Only six gliders landed in the proper zone, although most of them managed to get near it. But the gliders that got down without total disaster brought jeeps, antitank guns, and soldiers to join the paratroopers.

The 82nd Airborne's gliders carried part of the divisional staff, a signal detachment, two antiaircraft batteries, and jeeps, trailers, 57 mm. antitank guns, and ten tons of other equipment. In the clouds seven gliders broke away from their tows, and half a dozen gliders were shot down. Of 52 gliders, 37 reached the Landing Zone West, but not all pilots knew it; the Pathfinders' flaming T was not functioning. The landings were mostly outside the zone, and all but a dozen gliders were badly smashed. For all this, the number of casualties was remarkably light: 3 men killed and 23 wounded.

As the gliders came down, the paratroopers rushed forward to help—and to get those guns. The airborne artillery was in action long before artillery hit the beaches from the seaborne invasion.

No more airborne missions were flown during D day until late evening. Reinforcing the 101st Airborne came the first group of 32 Horsa gliders, with medics, vehicles, guns, and ammunition. Most of them got down into Landing Zone East without incident. The next mission carried reinforcements for the 82nd. The first half of that mission consisted of 76 gliders. Two hours later another hundred gliders set out. More jeeps, more 57 mm. guns, more ammunition, food, and equipment began coming in. This time, unlike in the first air drops, the airborne men had fighter protection. Some of the 82nd's gliders in error went into Zone East instead of Zone West, but most got down safely.

Safely was a debatable word, particularly in the 82nd's sector. During the afternoon troops of the U.S. 8th Infantry had landed on the invasion beach and driven the enemy from the southern part of landing Zone West. Colonel Edson Raff, who had come in by sea, brought units of the 82nd to push the Germans out of the drop zone. But the Germans still held the northern quarter of Drop Zone West that night. And the whole perimeter was a no-man's-land patrolled by elements from both armies and haunted by snipers, mortars, and one German 88 mm. gun that was operating near Fauville. Later, as the gliders continued to come in, the situation grew much worse.

As the first day wore on, the units of the 101st began to organize. By midnight General Taylor could account for half his force, although some units were scattered. The 501st, except for 3rd Battalion, was out of touch. The 502nd was holding a number of strong points with small numbers of men. Some of the men who were supposed to be with the 506th were with the 502nd, and so were 85 men of the 377th Parachute Field Artillery Battalion—with only one gun. Their other 11 guns had been lost.

The 101st Airborne managed to take most of its objectives quickly. St. Martin de Varreville fell, and then Pouppeville. Within a matter of hours the way was cleared for the troops from Utah beach to move inland. There still was the one catch: From Pouppeville all the way to Crisbecq, the ground behind the beaches had been flooded by the enemy; but this was not as dangerous as it might have been, since most German resistance in the 101st's area had been reduced to pockets.

This was a sharp contrast to the dispersion of the troops of the 82nd. About all that went according to plan for the 82nd was the capture of St. Mère Eglise: A quarter of the men of the 3rd Battalion managed to find each other in the darkness and captured that important crossroads before dawn on D day; and here General Ridgway set up his command post.

On the second day the scattering and the inability of the division to form up worried General Ridgway. On D+3 he estimated that he still controlled only 2,100 men, consisting of parts of the 507th and 508th Regiments. The basic problems preventing linkings were the flooding and the unluckiness of drops that brought these units down close to the assembly point of the German 91st Division.

As far as doctrine went, the 505th Parachute Infantry Regiment had the most successful drop. The 1st Battalion managed to organize within a few minutes and launch an attack, as ordered, on La Fiere bridge. Major Frederick Kellam led the attack until he was killed; then Major James McGinity, his executive officer, was there to take over.

General Gavin's experience was an indication of the confusion that reigned elsewhere. After Gavin dropped, he found himself in an orchard, where he ran into that flooded marshland no one had known about. It had all appeared on the aerial photos to be lush meadow. Soon aides had rounded up 40 men, and Gavin saw the red and green lights of the assembly points for the 507th and 508th, across the swamp. He sent Captain Hugo Olson to make contact and find out where they were. Olson returned to report that the water in the swamp was shoulder deep, but that on the other side he had found a railroad. Gavin looked at his map. They had dropped two miles north of the objective at La Fiere. The whole drop had been fouled up.

Gavin tried to organize the troops of the 507th, but with a hundred troopers he was not able to accomplish much. He led them to the railroad embankment and they started down the track for La Fiere.

They drew heavy fire from an island in the Merderet river, and finally Gavin set up his command post at a point where a road crossed the railroad, a few miles from Ste. Mère Eglise. Next day

General Ridgway came to the command post. At this point the division was still out of contact with army headquarters and had seen no sign of troops from the beachheads. Ridgway was not even certain the amphibious landings had ever made the beach. The division controlled Ste. Mère Eglise and had units spread out in all directions around it, but few of them were capable of repelling a strong attack, and none had expected to have to fight for more than a day without reinforcements.

The 2nd Battalion of the 505th was to occupy Neville au Plain, five miles north of Ste. Mère Eglise. But 2nd battalion was called to the defense of Ste. Mère Eglise when the Germans counterattacked, and so only one officer, Lieutenant Turner B. Turnbull, and 44 men were sent to take Neville au Plain. They did, and organized a defense point on high ground to the north, but were soon attacked by a whole German column and fought all day long. They held off the Germans and stopped the drive against Ste. Mère Eglise, but of the 44 troopers only 16 survived. That night they had to withdraw. Next morning the Germans resumed their move southward again against St. Mère Eglise; but in the nick of time troops from Utah beach showed up, and Ridgway was able to get in touch with General Lawton Collins, who sent a task force from the 704th Tank Battalion to reinforce the town. It had been a very narrow margin of success.

During D + 1, the gliders kept coming in, reinforcing the paratroops with men and weapons. Many of them still landed outside their zones, particularly in the 82nd area, because the disorganization of the division meant many of the markers were never put out. Still, jeeps, trailers with ammunition, and guns began to move along the roads even before the amphibious forces were able to help. Troops of the 325th and 401st Glider Regiments began to join the action. The 325th landed well, 90 percent of the regiment was ready to fight, and all its battalions soon reported in and moved to Chef du Pont, where the Germans had already evacuated. The 325th's action on D + 2 was a mission to ford the Merderet north of La Fiere bridge. The troopers ran into a hornet's nest—a superior force of Germans on the other side who drove them back.

The 82nd Airborne won its first Congressional Medal of Honor that day: As the Germans counterattacked the troops on the edge of the water, Private, First Class, Charles DeGlopper of the 325th stood up in plain sight with his automatic rifle and kept the Germans down so his comrades could fall back in order. He was killed by a sniper, but he had saved a hundred lives.

That day the troops from the beachhead began to pour into the area and to mop up the Germans, who had been nearly as fragmented south of Ste. Mère Eglise as the Americans. The airborne troops continued in action that was stubborn because of the hedgerows. The Germans had to be routed out, one by one, for each hedgerow might surround a field that had been turned into a miniature fortress. This was pure infantry warfare, and the airborne men could fight that sort of war too. They did, for 33 days, until July 8, when they were relieved for reorganization and rest.

Normandy, as it turned out, provided ammunition for the supporters of airborne operations—and for their detractors. The airborne troops had accomplished their mission. They had created a diversion—even more than expected in the case of the 82nd, because of the wide area over which the troops were scattered. They had captured the key points assigned to them and opened the way for the troops from the beaches. But they had done this raggedly; and they had not been able to function as divisions until one full day after landing, in the case of the 101st, and two full days, in the case of the 82nd. The degree of success was, in spite of General Gavin's criticism of several elements of his own division, due almost entirely to the will of the troopers to fight. They lost most of their heavy equipment, they were often reduced to the basic infantry tools of rifle and grenade.

Many holes in plans, training, and equipment appeared in the Normandy operations. The British plywood Horsa gliders were found to fracture and break up on landing. For example, the last glider mission of Operation Neptune (Normandy airborne operation) utilized 30 Horsas and 20 Wacos to carry troops of the 325th and 401st Glider Infantry Regiments. They landed in the same sort of terrain, and 16 of the Horsas were destroyed and 10 damaged in the landing while 15 soldiers were killed and 59 injured. Aboard the Wacos only four gliders were destroyed and 10 damaged, without injury to the troops.

The troop carrier pilots performed generally according to the intensity of their training. Some, when faced with heavy anti-aircraft fire, began to climb and raised their speed for the drops to 150 miles an hour, which guaranteed injury to troops and destruction of matériel. The lack of any direct air support hampered the forces faced by German armor.

The airborne men said they needed armor, at least light tanks. They needed more riflemen in the rifle companies, more engineers, and more artillery. Still, in the final analysis, the airborne divisions had proved themselves enough to warrant their retention and that was the important matter.

The war in the Southwest Pacific had proceeded slowly, largely because the bulk of matériel was going to Europe and to Admiral Nimitz' Central Pacific forces in 1942 and 1943. Thus General MacArthur could not move as he wished to do. But moving slowly, by the spring of 1944, MacArthur had control of Papua, the British half of New Guinea, the Admiralty Islands, and western New Britain. He was ready to attack the Japanese in Dutch New Guinea. The area he chose was called Hollandia, after a village on Humboldt Bay, which was more or less the center of the region. The Japanese resisted every foot of the way, but by May they had retreated, and Americans at home were reading about such strange places as Wakde and Sarmi and the Kumamba Islands, all points off the coast of Dutch New Guinea, which had become important in the war. The reason, of course, was not very complex: MacArthur had a dream—an obsession some called it—of returning to the Philippines to redeem the pledge he had made when driven out by the Japanese. His famous "I shall return" statement was regarded by the Japanese at the outset as braggadocio. It was important as much politically as militarily that the general live up to the promise. The Dutch East Indies were important because they supplied Japan with the petroleum necessary to oil her war machine. They were also important, because New Guinea controlled communications between Australia and the Philippines, and New Guinea was a point close enough to the Philippines for the launching of an invasion.

Much of this warfare on land was conducted in the jungles. Paratroops would have been of little advantage here, the concentrations of the enemy were too diffuse. But the paratroops were considered for various actions in the early months of 1944, and although for various reasons they were not employed in the winter and spring, there would be a time when they would go into action.

Japanese and Jungle Rot

While the airborne question was occupying the attention of Washington and the generals in Europe were talking about formation of an airborne army, in the Pacific, with little attention and less glamour, the 503rd Parachute Infantry Regiment was slogging away at tiresome, dangerous, dirty jobs.

There were some lighter moments, as when Company A's Technician, Fourth Grade, Tsigonis was presented with his Purple Heart and it was discovered that he had actually been lightly wounded by Lieutenant Fife—"dead-eyed Louie," they called him—who had mistaken Tsigonis for a Japanese on that night at Nadzab, on New Guinea. But there were moments of tragedy, as when they buried Colonel Kinsler, killed not in battle but in an accident.

The autumn of 1943 had been devoted to training and infantry problems: night marches, jumps, marksmanship. In November the rumor had it they were scheduled for a drop mission onto New Britain Island. The men were eager, ready to go again. The plan fell through, just at Christmas, and dampened that day for them in spite of the turkey and all the trimmings.

"Won't we ever jump again?" That was the question that went around the regiment.

New Year's brought celebrations, in spite of the price of black-market whiskey ($40 a bottle). In January it was back to training again, with emphasis on jungle and survival. Men from the Kansas prairie began to consider the jungle a part of their life. The regiment was shipped to Cairns, North Queensland, on January 25, but was moved immediately to Brisbane, where they took over the old 32nd Division's Camp Cable, all set up for them. For two months the men luxuriated in camp life; training was only for replacements. They stuffed on ice cream, drank Coca-Cola, and had plenty of beer. There were three-day passes and furloughs to Newcastle, which meant whiskey and girls.

All that came to an end on April 5, when the regiment shipped out in army transports; where, nobody knew. Some said Hawaii, some said China.

The ships took them to Port Moresby, but they did not stop there; the ships went to Milne Bay, New Guinea, but they did not disembark. Around the corner the ships pulled into Dobadura, New Guinea, and this was the end of the line.

A month went by. It rained, it rained again, and then it poured. Two more weeks went by and it rained some more. Was anything ever going to happen? the men asked.

Then, on the night of May 29, the troopers were issued combat equipment, and before dawn they were moving to the airstrip, Hollandia's Cyclops Airdrome. They were flown to a Dutch coconut plantation, where they strung up jungle hammocks—and waited.

Two more weeks went by. They believed they would fight on Biak, but the mission was called off. On June 14 they moved out, to the Tami river, to patrol against Japanese troops infiltrating from Wewak. They were in action, even if they had not jumped. This was straight infantry work. They patrolled for Japanese stragglers for two weeks. They took some prisoners, killed some enemy troops, and took some casualties. They began to wonder if MacArthur and his generals remembered they were airborne troops.

On June 30 they had the answer. They were issued parachutes and airborne equipment. The maps came out. It would be a jump onto Noemfoor Island (in Netherlands New Guinea), to reinforce the 158th Regimental Combat Team, which was to make a landing on July 2.

The regiment boarded planes just after 6:00 A.M. on July 3. Three hours and 25 minutes later they were approaching the drop zone, which was covered by a smoke screen. The pilots had been a long time in supply missions and had half forgotten the techniques of dropping parachutists. The formations were ragged, and the drop widely scattered. They jumped at 350 feet, and when they came down they found themselves on a shell-pocked coral strip, often landing hard on trucks, amphibious craft, bulldozers, and heavy equipment, some of it Japanese, some of it seaborne matérial that had come in with landing forces. There was no Japanese resistance, but still the regiment suffered 114 casualties, or almost 10 percent, because of the landings.

The 3rd Platoon of Company A was sent on a mission to secure nearby Manim Island. The troopers destroyed one pillbox, and killed eight Japanese soldiers. That was all the enemy there was. They had one casualty: Private Corley was shot through the face. The island was secure.

On Noemfoor the Japanese were harder to rout out. They had moved inland on D day, and the paratroopers had to find them. The patrols went out day and night. At night they used sign and countersign.

"Linger" was the sign.

"Longer" was the response.

Anyone who shouted "Linger" and then heard the response "Ronger" got his head down and his gun up.

The regiment took casualties. Private Dundas and Private Lanier were killed at Manaquari. Then E company's Private Anker was killed, and Finsterwald and Toupal. Every unit suffered, but for every American casualty there were 20 Japanese, as the stragglers were wiped out.

Sometimes the fighting was as fierce as that of the night of July 23, when a platoon of Company D ran into a superior Japanese force in the jungle. Lieutenant Arthur C. Vandivort crawled forward to direct the platoon and signaled them the movements of the enemy until he was shot by a sniper. Lieutenant Long's platoon was pinned down by machine-gun fire until he took a squad forward.

"Come on, men," he shouted. "There are just a few Japs up there. Let's get them."

The lieutenant moved out, and the men followed and overran the Japanese position. Lieutenant Long was killed, but the Americans counted 23 enemy dead.

Sergeant Ray Eubanks led a squad up a ridge deep in the jungle. They were stopped by Japanese fire. Eubanks took over the BAR (automatic rifle) and laid down a steady fire on the enemy until a bullet smashed the BAR and blew off his right forefinger. Another bullet caught him in the body. He ran forward and clubbed four Japanese soldiers to death with the butt of the BAR before he was shot down. When the others came up, they found 19 dead Japanese soldiers lying around him.

The end of August saw the end of action, and the 503rd went into camp six miles from the Kaniri Aerodrome. It was training again. The real training program was for the troop carrier pilots, who had to re-establish the old skills of airborne drop. With the movement into the Philippines that fall of 1944, it seemed likely the paratroopers would play an even more important role, and it was time to get ready.

Originally, the military planners in London had considered the invasion of France simultaneously in the north, across the English Channel, and from the south. The idea was attractive because it would force the Germans to split their defenses. But when it came down to actual operational planning in the spring of 1944, General Eisenhower discovered that even the United States' vaunted capacity to produce was strained by the two-ocean war and that it would be impossible to make a broad landing at Normandy and invade southern France at the same time. The vehicles and the ships were simply not available.

So Normandy and June 6 were the solutions, but the idea of the southern invasion, having been born, continued to have a life of its own, even after the idea was outmoded. A little later in the year it was to come to be, although some generals, particularly British, could never figure out quite why. Indeed, some histories of the war, telling the tale in sweeping terms, have not mentioned the invasion of the south of France at all! But the paratroops were to play a vital role in the operation, for whatever impact it had on the total picture. And glider troops—and the Nisei 442nd Regimental Combat Team from Hawaii suddenly found themselves glider troops—were also to play their part.

The War on the Gold Coast

When the Allied commanders had put in motion the plans for the second front in Normandy, General Eisenhower had wanted a third front, to threaten the German army in the south of France. The British had argued against it, and when it got down to details, there were not enough troops and planes and naval craft to make the effort at the same time that the Normandy invasion was launched.

But Eisenhower was insistent that a diversion be made to draw off some German military forces from the north. Major General Robert T. Frederick was put in command of what was called The First Airborne Task Force, with headquarters in Italy. The troops would be 10,000 American and British airborne soldiers. The British were the 2nd Parachute Brigade Group. The Americans were the 517th Combat Team, the 509th Battalion, the 1st batallion of the 551st Parachute Infantry, the 463rd Parachute Field Artillery, and the 550th Glider Infantry Battalion.

The whole was as hastily assembled as the name of the organization indicated. It was, in fact, a provisional airborne division, with very little unity of command, but in this instance the independence of various airborne regiments and combat teams would prove to be a distinct advantage.

The weak point was the glider operation. An Airborne Training Center was established at Rome, and there the glidermen learned their roles and practiced with troop carrier units. There was no time for dress rehearsals, but a course was established for the troop carrier planes. One of the units to become glider troops on short notice was the 442nd Combat Team, the Nisei organization from Hawaii which had so distinguished itself in the Italian campaign.

The first part of the mission consisted of a diversion to try to fool the Germans. Six planes took off from Italian fields and headed for Toulon. On the way the crewmen dropped window-long strips of aluminum foil that activated the German radar and indicated a large aerial force moving in. A false drop zone had been established northwest of Toulon, and the planes came in to drop 600 parachute dummies with electronic sound effects that would, for a time, simulate the noise of battle.

Meanwhile three teams of pathfinders of the real mission were in the air, to mark the drop zones and the landing zones for the airborne troops.

Behind them came nearly 400 planes, which had taken off from ten Italian airfields, carrying paratroopers or towing Waco or Horsa gliders.

From the beginning the drop showed that the paratroopers and their troop carrier pilots needed more practice and better communications. Only one pathfinder team made its drop zone. That meant there was, for practical purposes, no guidance in two-thirds of the drops and landings.

Yet these airborne landings were a vast improvement over Normandy. The diversionary effect of the false drop undoubtedly had something to do with the success. So did the guidance the planes received from shore stations and from naval vessels. Only one American heavy cruiser fired on them (unlike the barrage that had been laid up in Sicily). The enemy did not seem to suspect they were coming. And the pilots brought their planes in formation to the French coast and inland, with scarcely a hitch. There were difficulties in two zones because of the failure of the pathfinders, but the whole landing was by far the most successful ever undertaken by airborne units. Some parachutists missed their drop zones by 20 miles, which put them out of the main action, but more than half hit the drop zones. And even those who missed proved valuable to the common effort. As always, their presence confused the enemy. Further, most of them made contact with French Resistance forces and operated with them until they had a chance to return to the Allied lines.

The paratroopers had been hampered by haze and a developing overcast. By 9:00 A.M., when the gliders began moving in, the overcast had grown much heavier. A few gliders released prematurely (four crews were rescued by the navy), but most of the pilots proved cool and competent and put their gliders down very well. The Germans had put up *Rommelspargel* but without the enthusiasm shown by the Normandy defenders. Consequently, the poles and wires were so far apart that even in the landing zones they did not seriously hinder operations. The mines that were supposed to be triggered by the wires were not fused.

There were some errors and some tragedies. A planeload of paratroopers was dropped into the sea, and all drowned. One serial dropped its paratroops into the town of St. Tropez, which was crawling with Germans. Some of the tow plane pilots forgot the limitations of their tows. One pilot kept advancing his throttle until the horrified glider pilot behind him saw the airspeed indicator inching up above 150 mph—the "redline" mark, above which the glider was subject to such structural stress that it might break up. The glider pilot, Flight Officer Willie Haynes, looked off to his left and saw another glider break up in midair—the excessive speed had destroyed the wing. The glider went into the sea. There were no parachutes; Hayne could not release his glider from the tow. He spoke into his microphone to the pilot towing his glider.

"Listen, you son of a bitch, I'll give you til I count ten to slow this thing down and then I'm going to shoot your goddam right engine out."

"One, two. . . ."

Before Flight Officer Haynes reached the count of eight, the speed dropped below the red line.

Once the troops hit the ground, resistance was relatively light. They had come into an area where many of the troops were on rest from the Eastern front. They had to fight into Le Muy, but by 6:00 P.M. on D day they had taken La Mitan, La Motte, and Les Serres, and cut the roads from these points to the invasion coast. The enemy would have a hard time pushing reserves down toward the beaches. On D + 1 the 45th Division pushed inland and linked up.

Those troops who jumped on the wrong signal and landed in St. Tropez found the Germans more surprised than they. They moved fast and captured an antiaircraft battery, two coastal defense guns, and a garrison of 240 Germans. When the 3rd Division came probing into St. Tropez on the afternoon of D+1, the troopers greeted them, bottles in hand, and asked them to join the party.

The pressure was extreme by the airborne men to create an airborne army and then use it. The contention was that the airborne could make it possible to play leapfrog with the Germans: drop behind their lines, surge forward in front and concentrate in the drop area, and then, when all was consolidated, repeat the procedure. It sounded good, but the traditional generals were suspicious. They remembered how the 82nd Airborne had been so diffused in the Normandy drop that it had failed to capture several of its objectives, and how the 101st had failed to take some of its assigned bridges for the same reasons. The airborne answer was that the troops needed better weapons, bigger artillery, and more of it, and that in the airborne army concept this was included.

When Field Marshal Montgomery bogged down in northeast France and Belgium, and yet by a fluke the Allies managed to capture Antwerp, a chance came that seemed to welcome employment of the airborne army. Montgomery wanted to cross the Rhine over the Dutch bridge at Arnhem. The trouble was that he had two other major rivers to cross before he could get to Arnhem: the Meuse, or Maas as the Dutch call it, at Grave, and the Waal at Nijmegen. Montgomery wanted his 30 Corps to drive straight on through, but this seemed impossible because of the major bridges that must be crossed. Obviously, if the Germans could see what Montgomery planned, they would blow up the bridges, and the 30 Corps would be stopped somewhere. The answer was to seize these bridges swiftly as the operation started and the Germans did not know the objective. Paratroops were the logical choice for such a task. They would drop in the important areas in force and hold those bridges. The 30 Corps would then start from Belgium and drive right on up to the Zuider Zee. The result would be to cut off the German Sixteenth Army, which had already been isolated in the Pas de Calais area. Having crossed the Rhine, Field Marshal Montgomery would be in a position to drive down the east bank and seize the important steel producing cities of the Ruhr, located just along that river.

It all depended on the use of the roads and the bridges, for this was marsh and canal country. Control of bridges depended on surprise and tenacity. It was a big job, involving three large areas of land in two countries. The airborne army concept could certainly be tested here.

The Heart
of the Enemy

In the summer of 1944 General Eisenhower decided to create the First Allied Airborne Army. Immediately he ran into political flak, which included such abstruse problems as whether the move would affect the British chain of command. It seemed a good idea to put an Air Force general in command, since the basic problem was still coordination between troop carrier units and the airborne troops. Lieutenant General Lewis H. Brereton was chosen for the task and taken from the Ninth Air Force. He was enthusiastic about the job, because he was one of Billy Mitchell's boys and had been in the planning of that putative airborne strike in World War I.

In the change of organization General Ridgway was moved up to command the XVIII Corps (Airborne), and General Gavin succeeded him as commander of the 82nd Airborne Division. Also in the force were the 101st Airborne Division, the 17th, and British airborne troops. The planes would be flown by IX Troop Carrier Command and whatever RAF units might be available. That summer very few planes of any sort were available; the invasion of southern France and airdrop missions in France occupied most of the troop carrier planes, and the airborne troops did not even have C-47s available for training missions.

The trouble was caused by too much success. General George Patton was given command of the U.S. Third Army, and on August 1 he began to move. He pushed that army through Brittany to the Loire and began the encirclement of the Germans. He moved until he was stopped by Eisenhower for political reasons. Patton had reached Argentan, and he wanted to drive toward

Caen, where British Field Marshal Montgomery was operating lackadaisically.

". . . let me go on to Falaise and we will drive the British back into the sea for another Dunkirk . . ."

Eisenhower, the great placator, did not share his junior general's distaste for their Allies, and he stopped Patton and saved Montgomery's face—although some said that by so doing Eisenhower lengthened the war by many months.

All this while, IX Troop Carrier Command was called on to supply Patton and other forward elements by airdrop and forward landing. The planes carried gasoline in five-gallon jerry cans, they dropped supplies, they carried replacement troops, and they brought out casualties.

At this stage, however, it was Montgomery who made the proposal that brought the airborne troops back into action. He suggested that the airborne troops be sent into Holland in his sector, and then his British Second Army would follow.

The idea appealed to Eisenhower for several reasons. It was bold, involving the drop of troops nearly 70 miles inside the enemy lines. Intelligence reports indicated the German army in this area was fragmented by the need to send extra troops against Patton. Eisenhower was in trouble with Generals Marshall and Arnold back home for not being aggressive enough, and the British in London were seriously worried about the V-2 flying bombs that were being launched just then in Holland. The airborne mission could roll all these problems up into one victory. It would employ the 101st Airborne, the 82nd, and the British 1st Airborne Division. The 101st would capture the southern bridges around Eindhoven. The 82nd would take Nijmegen. The British would capture Arnhem.

In the American sector two points were most important: the high ground near Nijmegen—the highest ground in Holland, which must be wrested from the enemy's hands; and the Nijmegen bridge, across the Rhine river. That was not to say that other bridges were not vital. General Gavin was particularly aware of the need to seize them intact; he blamed himself for the heavy casualties and ineffectiveness of the 507th Parachute Infantry Regiment at Normandy, because he had not seized bridges that would have let the units of the division draw together quickly to present a united front.

The most important of these points was the Nijmegen bridge. Gavin assigned Colonel Roy Lindquist of the 508th Parachute Infantry Regiment to its capture. Lindquist was to commit his 1st Battalion to that purpose. But he also was to watch for the mans to react and drive from the Reichswald, on the right of the Maas river, up the main highway to Mook, Molenhoek, and Nijmegen by way of the flat ground east of the city.

The operation began in daylight on September 17, 1944. First off were the pathfinders from 101st Airborne Division. One C-47 was shot down over Belgium, and part of the 101st pathfinder section was lost. Only four parachutes emerged from the plane, and they were far from the zone. But they had been assigned Drop Zone A, and the second plane in that serial came in on target. A few minutes later the homing radio was assembled and in operation, and the letters T and A were set out on the ground, burning. The pathfinders for Drop Zones B and C jumped and within four minutes had their equipment working. When the troops of the 101st came in just before 1:00 P.M., they made successful landings. There was little opposition.

The 82nd pathfinders were equally effective. One group was to drop near Grave. The Germans put up heavy antiaircraft fire, but for this mission the airborne troops had air cover, and Allied fighters moved in to neutralize the guns. Both pathfinder teams assigned to Drop Zone O made successful landings. So did those at N, where the 505th would land, and T, where the 508th would drop.

The parachute troops dropped, came down, and began to assemble. Soon the gliders brought in headquarters elements, glider troops, and supplies. In mid-afternoon hundreds of gliders were in the air above this section of Holland. The 101st was flying the southern route, and it took 500 C-47s to deliver the parachute troops and the 70 gliders of the first wave. The German flak brought down 16 troop carrier planes, most of them after their parachutists had jumped or they had released their gliders. The reason was easy enough to see: This time the pilots held their courses and their speed, and at 100 miles an hour were, indeed, "sitting ducks" for the gunners.

If there had been serious criticism of the C-47 pilots in the past, it was erased this day. Most of the planes and pilots lost were the victims of enemy fire that hit them because the men were doing their jobs as ordered. One C-47 began to flame a few seconds before reaching the drop zone.

"Don't worry about me," the pilot told his flight leader. "I'm going to drop these troops in the DZ."

He did, and the plane crashed in flames almost immediately. There were no pilots' parachutes.

Another C-47 pilot heading for the drop zone was warned that shrapnel had torn up his right wing tanks and the gasoline was streaming out. He refused to turn back and seek an emergency airfield behind Allied lines. He made the drop right down the middle of the DZ, but he never got back to England.

This time 80 percent of the 101st's men landed safely in the proper zones. They scrambled free from parachutes and gliders— many of them shattered—and began to move to secure their bridges.

Colonel Sink's 506th Parachute Infantry Regiment came down in Drop Zone C, and the men were quickly organized into units of 15 or 20. First Battalion had the task of taking the bridges over the Wilhelmina Canal at Zon. Then the rest of the regiment was to move through the 1st Battalion and capture Eindhoven and its bridges over the Dommel river.

Within 45 minutes Major James LaPrade had 1st Battalion on its way, General Taylor with him. Meanwhile 2nd and 3rd Battalions were organizing on the ground, and gliders were coming in.

Colonel Sink remembered that as they came in, he had seen several tanks near Wolfswinkel, quite close to the drop zone. He was about to dispatch a patrol to investigate when American fighters came in low, saw the tanks, and knocked them out with .50 caliber machine guns and 75 mm. cannon.

Second Battalion started out for Zon. There was no opposition until the scouts reached the outskirts; then they were fired on by an 88 mm. gun. Private Thomas Lindsey knocked the gun out with one round from his bazooka, killing one German. Six others ran for the bridge, but Sergeant John Rice killed them with a tommy gun.

Second Battalion moved on. By this time they should have come through 1st Battalion, but LaPrade's men were nowhere to be seen. They had encountered a batch of 88s firing shrapnel and had been pinned down, taking many casualties. The net result was that the Germans had a little time to act, and as Colonel Sink reached a point 75 yards from a Zon bridge, it went up with a roar. The first objective had been missed, through no one's fault.

The leading elements of the regiment crossed the canal by swimming and by rowboat, but the engineers would have to re-build the bridge. The main pillar was undamaged, so the rebuild-ing should not take too long. Up came the engineers of the 326th Airborne Engineer Battalion, and in an hour and a half they had put a footbridge across the canal.

Two smaller wooden bridges had been blown two days earlier by the Germans. The footbridge was not strong enough to take many men at a time, so the progress of the regiment was badly delayed. It was midnight before the last man crossed.

Colonel Sink was supposed to press on to Eindhoven to make way for the British 30 Corps. He was also supposed to have Eindhoven under control that night. But the British had run into the same sort of trouble that the Americans had encountered and were only halfway to Eindhoven by evening. The capture of Eindhoven, they said, would have to wait until $D + 1$.

The 501st Parachute Infantry Regiment's mission was to se-cure four rail and highway bridges over the Aa river, and the Zuid Willems Vaart Canal at Vechel. First Battalion came down three miles northwest of the target, but the other two battalions landed in proper order. Within 45 minutes 3rd Battalion seized the town of Eerde and blocked the Vechel-St.Oedenrode highway, as planned. Second Battalion moved on Vechel. There was little opposition, and when the troopers came into the town some found it hard to remember there was a war on. Dutch people thronged around them, offering everything from chocolate to Genever gin.

They learned soon enough that the Germans were still in Holland. Moving out of the drop zone, the battalion had left a detail of 46 men, under Captain W. C. Burd, to guard supplies and take care of eight drop casualties. Burd was to wait for transportation to bring the men up. But after the battalion moved on, a large party of Germans appeared and began firing on the detachment. Captain Burd retreated to the shelter of a stone building. He sent a messenger off to Battalion headquarters, and Lieutenant Colonel Harry Kinnard asked Regiment for permission to send a company in relief. But Colonel Howard Johnson, the regimental commander, did not believe he could spare so many men. He let Kinnard send a platoon. That night the platoon moved back toward the drop zone for the rescue but was stopped 800 yards from the objective. At dawn it became apparent that the Germans had so large a force here that the platoon had to be either supported or pulled back. Regiment said pull back; Captain Burd and his detachment were captured.

First Battalion was ordered to take St. Oedenrode, a major junction point for German supply. After the drop Lieutenant Colonel Patrick Cassidy led the men north of the town and around the flank. Company B found a highway bridge near the town that had not been mentioned in the orders—and just in time; the troopers also met a German squad advancing to blow the bridge. A bazookaman put one round into the middle of the crowd. It hit the explosives and the whole German squad went up, satisfyingly, in little pieces. Company B routed one more German unit, and then St. Oedenrode was in 101st Division hands.

Third Battalion's Company H had been sent to take rail bridges over the Wilhelmina Canal at Best. These were important, now that the Zon bridges had been blown. Captain Robert E. Jones led the company out to the highway 400 yards of Best and ran into a storm of German resistance.

Shortly after the company arrived, so did 12 more truckloads of German troops, and Jones pulled back into the woods. Lieutenant Edward Wierzbowski took 2nd Platoon and the Engineer Platoon to get and hold the bridges. They set out at dusk, through a tree farm where hundreds of pines were planted in even rows. As they reached the first fire lane in the trees, a machine gun began firing on them. Wierzbowski moved back into the woods to the right, and then his men crawled through all the other fire breaks. They reached the dike at the edge of the canal. There before them was their bridge. It was dark, and rain was pelting them so hard it destroyed visibility. Wierzbowski went forward with one man, Private, First Class, Joe Mann, to reconnoiter. They overshot the bridge and ended up within the patrol area of a German sentry, who turned just as they ducked down. They found themselves pinned here.

When Wierzbowski failed to reappear in half an hour, the men of the company grew nervous. Then Germans suddenly appeared and began throwing their potato-masher grenades. Men scrambled up the dike bank. As they came to the top, they ran into German machine-gun and rifle fire and the American party stampeded for the woods. But this diversion did have the positive effect of freeing Wierzbowski and Mann. They came back, and Wierzbowski found he had 15 men and 3 officers left. He held the position, was reinforced, lost men, and held again. The Company H mission would require half the 101st Airborne Division and a squadron of British tanks to finish the job.

Wierzbowski did not know what strength and determination he faced. As dawn came up on D + 1 he saw his bridge clearly for the first time. It was a single span of concrete, a hundred feet long. Just south of the canal, 20 yards from the bridge, was a German barracks surrounded by dug-in positions. On the other side, 80 yards away, was another German position. Every time Wierzbowski's men moved, they drew fire.

As Wierzbowski watched that morning, Germans straggled into this American position. His men ambushed one party and killed 35 Germans.

At 10:00 they saw a German soldier and a civilian walk up to the far side of the bridge and stand there, talking for 20 minutes. Then, at 11:00, the span shook, a tremendous explosion rent the air, and everyone back on the canal bank ducked as steel and concrete from the bridge began falling all around them. Wierzbowski's objective had just gone up in smoke. Private, First Class, Mann and another paratrooper, Private Hoyle, saw a German 88 mm. dump 100 yards away and took a bazooka out there. The resulting explosion was not as spectacular as that of the bridge, but it was much more satisfying to the Americans. The two men came under attack and killed six Germans, but Mann was hit twice by rifle fire. Private Hoyle took the bazooka forward and knocked out an 88 mm. gun.

With each encounter Wierzbowski's unit grew smaller. In the middle of the morning they were strafed by American P-47s, but without casualties. In the afternoon Lieutenant Watson of the engineers went out to the front of the position and was hit in the abdomen by rifle fire. Private, First Class, James Orvac crawled out and treated him, and Wierzbowski came out and dragged the lieutenant back to the lines.

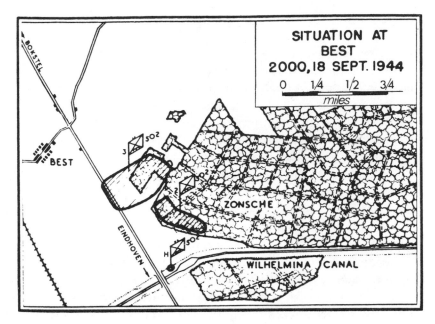

MAP 7

The Germans began shelling them. Private Luther was killed by a fragment. Private Northrup was hit in the spine. Mann got hit twice more and had both his arms in slings.

Wierzbowski was in real trouble, surrounded and running out of medical supplies. Lieutenant Otto Laier and Sergeant Betras tried to break through to get assistance from the company. They were ambushed, and Lieutenant Laier was wounded and captured. Betras made it back.

Late in the day it seemed their troubles were over when a British armored car and a reconnaissance car appeared on the other side of the canal. The Germans fired, and the British moved around behind a building for cover and then blazed away with their machine guns. The Germans quieted down. Corporal Daniel Corman found a small boat on the bank of the canal and rowed across, met the British, and secured a first-aid kit—but also the bad news that this was only a patrol. Lieutenant Wierzbowski yelled across the canal at the British to call Division on the radio and ask for help. The car couldn't raise Division, so Wierzbowski decided to take his men to the safety of the armored car. But the British had to be moving, they said. They told him to sit tight: Help would be along soon.

Three privates, Laino, Koller, and Waldt, went out foraging and captured three German medics and a wounded officer. Wierzbowski put the medics to work on the American wounded.

Things again seemed to look up when a patrol from Company E stumbled onto their position and the patrol leader promised to get help. But the message was mixed up at Regiment and no help came until a platoon from Company D showed up, quite by accident, and decided to stay the night. This group was attacked on the flank that night, fled across the canal, and disappeared. Wierzbowski and his men were alone again. The situation looked dark. Lieutenant Watson was in bad shape; Private Northrup was dying from loss of blood and they had no plasma.

In the morning Wierzbowski's group was attacked by the Germans, who came to within 20 feet before Sergeant Betras began throwing grenades. The Germans were throwing them too, and although the Americans tossed out several potato-mashers that had landed in their trench, one blew up in Laino's face, knocking out one eye and blinding the other. Koller was hit in the temple. Mann was sitting against the back of a trench with six other men when he saw a grenade come over and felt it land behind him. Both his arms were bound up from the wounds of the day before.

"Grenade!" Mann yelled, and he lay back and took the explosion with his body.

The grenade blew his back apart. Three other men were wounded by fragments, although none seriously. But Mann was dying, and he knew it.

"My back's gone," he said. A minute later he died. (For this act of gallantry he was posthumously awarded the Congressional Medal of Honor.)

The Germans kept coming until the American supply of grenades was exhausted and only three men were still unhurt. Wierzbowski surrendered. But later in the day, when 2nd Battalion attacked here, Wierzbowski and his men overpowered and captured the Germans who were guarding them and made the Germans prisoners.

At Vechel the 501st's Company E settled down on the night of D day. The defensive perimeter was nicely organized. Or they thought so. But in the middle of the night fog settled in, and a company of Germans moved down the east bank of the canal and attacked. Fighting centered around a warehouse and was so fierce that 7 men were killed and 26 wounded, and it seemed the Germans would overrun the company. But Lieutenant Joseph C. McGregor, though wounded, held off the enemy with a tommy gun until his men managed to establish a new perimeter. He stayed out there in front until he was dragged to safety.

Two other German attacks were launched against Vechel that night but were beaten off. Next morning Colonel Johnson moved 3rd Battalion to Bechel to help, and the situation eased.

On D+1 Colonel Sink started the 506th toward Eindhoven, his major objective. He expected trouble. Eindhoven was sure to house a large nest of Germans, who could be expected to react as swiftly as a swarm of bees.

The regiment's fighting power—that of the whole division— was strengthened that day by the arrival of more than 400 gliders carrying men, ammunition, and even bulldozers. On the morning of D+1, 3rd Battalion led as the 506th began to move. The men did not move far. Only 600 yards out the Americans came under German fire. All the way to the edge of Eindhoven, the battalion fought Germans. On the outskirts it was stopped by fire down the road from German 88s, and the city was full of snipers.

Colonel Sink came up to the stalled battalion. He decided to send 2nd Battalion down an adjoining road to flank the Germans and knock out the two 88s that were holding up 3rd Battalion Lieutenant Russell Hall's platoon was given the job. A Dutchman offered to guide them to the guns, and they took him along with the rifle grenadiers, Privates Homer Smith and Robert Sherwood in front, and tommy gunners Corporal Marion Grodowski, Corporal Willard Sharp, Corporal Robert James, and Private Clarence Shrout right after them.

The guns were located in a block of Dutch houses, and the Americans moved up through backyards and then around to the front. Not a shot was fired until Sergeant George Martin saw a German walking on the street. He shot and missed. Three other

Germans came walking up casually. Lieutenant Hall and Taylor and Borden jumped out, 10 feet behind them, yelling.

The Germans were completely unnerved and offered no resistance to capture.

Riflemen Sherwood and Taylor saw the first 88 at a crossroads, 150 yards away. Taylor fired a clip from his M-1, and then it jammed. He wounded two Germans, but four ducked. The Germans began firing at them with the 88, and the first shell nicked a building just over their heads. Sherwood fired two grenades and Smith fired one. The 88 was hit and quit firing. But a German officer came up to the gun, leading more men. Taylor and the mortar squad began firing. The officer was wounded and ducked into a house. Sherwood sent a grenade after him and the house was silent after that. He did not know it, but his grenade had wounded 10 Germans inside.

When another patrol attacked the second gun, the Germans blew it up with a grenade and tried to run, but those who were not killed were captured. The troops moved all through the town and around it.

Soon the Americans moved into the center of Eindhoven. Colonel Chase, the regimental executive officer, climbed the tall steeple of the Woensel church for a look around. General Taylor came up. Chase reported that the regiment had taken all four bridges over the Dommel river.

"Impossible," said General Taylor. It was too good to be true. He climbed up for a look. There they were, those beautiful bridges. The 101st had taken a major point virtually without fighting for it, and the road was clear for the British 30 Corps when it came up.

At noon those two armored vehicles of the patrol that had given Lieutenant Wierzbowski a brief lift of morale the day before showed up. Six hours later the tanks of the Guards Armoured Division came clanking over the road and pushed through the city, and the next day they moved to St. Oedenrode and to Grave, into the territory assigned to the 82nd Airborne Division. The 101st's mission had been completed.

Trouble
at Nijmegen

The 82nd Airborne had flown over the northern route, which brought them across Dutch islands fortified with German antiaircraft guns and along a flight path near the Reichswald forest, just across the border in Germany. As everyone knew, the area would be heavily fortified. They were, for the first time, striking on the border of Germany proper.

The 82nd's planes and gliders came even closer to the Reichswald forest when they made the turn at Grave. The Germans did not disappoint them. They sent up a barrage; 10 planes were shot down and 118 were hit by flak.

In the drop zone the 504th Parachute Infantry Battalion had a good drop, and the men of 1st Battalion, for example, were on the ground at 1:20 P.M. In Company B only one man was injured: Private, First Class, Henry Hom sprained his shoulder. The drop performance was a great improvement over Normandy, and only one planeload of men dropped north of the drop zone. Their leader, Lieutenant Keating, brought these men in quickly with no harm done.

The men of the 1st Battalion assembled near a windmill and then began moving. One objective assigned to Company B was Bridge 7, a kilometer east of the village of Heuman, which would be used by the British column expected to come up on the way to Nijmegen and Arnhem. The bridge was 300 feet long, and 75 feet of it extended over water.

The men moved in columns of twos, with Private, First Class, Harris Duke and Private, First Class, Herman Wagner out as scouts, 100 yards in the lead.

All told, this group consisted of 95 men. They had 10 light machine guns, 7 BARs, 7 bazookas, and two 60 mm. mortars. They had found plenty of ammunition. Their radios (SCR 300) had burst transmitters in the jump, but they had several smaller ones (SCR 536).

They traveled east along a paved road flanked by two-foot ditches. The land on either side was apple orchards. All went well until 3:00 P.M., when the Americans were greeted by small-arms fire about 100 yards from the bridge. It seemed to be coming from rifles and Schmeisser machine pistols.

Lieutenant William Meerman of 3rd Platoon was up front with his men when the German ambush exploded. Sergeant Laurence Blazzeni was killed. The others dropped as the firing began and then were pinned down on the road, protected only by a slight rise—and then only as long as they did not move.

Second Platoon moved around to the right, where the road dipped down. Lieutenant Marcus led eight men up to the dike on the edge of the river and there set up a light machine-gun to cover the bridge. A second machine gun was established on the road along the dike.

As the Americans moved, machine gun fire began to come from a house on an island in the stream. Technician, Fifth Grade, Larrabee and Private, First Class, Robert Jetton fired four bazooka rounds at the house, but none of them exploded; they probably had been damaged in the airdrop. The men fired four rifle grenades. Two of them exploded.

Lieutenant Marcus decided to cross the bridge. He took a squad to the dike, which was about five meters high. As they clambered up, the American machine guns covered them. They crossed the bridge, but Technician, Fourth Grade, Orie Burnett, the radio operator, was killed on the bridge, and Lieutenant Marcus was wounded and pinned down. The others found refuge in German foxholes on the other side.

Sergeant Jerry Murphy began running across the bridge but was shot down at the far end. The Germans were picking off the officers and noncoms. The privates made it safely, but every time an officer or a sergeant tried to cross, the fire was vicious.

Captain Helgeson sent men from the 1st Platoon up on the dike behind the bridge and occupied more German foxholes. The squad set up a base of fire to cover the crossing of the others. Then Helgeson sent a squad from 3rd Platoon to move forward with a machine gun to fire on the house on the island. A BAR was stationed 25 yards away with the same mission, and Lieutenant Henry Dunavant, the executive officer, was dispatched with two mortars to fire on the house. The combined effort soon had the enemy pinned down, and the troops began moving up onto the bridge.

At 5:00 P.M. Lieutenant Meerman launched an attack on the island, whose buildings consisted of the house and a powerhouse. They moved around behind the powerhouse, but as they emerged at the corner, the Germans began firing. They ducked back.

It seemed to be an impasse. Lieutenant Meerman so reported to Captain Helgeson, who radioed Battalion. There the 1st Battalion commander, Major Harrison, said they had to clear out that enemy resistance before dark.

It couldn't be done, said Helgeson. He would not throw his men away. He would attack at dusk, 7:30. Harrison agreed to that plan, as long as it was before dark.

By 5:00 only three men had made it across the bridge safely. There were several wounded on the other side, and Lieutenant Smith found a boat and took six men and a medic over. The Germans fired at them, but there were no casualties. An hour later Sergeant John Kellog took a patrol out to occupy two houses on the west side of the canal, north of the bridge. They did, and they too began firing on the house on the island.

The shadows grew longer, and at 7:30 darkness began to settle. Lieutenant Meerman led nine men from behind the powerhouse, covered by the tall reeds and the darkness. The Germans began to fire, and all the American positions fired on the house. The enemy apparently could not see any targets, for the firing from the house dropped off.

Meerman's group moved up until the men could throw grenades into the German positions. Private Edward Schultz fired rifle grenades, while others moved up and overran one German machine-gun position in front of the house. Two men with BARs came up, and Sergeant Dustin placed them on the edge of the wood to fire down the path to the house. As the lieutenant and his men approached the house, they overran empty German positions. Near the house they encountered a dugout, occupied. Sergeant Dustin threw one grenade through a window of the house, and another at the entrance to the dugout when he saw a German head come up there. He called on the Germans to surrender.

A boy in civilian clothes came out and said there were two officers, a dozen enlisted men, and five civilians in the dugout. They wanted to surrender but were afraid they would be shot if they came out. Sergeant Dustin went down after them. He found one officer who could speak English and told him to tell his men to surrender. They would not be hurt. In a few minutes the dugout emptied; the Germans came up with their hands in the air. Then Dustin took the officer to the house and repeated the order. More men came out. Altogether they took 40 prisoners.

At 11:00 P.M. the Americans had the house, the powerhouse, and the bridge across the canal, intact.

After Captain Helgeson had committed Lieutenant Meerman and his men to capture of the island house, he took 40 men in three boats across the Waal river. On the north bank they met Major Harrison, who sent them up to capture the north end of the railroad bridge across the Waal.

Lieutenant Smith led an assault squad out at 6:15 that night. They got to within 400 yards of the bridge, when heavy fire came in from the left. The Germans had two machine guns, on the south end of the bridge, firing across the river. It was apparent to Smith that a successful assault was going to take more men.

Captain Helgeson radioed for help. He reached 3rd Platoon. They announced that they were coming.

Meantime Lieutenant Smith was in trouble. Four BARs had jammed. He had one light machine gun and one box of ammunition for it. It was getting dark.

At dusk they saw about 40 men run across the bridge but could not make out their uniforms or helmets. Smith moved up and found a platoon of Americans, sitting, smoking cigarettes. They were lucky; the Germans had retired to a garden up the road. These were men of 3rd Battalion, who had no idea of what was happening here. Smith sent them across the bridge to find their objective and their command post, and Helgeson posted a perimeter defense on the bridge. Soon he was called up to help 3rd Battalion secure a road bridge, and he moved there. At about

1:00 A.M., after the British put six tanks across that bridge, the Americans moved back to the railroad bridge. There they found the Germans had been reinforced and had pushed the Americans off the north end of the bridge. The Germans were preparing to blow up the railroad bridge. Captain Helgeson called for reinforcements from his company, and they came. The Americans began firing from a number of positions, and Helgeson found a member of the Dutch underground who spoke German. The Dutchman moved to the edge of the bridge and called on the Germans to surrender. They did, and the bridge was secured without more fighting.

For three days 1st Battalion held these positions. Early on the morning of September 20, the Germans sent a patrol of 10 Luftwaffe troops into B Company's area to blow up the bridge across the canal, but B Company was alert. One German was killed and nine were captured. On September 20 the Americans were relieved by the Coldstream Guards.

Company E of the 504th Parachute Infrantry Regiment dropped on the south side of the Maas, three quarters of a mile from Velp. Their assigned bridge was formidable: It mounted a flak tower with a 20 mm. gun that could be depressed onto the road. Fire from the tower was heavy, until a bazookaman fired two rounds of ammunition through a vent at the top. The fire stopped then.

The company moved on Grave, where the Germans were established. Slowly they moved ahead. They were stopped at a road junction where the Germans had set up a machine gun. The Americans set up a roadblock and mined the road. A tank came up from the south. The driver seemed to see the disturbance the mines had made in the road: He stopped. The Americans began to train their bazookas. Then someone shouted.

"Don't shoot, it's a British tank."

It wasn't; it was a German Mark III, but several men moved up onto the road. The tank's two machine guns began to sputter. The 74 mm. gun also moved and fired. Lieutenant Files was killed. Lieutenant Murphy was wounded, and so were 12 enlisted men before Private, First Class, Lyman Brainard and Private Paul Kunde began firing their bazooka. The first shot was short, but the

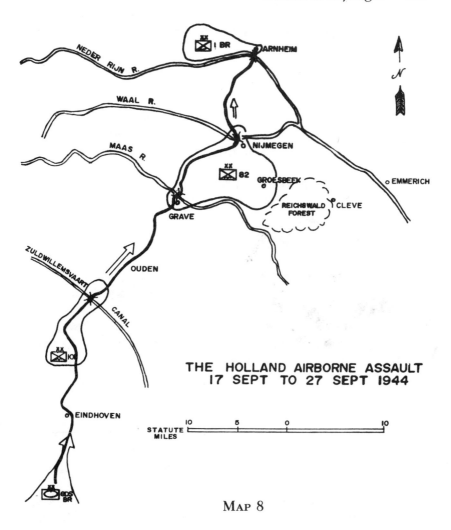

THE HOLLAND AIRBORNE ASSAULT
17 SEPT TO 27 SEPT 1944

MAP 8

second was so close that the tank backed up, turned around, and moved south.

That night Company E dug in along the road, facing south toward Grave. A German patrol came along, but Private Kunde threw a grenade and the patrol disappeared, leaving blood on the road.

The night was quiet then until about an hour before midnight. Raucous noises began coming from Grave.

It sounded like singing. Lieutenant Sharp and Sergeant Coppola moved forward.

". . . It's a long way to Tipperary, it's a long way from home . . ."

They looked at one another and began moving toward Grave. They saw flashlights, and German trucks, and German troops burning papers. They walked down the street, and the Germans did not even look up. From the town the singing continued, punctuated with shouts and laughter. Sharp and Coppola went back to report that the Germans were preparing to pull out.

Just after midnight "Tipperary" grew louder, and it was followed by the Dutch national anthem and shouting. Out of the town sped a sedan with two civilians in it. It raced to the mine field, hit a mine, and blew up. One man was killed, and the other injured. The Americans moved to take them out of the wrecked vehicle. Someone came from the town to identify them; they were a pair of Dutch Nazis trying to escape their townsmen.

In the early hours of morning all was quiet, except the racket from the town, until dawn. Then the noise stopped. At 5:30 A.M. a German motorcycle came up from the southwest at high speed and hit a mine. The motorcycle and its rider blew into little pieces.

At 6:00 A.M. the company was in Grave, the singers of the night before were out in force, apparently little the worse for wear, and the Grave operation was ended successfully.

Not all the units of the 504th or the other parachute regiments had luck as good as the 1st Battalion that day. Captain Helgeson's bridge was called No. 7. It and E Company's bridge over the Maas gave the British 30 Corps a chance to come up. But the 82nd had been given three other important bridges to take.

One of these was No. 8, across the Maas, further north. No. 9 was the bridge at Hatert, and No. 10 was the big railroad and road bridge at Honinghutie.

Troops of the 504th moved up nearly to bridge No. 8 when, almost under their noses, it went up with a roar. The Germans had blown it very effectively. The same thing happened at bridge No. 9. Bridge No. 10 was the most important of all, because it was the only one between Grave and Nijmegen that the Americans were sure would carry heavy armor. The 508th was sent in strength against this bridge.

The Germans obviously knew the importance of the bridge and had protected it with a defense of linked pillboxes, trenches, and barbed wire, with interlocking fields of fire. Lieutenant Lloyd Polette's platoon was pinned down here and called for help. But before it could arrive, the Germans managed to blow up the railroad bridge and damage the road bridge until it was not safe for armor. The 504th's bridge No. 7, then, became the key crossing in the first part of the Allied drive to link up with the British 1st Airborne Division at Arnhem.

General Gavin expected the strongest German resistance to come from the Reichswald, because for the first time the Allies were striking on the edge of Germany. He also knew that his most important objective was the Nijmegen bridge, which was now the key to advance across the Rhine. But since they expected the bridge to be stoutly defended, Gavin and his men planned to delay capture of it until matters were well in hand.

Thus Colonel Roy E. Lindquist, commander of the 508th, had the equivocal orders to commit his 1st Battalion against the bridge after landing, but to be sure that he did not dilute his force in case of counterattack from the Reichswald. In other words, he was to look both ways simultaneously.

Shortly after landing Colonel Lindquist was in touch with an agent of the Dutch underground, who said the battalion could be taken through the back streets of the city instead of making the long trek over the flat ground. Thus they could reach the bridge much more quickly and seize it before the Germans awakened to their presence.

Lindquist weighed the problems. He had to protect the glider landing zone, which lay off toward the Reichswald. All the division's artillery was to land here on D—1, and the division would need its artillery badly. But the opportunity to seize the bridge quickly by stealth was very attractive. He decided to send the 1st Battalion in. Major Jonathan Adams dispatched Company A behind the Dutch underground agent, who undertook to lead them to the stations. The Dutchman took the Americans to a crossroads short of the bridge and left them there. No one ever saw him again, a most suspicious circumstance in view of what happened next.

Company A got involved in street fighting, managed to destroy a building Adams thought was the control station for bridge demolition, and then was cut off from the rest of the regiment for the next two days.

Colonel Lindquist ordered his 3rd Battalion to move to the bridge from the south, and Lieutenant Colonel Louis Mendez sent a platoon out on reconnaissance. Soon Company G moved up and engaged the Germans.

By morning of D + 1 reports from the fighting troops indicated that all was not as it should be. Intelligence had said the Germans probably would offer little resistance and if they did, it would be ineffectual because they had pulled all their available armor south. But suddenly the Americans were facing Tiger tanks and 88s and heavy mortar fire. Allied intelligence had underestimated the enemy; it had not known the Germans had put command of Holland under Field Marshal Model. General Kurt Student had rounded up parachutists and formed the First Parachute Army. General von Zangen's Fifteenth Army had escaped from the British at Calais, not as dispirited as intelligence indicated, and had turned. Two entire panzer divisions unknown to the Americans, divisions that had been sent back to the Reichswald for rest from the Eastern front, had been refitted and were ready to go.

So instead of walking into an easy victory, the 82nd found itself faced by a vigorous counterattack.

The Germans had sensed that the Nijmegen bridge was a key to the whole Allied operation. This was true in that all the bridges were keys. If the 101st had not taken any of its bridges, and if the bridges across the Waal had all been blown up, the troops coming from the west could not have possibly made progress. Field Marshal Model had determined to hold the Nijmegen bridge, and he sent nearly 1,000 troops into the area to do it. Others argued with Model that the bridge should be blown, but the Field Marshal was not used to German defeat. He said hold; they would need the bridge to supply the troops that would drive the Allies into the sea. The Germans began building defenses, with 88s and other heavy weapons.

General Gavin became fully occupied with the defense of the

glider landing zone against attacks from the Reichswald. That zone must be kept clear; the division was waiting for the 376th Field Artillery, which would come in that afternoon. Troops of the 508th Parachute Infantry were brought back to the landing zone, and Gavin committed his reserves to the defense of the zone.

The landings began at 2:00 P.M. The German infantry held part of the zone, but half an hour later the last glider was down, and the recovery rate of men and equipment was high. The 319th Glider Field Artillery, for example, saved all 12 of its howitzers and 26 of 34 jeeps. Most important at the moment, Battery D of the 80th Airborne Anti-Aircraft Battalion recovered all eight of its 57 mm. antitank guns.

Late that afternoon the first parachute resupply mission arrived—135 B-24s, dropping parachute bundles. Many landed in no-man's-land between the Americans and Germans, but that night the Americans moved into the field and recovered 80 percent of the drop.

On D + 2 the British Guards Armoured Division began moving up through the 82nd's positions, much to Gavin's relief. So far he had been spared a major German armored attack, but he was half expecting one.

Elements of the 508th were still tied down at the south end of the Nijmegen bridge, and it seemed that the bridge would never fall. The German 88s controlled the road. Gavin decided he must make an assault by boat to attack the far end of the bridge. He planned the crossing for the morning of September 20, but late on the afternoon of the nineteenth General Browning and the British 1st Airborne Division were in trouble at Arnhem, site of the deepest penetration of the German-held area. Browning told Gavin the crossing had to be made that day—at the latest on the next. The British airborne division could not hold out another day without help; it was bearing the brunt of the German armor attack. The attempt was moved up; the 82nd would move that night. At about 11:00 A.M. the action began. But it was delayed; meanwhile the Germans overran two important 82nd positions at Mook and Beek, and Gavin had to turn his attention there.

All along the line in fact, the German strength was building up. The 101st was beating off attacks at St. Oedenrode. The

British were taking a beating up at Arnhem. Gavin left the seizure of the bridge to Colonel Tucker and the 504th. The paratroops made the crossing, landed, and began fighting. At 6:00 P.M. they reached the north end of the highway bridge, and troops of the 508th at the south end moved from their side. Soon the first tank of the Grenadier Guards crossed the bridge and headed for Arnhem to relieve the British 1st Airborne.

As the armor began to roll, German General Heinz Harmel watched. With him was an engineer with a detonator box. The Germans had wired the Nijmegen bridge months before and had painted the wiring to match the color of the bridge structure. Thus the captors of the bridge were to see no new black wires that obviously must be cut. When the British tanks appeared, Harmel ordered the engineer to push the detonator home. He did. Nothing happened. Again, ordered the general, and again the plunger went down. Nothing happened. The wires *had* been cut.

The tanks of the Grenadiers moved to the bridge, destroyed the two 88s on the north shore, and continued.

All day on September 20 Field Marshal Model sent his troops storming against the airborne. He intended to destroy all three divisions.

The British took the worst of it and suffered most. They were steadily compressed into a smaller area, most of them west of Arnhem. Bad weather prevented airdrops from resupplying them or reinforcements from parachuting in on D+3. On September 22 the armor moved up, but it was D+6 before the 325th Glider Infantry was able to join the 82nd and other reinforcements came to strengthen the 101st. The British 1st Airborne never was properly reinforced. The pressure of the Germans on the ground, the weather, and then the Luftwaffe hindered the operation all the way. On the night of September 25 the remnants of the division withdrew to the southern bank of the Rhine. The remainder of the operation became more of a regular infantry movement, less dependent on airborne. By D+30 the specific involvement of the airborne had more or less ended, although such was the need for seasoned troops that the 101st and the 82nd were kept in the line for weeks, under British command. Finally they were relieved.

The newspaper stories that got out about the operation in Holland indicated that the British airborne forces had won an enormous victory, and they said virtually nothing about the operations of the 101st and the 82nd. That was galling to the officers and their men. The British 1st Airborne had fought gallantly but had sustained a total of 6,986 casualties and had been forced out of its position. The 82nd had suffered 2,909 casualties and held its positions, and the 101st had taken 2,338 casualties and held.

It had been a difficult fight all the way through, but no one had expected a picnic. And although the American airborne men were resentful of the British seizing credit, at Eisenhower's headquarters and in Washington there was no doubt about what had happened. Generals Gavin and Taylor could reassure themselves with the knowledge that wars were not won in the newspapers. In its way the struggle—Operation MARKET-GARDEN—was a spectacular success. The airborne forces had again done all that was expected of them; the failure had been that of the Second Army to push forward past Nijmegen to Arnhem to relieve the 1st Airborne Division. Earlier Eisenhower had questioned the whole concept of airborne divisions, let alone an airborne army. But in Holland the First Allied Airborne Army had done its job better than any other unit.

The airborne troops had earned their spurs at Normandy. In Holland they cemented their place in the American military system.

The plan to put Montgomery across the Rhine and let him speed down the east bank, turned out to be the next thing to a disaster. The Americans had managed to take their bridges across the Meuse (Maas) and the Waal, but the British airborne division failed to take the Arnhem bridge and eventually had to be withdrawn. The Allies were left with a wedge 60 miles deep in the German lines, but they had not crossed the Rhine.

Montgomery spent most of that winter (and the rest of his life) telling the world that if his plan had been followed and he had been given the go-ahead, he would have defeated the Germans in a few months. The fact was, however, that Montgomery was incapable of making a move unless he had total superiority. He was hardly the man to entrust with a plan that involved swift action and flexibility. General George Patton, who had wanted to drive on and do what Montgomery said he was going to do, was restrained in the interest of Allied solidarity. Montgomery had always held that Eisenhower's plan of driving to Germany on a broad front was wrong. Patton would have agreed with him. The Eisenhower plan was more political than miliary. It would never do to have the Americans take Germany. Or the British for that matter. The Americans, British, French, and everyone else with a finger in the military pie must take Germany together, to preserve the political front.

So the war bogged down. The Allies advanced, but slowly. Near the end of 1944, they had become almost stationary, on a line that ran from the border of Luxembourg, up roughly along the German border with Belgium, to a point near Liège. The Americans were in the line, and with Christmas approaching they had become very leisurely. Many senior officers were in London for the holidays. Most of the experienced troops were in camp and had been replaced along the line by untried divisions. The situation that existed was very much as it had been at the outbreak of war in 1914 and again in 1939. The Germans were sitting on their side of the border, and the Allies were sitting on the west of it. The Allies were not much concerned. They knew they had given the German western armies a bad trouncing in the past few months, and they did not believe Hitler had the men or the equipment to launch a counteroffensive, particularly since the Allies controlled the air over France, Belgium, and along the front. The Allied generals, in other words, underrated their enemy and proved that generals do not always learn from military history. They left the line fragile and virtually unguarded. It was the same line that had led to German blitzkrieg twice before. The plan was still the same: drive through Belgium to the sea, cutting off all those Allied troops north and east of the wedge.

The Winter War

When the 101st and the 82nd Airborne Divisions were released from the sector near the Reichswald in mid-November 1944, they were sent for reorganization and rest to Rheims. There they settled down in camps built by the French and refurbished by the Germans.

The Allied drive bogged down. The reasons have been debated by many books of history, biography, and reminiscence since the war, but one fact is inescapable: By the end of November the Germans were pulling themselves together, and the Allied performance was stagnant.

The British-American buildup of men and matériel continued, and actually there could be no doubt as to the eventual outcome of the war, given the staggering defeats of the Germans on the Eastern front. But in the West there seemed to be opportunity for the Germans to create enough difficulty to achieve a negotiated peace. That was the hope of most of the German leaders. Not many generals in the winter of 1944–45 had a great deal of faith in Hitler's promises of victory, or even in his later hope of stalemate.

As the airborne troops regrouped in November, General Ridgway's XVIII Airborne Corps headquarters was located at Epernay. The divisions were nearby. In the next move, General Brereton indicated, airborne troops would be dropped and flown in by glider to seize bridgeheads across the Rhine in the assault on Hitler's Germany.

Unknown to Allied intelligence, the Germans had a fine appreciation of the condition of the Western front. In mid-December General Ridgway was in England on routine business, consulting with Eisenhower's headquarters. General Taylor was in Washington. The Allies had relaxed; hundreds of the veterans of Normandy and Holland were on leave in Paris or England. As everyone knew, including the German generals, the Wehrmacht was on the verge of collapse.

But unknown to the Allies, for two months Hitler had planned a breakthrough to Antwerp. Production of guns, tanks, and planes was stepped up, and in spite of the bombing, the Germans apparently began to recover strength. Hitler planned to throw 30 divisions into the battle.

The Germans, under Lieutenant General Sepp Dietrich, would drive a wedge between Montgomery's British army and the American First Army, commanded by General Courtney Hodges. After having captured Antwerp, Hitler had no further plan. His generals decided he must be expecting the Allies to seek a peace.

This sort of reasoning was beyond the comprehension of the Allied military minds, because militarily it made no sense. So, in mid-December, the Allies had given leave to their most experienced troops, and General Hodge's First Army was manned by an unusually large number of replacements. The U.S. 99th Division had arrived in Europe a month earlier. The 106th was basically untried. The 28th had been fighting hard in the Huertgen forest and was re)tting. The 14th Cavalry Regiment was the best prepared of the lot along the ragged line facing Germany.

On December 15 all was ready for the German drive. The meteorologists forecast several days of foul weather, so the Allied air fleet could not attack the armored columns, which were peculiarly vulnerable to low-level bombardment and strafing. Before dawn the German armor was on the way, moving against the weakest part of the American line and the untried 99th Division.

By the end of the day the penetration in the Ardennes forest was serious enough to draw the attention of Supreme Headquarters Allied Expeditionary Forces (SHAEF). The XVIII Airborne Corps would have to be moved into action—not as airborne troops, but as infantry to stem the German advance. As senior officer present, General Gavin was in command. He sent urgent calls to Paris and London for his officers and troops. Then he ordered the divisions to move.

The 82nd Airborne moved out first, to find the focal point of the 1st SS Panzer Division column that was leading the breakthrough.

The 2nd Battalion of the 505th Parachute Infantry Regiment got the word at 2:00 on the morning of December 17. It was to move by truck from Camp Sissons for a place somewhere in Belgium. The leader, Lieutenant Colonel Benjamin Vandervoort, was in England, and the senior officer present was Captain Taylor Smith, his executive officer, who had the battalion in training during this "quiet" period. At 8:00 on December 18 all the intelligence officers knew was that there was a German breakthrough somewhere in Belgium, and the enemy were headed for the town of Bastogne.

Halfway, the 2nd Battalion destination was changed to Houffalize. They sped on, and arrived at Houffalize to learn that the Germans were on their way with an armored column. The Battalion turned, and managed to move its last truck out of Houffalize just as the German armor appeared at the edge of the town. The battalion sped to Werbomont and there took up a defensive position. Civilians began filtering through the position, heading back toward the interior and France. The dreaded Germans were coming, just as in 1940, they said. The war was lost.

The German advance had indeed been spectacular. In a matter of hours the panzer forces had penetrated deep behind the American lines, taking bridges and capturing hundreds of vehicles, guns, and thousands of American troops. The column leader, SS Colonel Jochen Peiper, was driving fast, and Werbomont was his next objective.

On the morning of December 19 Lieutenant Colonel Vandervoort reached the battalion after a frantic trip from England. The American defense was just getting organized. General Ridgway had returned and moved his XVIII Airborne Corps headquarters to Werbomont. The mission now was to turn back the German advance, stop Peiper's column, and prevent the German infantry from moving in behind him and enveloping the front. The 82nd's mission was to take Trois Ponts and Vielsalm, and to open the road to St. Vith, the headquarters of the 7th Armored Division.

The 504th would go to Trois Ponts. The 505th was to connect

and take the front to Grand Halleux on the south. The 508th was to center on Vielsalm and Thier Dumont and protect the western flank.

Colonel Vandervoort was called to the 505th Regimental Command Post. He took Captain Charles Sammon along. Awaiting them with orders for the regiment was Brigadier General Ira Swift of Division. They were to move east along the Trois Ponts road, the general said. No one knew what they would encounter: The Germans could be anywhere. They were to take Trois Ponts. Afterwards they should seize the high ground over the Salm river and put one company up there to hold it. The rest of the battalion was not to cross, but to hold the Trois Ponts side—if the enemy did not have it.

Vandervoort went back to camp and moved his men out. They reached Trois Ponts and found the engineers of First Army still there. They set up a Battalion Command Post without incident. The Germans had not arrived. The commander then sent E Company across the railroad bridge to the high ground, where the men dug in. Still there was no contact with the Germans.

E Company was in place by 7:00 P.M. Fifty minutes later a German self-propelled gun appeared on the road, coming toward the bridge at full speed and virtually ran into the company. One of the bazooka teams knocked it out.

E Company patrols moved up and down the east bank of the Salm. On the left, or south, they met troops of the 3rd Armored Division. But on the right, to the north, they found no one. That meant a possible German flank attack.

The men laid a mine field around their position and waited.

The night went by without attack. On the morning of December 21 a German half-track appeared, but it hit a mine and was blown out of action. Seeing the armor coming, Lt. William Murddagh called for help from Battalion; he had bazookas and the mines, but no antitank defenses. Battalion sent a jeep and a 57 mm. antitank gun to the railroad bridge, but they could not get across. The road bridge had been blown, but not very thoroughly; so the engineers managed to repair the span and get the jeep and gun over, just before the bridge caved in from the weight.

At 9:45 A.M. the Germans attacked again, this time with infantry. It had begun to snow, but the ground was not frozen, and the snow became slushy, a very definite advantage for the defenders of the east bank of the Salm. A patrol brought in papers from dead Germans and these gave the bad news: They were facing the 1st Reconnaissance Battalion of the 1st SS Panzer Division. From engineers of the First Army, the 505th had already learned that this unit had ambushed an American convoy outside Stavelot four days earlier, rounded up the prisoners, and massacred them in the fields with machine-gun and Schmeisser fire. That information did not incline the men of E Company to take prisoners, and it helped set the tone of action for the next few days.

But whether the Americans could take anything remained to be seen. The strength of the unit facing them was presumably 800 men. E Company consisted of 110 men.

The Germans attacked. E Company sent a platoon to the flank and slowed the Germans. But even on the slippery ground there were too many Germans, as Colonel Vandervoort could see from across the river. He sent a platoon of F Company across the bridge to help, and ammunition-carrying parties to take up supplies and bring back casualties so they would not slow the men down.

By the time the platoon crossed, the Americans counted 15 German tanks firing into E Company. The 57 mm. gun knocked out two tanks and held the rest back. But the Germans swarmed forward, overrunning the American positions and engaging in firefights at each point. At 12:30 Colonel Vandervoort sent the rest of F Company across the bridge to E Company's right, where the major German strength seemed to be moving.

For the third time German troops launched an assault against E Company, charging forward across the snowy ground like madmen. The Americans mowed them down and counterattacked with one platoon. The Germans retreated. Vandervoort sent the word to Regiment that he was facing the 1st SS Panzers but could hold. The commander, Colonel W. E. Ekman, was skeptical of Vandervoort's ability to hold against these crack German troops. He warned that the battalion would have to pull back; the cost was too high. Vandervoort did not move. Instead, he sent D Company—his battalion reserve—across the river to outflank the Germans.

Lieutenant Jake Wurtich was manning the 57 mm. gun with E

Company. The gun grew hot, but he kept firing until it was knocked out and he was killed.

The battle broke down into hand-to-hand fighting, the sort of encounter taught in the obstacle courses and hand-to-hand combat sessions of infantry school. The Germans had found it so easy to smash through the green troops of the 99th Division that they expected the present tactics to succeed. But this time they faced tough soldiers who met them with rifles, bayonet, and trench knife. E and F Companies still held.

When Colonel Vandervoort refused to withdraw, General Swift came from Division. He found the town of Trois Ponts under fire and prepared to tell Vandervoort to withdraw. But there was no way to withdraw—the whole battalion was committed and battling on the east bank of the river. Swift was obdurate. On the battalion level, Vandervoort accepted the order. Regiment could give him no support, so he must pull back.

He went across the river to D Company, and when he saw how strong the enemy was, he issued the order: "Let's get the hell out of here."

The word went to the companies.

Here, from an after-action interview by the U.S. Army Historical Section:

> ... Even though they were outnumbered, they were very confident, frowning on a withdrawal order. Even though the company commanders knew it was unsound, the disengaging action began. All of F Company, what was left of E Company, and one platoon of D Company came over the top of the cliff, some men making leaps of ten to twenty feet at a time, with the enemy right behind them ...

The Germans did not try to cross the river, although they had a rout—one created, in effect, by American Division headquarters. They moved into E Company's positions and raked Trois Ponts with small-arms fire. But here, Vandervoort held. He had lost two antitank guns, two jeeps and mortars, light machine guns, and rifles.

General Ridgway came from Division Command Post, and

Vandervoort explained the situation. Gavin had been asked if he could not keep the 1st SS Panzers from linking up with Peiper's force, which was at Stoumont-la-Gleize. Trois Ponts must hold, if that was to be done. Vandervoort said they would hold, and Gavin went back to Division to move the rest of the 505th up along the

On the nineteenth Colonel Tucker's 504th was ordered to move to Rahier and Cheneux and link up with the 505th at Trois Ponts. The 1st Battalion was to take the towns of Brume, Rahier, and Cheneux. Just outside Rahier, on the Cheneux road, Companies B and C ran into the enemy. Along the way Company B had picked up a German 77 mm. self-propelled howitzer. They used this to knock out the German unit's machine gun, and then another, 300 yards further along. But as they neared Cheneux, they came under attack by stronger German forces. Two American platoons together were working up along the sides of the road. While one moved, the other covered with fire. But from Cheneux came German fire from a heavy mortar and two 20 mm. flak wagons—portable antiaircraft guns that could be trained against infantry as well. The initial blast killed six men and knocked out the radio. The captured 77 mm. half-track gun was brought up on the road and returned the German fire, but the rate of 20 mm. fire increased and the half-track moved back. The third platoon moved out ahead of the other two but was pinned down 10 yards from the enemy position. The Germans had two heavy machine guns there, a 20 mm. gun, and a squad of riflemen. The area was a maze of barbed wire.

At 5:00 P.M. Captain Helgeson ordered his company back 200 yards. The platoons withdrew, one at a time, and set up a defense on the edge of the wood.

An hour later Helgeson conferred with Lieutenant Colonel Harrison, the battalion commander, who conferred with Colonel Tucker. The colonel ordered a night attack on Cheneux. Companies B and C would make the assault.

At 7:30 they started. Company C had to attack through a system of barbed-wire fences. Company B had to cross 400 yards of flat, where the enemy had perfect fields of fire. Company B came out of the woods in skirmish formation and moved to a point 200 yards from the edge of Cheneux. It seemed easy. Then the troopers' world erupted with a barrage of 20 mm. fire, machine guns, mortars, and artillery, followed by rifle fire. The men had no cover, and they began to fall "like flies," as Staff Sergeant James M. Boyd said bitterly. They were supposed to have weapons support from the road. It never showed up, and in a matter of moments the first two waves of attackers were almost completely wiped out.

Company C moved up, and as the men hit the first barbed-wire fences, the German machine guns began firing on them. The men dropped. The whole first assault wave was pinned down. The second wave moved up to build up the firing line. Someone from Company B yelled "Come on!" and they came, through the barbed wire fences. Nobody had any wire cutters. They bogged down again.

Staff Sergeant Walsh of Company B stood up.

"Let's get the sons of bitches!" he yelled, and he began to move. Behind him came the men of the company, screaming and yelling as they drove toward the enemy roadblock. They fired until their ammunition was gone, then they used their rifles as clubs and pulled out their trench knives.

Sergeant Walsh crept up to within 20 yards of a 20 mm. flak wagon and picked up a grenade. He had been wounded in the wrist and could not pull the pin. He crawled back and got the pin free. Holding it in place he crawled closer to the wagon again and hurled the grenade. Exit one flak wagon.

Private Barkley of Company C moved in on the side of another flak wagon. His ammunition was gone. He crawled forward with his trench knife, climbed up on the flak wagon, and cut the German gunner's throat.

The riflemen killed some 20 Germans in hand-to-hand fighting and held the roadblock. The American guns moved forward and began to fire into the German position. By 10:00 P.M. the battalion held the edge of the town, with the Germans in possession of the buildings inside.

By this time, all the officers of Company B were out of action, killed or wounded. Staff Sergeant Clyde Farrier became the commander. He led a patrol to try to knock out two houses where the enemy was holed up. They made two attempts, but a 20 mm. flak gun kept them off.

From Regiment came the word that Company G of 3rd Battalion would move through and clean out the town. With a platoon of the 307th Engineers, the remnants of Companies B and C took up positions on the high ground around the town. The Germans who could, moved out at 11:00. At 3:00 A.M. on December 21, when elements of 3rd Battalion arrived, the town was clear for the Americans to set up. Company B and Company C counted heads for Regiment. No officers and 18 men were left of Company B, and 3 officers and 38 men remained of the 8 officers and 119 men of Company C. But the town and its important bridge across the Ambleve river had been taken by 3rd Battalion, and the men had captured 14 flak wagons, a battery of 105 mm. howitzers, and so many vehicles that when General Gavin showed up next day, the men told him they were now the 504th Parachute Armored Regiment.

At Trois Ponts on the night of December 21, Colonel Vandervoort of the 505th's 2nd Battalion saw that E Company had been virtually destroyed in the action of December 20–21. Only 50 of the 110 men had made it back over the Salm. But D and F Companies had stopped the Germans. They let the enemy ford the river, which was very narrow, and almost reach the west bank. Then the Americans opened up with rifles, machine guns, BARs— everything that would shoot. Some swam back to the east bank, but wounded and dead were swept downstream, and the Germans who made the western shore were taken prisoner.

A German officer made the top of the hill on the east bank, saw one of the jeeps there and began to drive it away. The men of 2nd Battalion saw, and a .50 caliber machine gun opened up. The officer fell out of the jeep as it began to burn.

At 1:30 the Germans launched another attack. Germans moved down the bank and one group started across in a rubber boat. The battalion waited, then opened fire. None of the Germans escaped. But that did not deter the others from attacking again. They attacked all day long until dusk.

That night the 504th moved up on the left of the battalion. Next morning the battalion began to probe the east bank of the Salm but could not ascertain the German intentions.

The line now roughly formed a right angle, with the vertical axis on the Salm river, from Thier Dumont on the south to Cheneux on the north and Regne on the west. The German armored column was moving down behind the Americans from Cheneux and Rahier, and the 2nd and the 9th SS Divisions were getting ready to drive straight up from the south. The 504th and 505th Regiments were in the Salm line. The 508th held the bottom of that line as well as the horizontal axis halfway to Hebronville, where it linked with the 325th Glider Infantry. The German 1st SS Division and 9th SS Division were on the east, and the 2nd SS was on the south. They were preparing a drive north to roll the American line back toward La Glaze, envelop it, and destroy the 82nd Airborne.

Desperate Christmas

The 101st Airborne Division had moved to Bastogne on that first warning that the Germans were moving fast. They got there just hours before the Germans. That they got there at all was a considerable tribute to the American powers of rapid recuperation from total surprise.

General Taylor was in the Pentagon conferring with General Marshall on the future of the airborne, because a number of high officers in Europe were still raising irritating questions. General Ridgway, the XVIII Corps commander, was in London with his staff. In a matter of hours Taylor was in the air and Ridgway had 55 planes, loaded with that staff and men on leave en route to France. He had left orders for Major General William Miley to get his 17th Airborne Division moving too.

By December 20 the 101st was in place, and the men were digging in. The Germans launched attacks at Neffe and Mont, but the 501st Parachute Infantry stopped them. On the night of December 20, however, the Germans cut the road to Neufchâteau and surrounded Bastogne, just half an hour after General McAuliffe had come along that road. McAuliffe had gone to Neufchateau to report on the situation to VIII Corps. Almost while he was talking, three German divisions were already surrounding the area, and the 116th Panzers came up to make the ring complete.

McAuliffe had part of the 10th Armored Division, and some other troops, in the encircled area. But he was on his own. On December 21 General Middleton, the commander of VIII Corps, ordered McAuliffe to hold Bastogne at all costs. General McAuliffe knew what that order meant. He was stuck within a two-and-a-half-mile circle around Bastogne, with Germans all around.

For two days, December 21 and 22, the Germans pushed up as though they were going to move right ahead. But the frontal attack of Panzer Lehr Division was stopped. The Germans then decided to move around the enclave in concentric circles and choke it to death. As they prepared, the attacks diminished and the Americans were able to dig in deeper and consider tactics.

Intelligence had some more than usually interesting reports to indicate what to expect. Corpses had been found within the perimeter wearing civilian clothes—and German army dog tags. Other reports told of attacks by soldiers wearing American uniforms and driving American vehicles, even Sherman tanks. So McAuliffe and his staff sent the word down to the regiments and the battalions: They could expect anything from the Germans.

On December 21, troops a mile and a half southwest of Bastogne, at Isle le Pré, ran into a large German force riding American vehicles and wearing American uniforms. The 33rd Field Artillery sent a column out and found itself followed by another column of "Americans." These were Germans. They began firing, then slipped off into the woods of the Bois de Fragotte, where the Americans fought an inconclusive engagement with them.

The Germans still believed Bastogne to be an easy nut to crack. At 11:30 on the morning of December 22, a German major, a captain, and two enlisted men came up the road from the south, carrying a white flag. They were met by three troopers. Private First Class Ernest Premetz, of the 327th Medical Detachment, could speak German. The German captain could speak English. Between them they established that the Germans were there to parley.

As the Germans were blindfolded and taken to McAuliffe's command post, the rumor was out that the enemy was about to surrender. That figured, said the paratroopers, who had no particular respect for German might after Normandy and Holland. But the Germans carried a message from Lieutenant General Heinrich von Leuttwitz, commander of the XXXXVII Panzer Corps.

December 22nd 1944

To the U.S.A. Commander of the encircled town of Bastogne.

The fortune of war is changing. This time the U.S.A. forces in and near Bastogne have been encircled by strong German armored units. . . .

There is only one possibility to save the encircled U.S.A. troops from total annihilation: that is the honorable surrender of the encircled town. In order to think it over a term of two hours will be granted beginning with the presentation of this note.

If this proposal should be rejected one German Artillery Corps and six heavy A.A. Battalions are ready to annihilate the U.S.A. troops in and near Bastogne. The order for firing will be given immediately after this two hours' term.

All the serious civilian losses caused by this artillery fire would not correspond with the well-known American humanity.

The German Commander

They delivered the message to Major Alvin Jones, who brought it to the general. As he entered, McAuliffe asked what was in the document.

A demand for surrender, said the couriers.

"Aw nuts," said the general, and laughed.

The paratroopers were used to fighting while surrounded, but when McAuliffe saw the document he realized it needed a reply. He sat with pencil in hand, pondering a message that might go down in history. What should he say?

Colonel Harry Kinnard, Divisional G-3, (operations officer) said that McAuliffe's first reaction was the proper answer, and every man in the room agreed. He wrote.

"NUTS."

Colonel Harper, commander of the 327 Glider Infantry, took the message back to the German officers, who were blindfolded and standing at the edge of the wood. It was 1:50.

"I have the American commander's reply."

"Is it written or verbal?" asked the German captain.

"Written. I will stick it in your hand."

The captain translated the message. The major did not understand.

"Is the reply negative or affirmative? If it is the latter I will negotiate further."

"It is decidedly not affirmative."

The German major nodded. Colonel Harper then took the two officers in his jeep back to the main road, where the German enlisted men waited, and removed the blindfolds. The colonel spoke.

"If you don't understand what Nuts means, in plain English it is the same as Go to Hell. And I will tell you something else: If you continue this attack we will kill every goddam German that tries to break into this city."

"We will kill many Americans," said the captain, bowing stiffly. "This is war."

"On your way, Bud. And good luck to you."

So the Germans walked down the road, their white flag drooping, and Colonel Harper went back to his command post, regretting the slip of the tongue. Good luck indeed! He would see them in hell.

The two hours went by, but no attack materialized except two sorties against the 327th's Company F, which were beaten back by small-arms fire.

But that night the Luftwaffe came to bomb the city. The Germans were, as the soldiers put it, "going for broke."

At McAuliffe's command post there was worry behind the bravado; the reply to the Germans had been all very well for morale. It was high, anyhow. The 105 mm. batteries were completely dug into circular gun pits. But the 463rd Field Artillery Battalion in support of the 327th had only 200 rounds of ammunition left, and that was about average. Ten rounds per gun was the level of supply. At the same time, small-arms ammunition was running out. All day on the twenty-second McAuliffe waited for resupply. But the weather was too bad for the troop carrier planes to fly, and it was impossible for them to make their drops. No supply came on December 22.

McAuliffe needed 104 airplane loads of ammunition and ra-

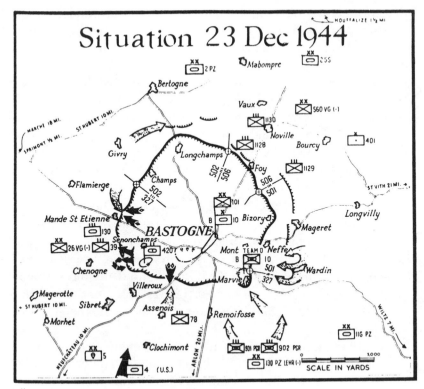

MAP 9

tions. Without them he could hold out only for a matter of hours.

At 9:35 on the morning of December 23, the C-47s came.

Two pathfinder teams dropped in the area of the 327th and said the supply planes would come in 90 minutes. The drop zones were set up, and the planes began to fly over, 16 in the first flight. By 4:00 that afternoon the troop carrier command had sent in 241 planes and 1400 bundles—144 tons of supplies in a mile-square drop zone. The recovery was 95 percent, as jeeps rushed from one bundle to the next and hurried them off to the units. Before dark the artillery was firing ammunition from the new supplies.

They had come just in time. At 5:25 that night the 2nd Battalion of the 327th was hit by shellfire from enemy tanks, and ten minutes later the tanks moved forward, followed by infantry. They were striking at Marvie. Within half an hour a major attack developed and a platoon of Company G was surrounded in a hill south of Marvie. This fight gave one lesson in the high price of timidity. Colonel Harper had asked for a tank on that hill, and a 57 mm. self-propelled gun had been sent up. But the gun came just as the Germans began to attack. The first few rounds of artillery were enough for the gunners, and they turned around and sped into Marvie with the gun. The American defenders thought it was a German gun and poured a rain of fire into it, killing the crew and wrecking the 57 mm. gun. At least then it served the useful purpose of blocking the road and causing two following German tanks to retreat.

This German attack developed in frenzy. The infantry came yelling and firing up the road, shooting flares in the darkness. Tracers were going in all directions. A self-propelled gun, charging up along the Wiltz Road, came abreast of an American tank— which sent it up in flames. That fire lighted up the farmhouse behind. The Germans then turned their artillery on the farmhouse and set the hayloft afire. The light was so bright the Americans had to fall back 100 yards.

On the slopes of Hill 500 Lieutenant Stanley Morrison and his men of Company G of the 327th were dug in. The Germans were all around them—tanks, and infantrymen in the first white snow-suits the Americans had seen. Colonel Harper called him on the field phone.

"What's your situation?"

"I see tanks just outside my window," said Morrison. "It looks like they have us."

Then the line went dead. That was the end of the platoon, overwhelmed by the 901st Panzergrenadier Regiment.

By 8:00 the Germans had worked their way into the south end of Marvie. Two U.S. tanks came up and harried the Germans, holding them back since they could not move their armor up because of the destroyed American half-track in the road. The Germans might have broken through, but they did not attack the line, and Company A of the 501st Parachute Infantry moved up to help. The line was patched up north of lost Hill 500. By 1:00 A.M. on December 24 the breach was closed. Twice before dawn the Germans attacked. But the Americans held, although on one assault two German tanks came within 50 yards of the foxholes before they were turned back by bazooka fire.

The fighting continued about Bastogne that night. Two German tanks got into the town and shot up houses but did not do much damage. Near midnight, a German armored column headed up toward Marvie on the south road, but the lead tank was again halted by the wrecked American half-track that blocked the road. Trying to turn around, the tank was knocked out by a pair of Shermans. The other German armor was stalled behind.

Soon after dawn Colonel Harper checked his lines and found that his men still held most of Marvie, although the Germans had some houses in the south. Unfortunately, the U.S. Air Force didn't know it. That afternoon six P-47s bombed the village and strafed the houses, although the Americans had identifying markers at the front of the U.S. position. The Germans camouflaged tanks and half-tracks as haystacks and generally kept under cover. At 4:45 the P-47s came back and attacked Marvie again, and then Luftwaffe planes came in to strike Bastogne again.

That afternoon Harper was informed that he was responsible for the perimeter of over half the division territory. All seemed safe enough because it was heavily wooded country, not suitable for a swift armor attack—except one area. The Wiltz road moved through a narrow corridor, and that might be dangerous. Also in the northwest the countryside was rolling without much tree cover. McAuliffe and his staff wondered, but they were half expecting a major German move on Christmas Eve or Christmas Day.

But that night, the besieged discovered that the supplies had not been altogether what they needed. They had plenty of .50 caliber ammunition but not enough .30 caliber for the M-1s. They needed penicillin and litters for the wounded, and 75 mm. pack howitzer ammunition.

The resupply continued on December 24 as IX Troop Carrier Command dropped 159 tons of supplies to the 101st. The defenders had been scrounging about in the ruined defenses for old supplies left by the original U.S. units in garrison there. They found jam and flour, and 2,000 burlap bags that were invaluable to the troopers in the line, who had not been issued arctic boots.

On Christmas Day the weather was so foul that resupply had to be canceled. The Germans attacked with armor, and the artillery began using up its precious shells. On the twenty-sixth the need was desperate again, and flying weather from England was impossible. They used gliders, then, to bring in ammunition from French fields. Later, 301 planes took off from England in vile weather, carrying 320 tons of supply for the 101st. Next day, resupply was again questionable. Thirty-five gliders came in, but the Germans had ringed Bastogne with guns. They increased the antiaircraft fire in the area, which caused heavy plane loss. Even so, the troop carriers flew 188 missions that day and dropped 162 more tons of supplies.

That evening Major General Hugh Gaffey forced a corridor through the German lines to Bastogne from Arlon, and the 4th Armored Division relieved the 101st just in time. The German drive was bogged down.

Meanwhile, in the 82nd Airborne sector, on December 23 the Germans had begun their attack to drive to Liège, through Werbomont, from the south. The 325th Glider Infantry felt the first brunt of it that morning. The 2nd SS launched an attack, but the 325th drove it back. Here, too, the Germans were surprised. Up to now they, like the 1st SS, had found the Americans easy to handle. They settled down south of the line, and their artillery mortars and tanks began to pound the little crossroads village of Regne. Late in the afternoon two panzer companies lumbered into position and began to move. Behind them came the whole 4th Panzergrenadier Regiment. The 325th stood as long as possible. Finally Colonel Billingslea ordered the men out and the 44 men left of the 116 who had been sent to hold the crossroads came.

The 2nd Battalion of the 504th Parachute Infantry was next to feel the pressure. Major E. N. Wellems had brought them from Cheneux to Lierneux to back up the 325th. Then, General Gavin took a trip to Manhay, west of the division's line of responsibility, where the 3rd Armored Division command post was supposed to be. He found the place deserted. Without notice, 3rd Armored had retreated, leaving the whole western flank of the 82nd exposed. Gavin went back to XVIII Airborne Corps headquarters to complain. The chief of staff had no help for him. The situation threatened to develop into a disaster. There were no reserves to send, he said. But it was not quite so bad as that; within a few hours Gavin had his help: Corps had been given Combat Command B of the 9th Armored Division to move to the 82nd's right flank.

On December 24 Corps headquarters ordered the withdrawal of the division to a line running from Manhay to Trois Ponts in the northeast. This would give time to prepare for a German attack.

The 504th regimental plan called for one platoon per company to cover the rear while the remainder pulled away. The covering force was to remain in position until 4:00 on Christmas morning and then withdraw north. The plan worked beautifully for all except the platoon of Lieutenant Lamm of 2nd Battalion, which found itself surrounded in the Vielsalm area, where German troops had forded the river to attack just as the others had withdrawn. Lamm had to fight his way out. The platoon losses were two officers and eight men missing, two men killed, and one officer and eight men wounded.

As the covering force withdrew, Corporal Frederick Robbins was posted at the Odrimont crossroads with one rifleman and a radio operator to inform Battalion of activity. He saw an enemy motorized column moving toward them and, just before he pulled out, gave the coordinates to the artillery. Shells began to rain down on the German panzers.

On Christmas Day, then, the 504th was in its new line, patrolling to capture prisoners and stringing barbed wire and mine fields out front. The machine guns prepared fields of fire. The artillery zeroed in on the roads. For the first time since the panic began, the unit commanders had a chance to reconnoiter and plan their battle.

Lieutenant Colonel Wellems, commander of 2nd Battalion, sent one platoon of Company D to Floret. This would be the combat outpost. The assignment was drawn by Lieutenant Harry Rollins, who had 41 men. He sent Sergeant Harold Dunnagan with a reinforced squad to set up a roadblock and a mine field on one road out of Floret. A second squad, under Corporal Jack Larison, had the same assignment at another roadblock. The mortar squad, under Private, First Class, Bert Davis, would support

Larison. The command post would remain in Floret.

By midnight on Christmas Day the men were in place. An hour later the Germans showed up at Dunnagan's outpost on the main road. The first sign was a patrol of six German riflemen. Dunnagan opened fire at 75 yards, with a machine gun and M-1 rifles. The Germans drew back, leaving one man wounded in the road. He screamed and groaned, apparently shot in the abdomen. As long as the moon was up the Germans made no attempt to rescue him, but when daylight came at 7:30 on December 26, the man was gone.

All was quiet at Dunnagan's post until 10:00. Then the field telephone linking the outpost with the command post went dead. Corporal Emmett Coffin, signalman, and Private Luther Kranz, the platoon runner, were sent to repair the line. They found the break and repaired it, but as they started back for the roadblock, a German mortar shell struck between them. Krantz was killed. Coffin was wounded.

At 12:00 the outpost was attacked from the woods on the right flank. The Germans had moved around to come up with the sun at their backs. They were well-armed, with MG 42s and Schmeisser automatic pistols. The opened fire, and Dunnagan returned it. Then another German force appeared on the road.

Dunnagan called up Lieutenant Rollins, who ordered the roadblock evacuated. They were to pull back to join the platoon at Floret. Larison's squad had a radio, and at 1:00 P.M. Larison called for artillery fire into those woods and then onto Dunnagan's roadblock, which the Germans had taken over. But the Germans kept moving more troops into the area. An hour later, Rollins called up D Company and asked for permission to withdraw. The word went to Battalion; Wellems said hold.

Larison and his men saw a German coming up in a wagon. They opened up on the wagon but did not shoot at the horse or man; they wanted a prisoner. The German raised his hands and came into the roadblock. Larison looked into the wagon. It held two MG 42s and eight Karbiner 98s. The men destroyed them, and Larison took the prisoner back to the platoon command post. The prisoner said he was from the 9th SS Division and that the German unit was planning a night attack.

Lieutenant Rollins brought Larison's squad back from the

roadblock to the command post, and the mortar squad withdrew to the rear of the post.

At 5:30 the attack began with a barrage of Nebelwerfers, mortars, and 88s. The troops worked up on three sides and attacked. Rollins estimated that he faced a battalion. He called for artillery support, but none came. The platoon returned fire as the Germans came in, but without support it could not hold. Rollins sent the men back, four and five at a time.

Platoon Sergeant Charles Anderson crawled back to the mortar squad to cover the retreat with his tommy gun. All the mortarmen moved out, except Private, First Class, Davis and Private Connor Dilbeck. They said they would stay until they ran out of ammunition. The Germans began crawling up onto the mortar position. A 20 mm. flak wagon came up, and the mortarmen then withdrew.

The German platoon that had cut off the mortar squad also cut off the line of retreat from the command post. Lieutenant Rollins and the three riflemen in the post were lost. Larison's squad was overrun, and five of his men were killed or captured.

As the remnants of the platoon moved back, they came into Company E's position. The Germans, believing they had routed the Americans, rushed after them. Company E met them with machine guns, BARs, and M-1s. The Germans dropped fast, and the assault was pulled back. The battalion had held on the Floret sector.

In the 505th's area, around Bru, southwest of Trois Ponts, the military situation appeared confused. On the night of December 24 Colonel Vandervoort and Captain Sammon set out on foot for a reconnaissance of Bru. They heard a noise as they walked along the road, they challenged, had no response, and opened fire. Someone fired back. They went back for the colonel's jeep, which was equipped with a light machine gun, and sprayed the area. There was no answer. Later they learned they had run upon a handful of Germans from Colonel Peiper's armored column, which was now bogged down in the midst of the Americans and had run out of gas. The Germans had abandoned their vehicles and were making for the Salm river to cross into the safety of their own lines.

All day long on the twenty-fifth the 505th captured handfuls of

German prisoners from the Peiper unit. At one point a battalion-sized force attacked the Americans from the rear, then fought its way through to the Salm.

The 508th had the most difficult withdrawal. The regiment had to pull back seven miles to reach the positions assigned by division headquarters. On the other side of the river they faced the 19th Panzergrenadier Regiment, one of the most aggressive of the German units. The plan called for the 508th to leave a small force to cover and move the rest out on Christmas Eve. The plan worked beautifully. The Germans slept on, not knowing, except in one area: The 19th decided to cross the river at Vielsalm, just as the men of the 508th were beginning to move.

Lieutenant George Lamm had been assigned to cover the withdrawal, and he found his platoon surrounded by German infantry. The Americans had to fight their way out. The casualties were high, but they made it back.

On Christmas, then, the 508th was also dug in along its new line. The division was holding the sector from Vaux Chavannes to Trois Ponts, although the town itself was evacuated.

On the night of December 25 the Germans struck the 508th at the boundary of 2nd and 3rd Battalions. The German troops had no armor. They were driven back.

On the night of December 26 a battalion of the 62nd Volks-grenadiers attacked. This time they were preceded by German fighter planes strafing the mortar positions of the regiment, as well as bombardment by 88s. The Germans came in yelling and screaming, but the paratroopers were not green; they did some yelling and screaming themselves. The situation seemed to be under control until elements of the 9th SS Panzer Division attacked on the boundary of the battalions. The full force hit the left flank of 3rd Battalion and overran H Company. I Company, which had been in reserve, came to the rescue. F Company, on the right flank of 2nd Battalion, counterattacked, and the remnants of H Company attacked from the rear. The Germans retreated. In this wild fight the regiment lost 15 men, killed or wounded. Next day the Americans counted 62 dead Germans in the H company position and 50 more in front of H Company. The men of 508th had completely wiped out a battalion of the 9th SS Panzers.

Later, when the town of Goronne was captured, civilians reported that for three days after that assault German ambulances were overrunning the city, moving out the wounded from the battle. This was the last attack of the 9th SS Panzers on the 508th. The German roll-up had been stopped on Christmas. The 82nd Division had held, too.

The favorite position of paratroopers has always been the front-leaning rest. Push-ups follow.

Getting the feel of it.

A trainee jumps from the 34-foot tower at Fort Bragg, North Carolina. Most jump training is now conducted at Fort Benning, Georgia.

Learning to disengage from the chute.

Airdrop.

A World War II paratrooper rigged
to carry extra equipment.

A World War II paratroop officer ready to board.

The Normandy airdrop.

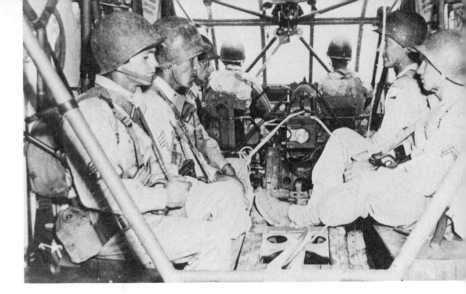

Glidermen of the 82nd Airborne Division during a World War II assault.

Sometimes the gliders came down hard.

In Operation MARKET-GARDEN, paratroopers of the 82nd Airborne Division made an assault into Holland, September 17, 1944, as part of the First Allied Airborne Army. More than 50,000 American, British, and Polish paratroopers took part in this airborne invasion, the largest in history.

Covering fire provided by a water-cooled .30 caliber machine gun left over from World War I. This weapon is no longer used by the Army.

A 75 mm. pack howitzer.

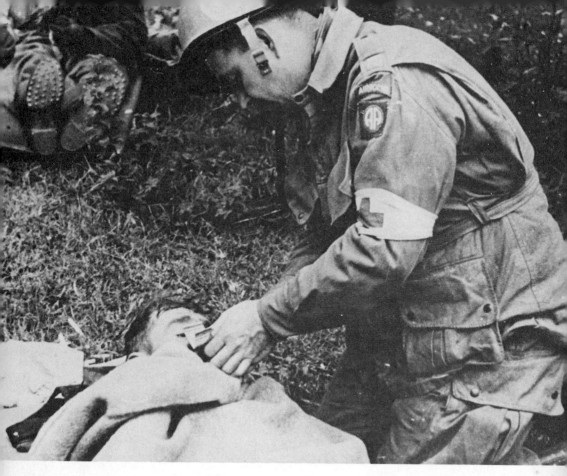

An 82nd Airborne Division medic treats a wounded paratrooper during World War II. The division made four parachute assaults in Europe and suffered more than 5,000 casualties during the Normandy invasion alone.

Marching through France.

The results of house-to-house fighting.

Showgirls of the Jack Benny USO troupe with men of the 11th Airborne Division at Dobodura, New Guinea on August 1, 1944.

Paratroopers of the 17th Airborne Division get together with their generals in Mourmelon, France prior to a jump beyond the Rhine River into Germany, March 24, 1945.

Ready to go.

Glider troops of the 17th Airborne Division, First Allied Airborne Army, leave their gliders near Wesel, Germany and prepare for enemy resistance.

Captured Germans.

Private James Harper, a member of Company G, 187th Regiment, 11th Airborne Division, rests beside a dud para-bomb during a lull in the fighting in Luzon, April 9, 1945.

Members of the all-black 555th Parachute Infantry Battalion are briefed before takeoff from Fort Dix, New Jersey in 1947.

Men of Company L, 187th Regimental Combat Team, dig in along the ridge of Hill 299, East Munsan-Ni, Korea, in preparation for covering a charge over the ridge line by Company F, March 28, 1951.

Brigadier General Frank S. Bowen, Jr., commanding general of the 187th Regimental Combat Team, and his staff communicate with the battalion commanders at Munsan-Ni, Korea, March 23, 1951.

The Ready Force of the 101st Airborne Division, ready to move out during an exercise at Fort Campbell, Kentucky, in May 1965.

Members of the 82nd question a suspected rebel in downtown Santo Domingo during the 1965 uprising. U.S. troops were sent to the Dominican Republic to open a corridor for the possible evacuation of American citizens.

Troopers of the 82nd "All-Americans" entering a transport.

Vietnam copter operation.

Two members of 2nd Battalion, 327th Infantry, 101st Airborne Division, direct troop-carrying UH-1D helicopters onto an airstrip in the Ashau valley. August 1968.

A paratrooper of the 82nd helps a wounded Vietnamese soldier following an intense firefight in the Mekong Delta in 1969. The 3rd Brigade spent 22 months in Vietnam after being sent there during the 1968 Tet Offensive.

Units of the 82nd were called upon during civil disturbances in Washington in April 1968.

Modern paratroopers defend their position with an M-60 machine gun in a simulated gas-contaminated environment.

A team from the 82nd's Company E, 325th Infantry, trains with the TOW, a weapon capable of penetrating any known armor.

An infantry fire team provides cover as paratroopers of the 82nd Airborne Division descend in a parachute assault at Fort Bragg's Sicily drop zone. The fire team employs the M-16A1 rifle and the M-203 grenade launcher.

On the Offensive

On December 23 half the 17th Airborne Division was brought to back up the defenses of Bastogne. One battalion of the 513th Parachute Infantry was to defend the bridge at Stenay, one the bridge at Verdun, and one was to be kept in reserve at Buzancy. After landing near Rheims these troops were moved by motor vehicle. The 194th Glider Infantry was brought to Cheremy, and the 193rd Glider Infantry to Boulzicourt. The 507th Parachute Infantry prepared to move in reserve. Major General William M. Miley, commander of the 17th, was given responsibility for the whole line of the Meuse.

The orders came on January 2. The 194th moved up through a line of villages—Rechrival, Hubremont, Millomont—and then encountered stiff resistance that stopped them and drove them back. The 1st Battalion was hit by armored force as it came down the St. Hubert–Bastogne highway. The 2nd Battalion ran into a large unit of German infantry at Mande-St. Etienne, staged a bayonet attack, and killed more than 200 Germans in hand-to-hand fighting. It was a bloody christening for green troops. The men of the 17th Airborne knew what to do even though the division had not before been in battle.

The 17th, like all the other American units, was hampered by bad weather. The Germans knew the terrain, and the Americans did not. The fog and heavy overcast prevented accurate American artillery observation, but the troops were under heavy bombardment and the battalions lost many casualties to shelling. Lieutenant Bruce Robbins of 2nd Battalion received a direct hit by an 88 shell. All this while Twelfth Army Group headquarters was complaining because the 17th Division was not moving. There were no Germans out there, said army headquarters; what was stopping them?

General Miley rejoined that there were not only Germans out there, but Germans with 88s and 105s and plenty of tanks and infantry. From its point of prescience, Army still insisted there could be no Germans there; intelligence told them so. At this time the 194th Glider Infantry had been virtually encircled.

Miley knew that the Germans were still dug in where the green troops had failed to dislodge them.

What he did not know was that as he reported, 2nd Battalion of the 513th had stopped right in the middle of a hive of those nonexistent Germans. Green troops or seasoned would have made little difference here.

Lieutenant Colonel Allen Miller, commander of the 513th's 2nd Battalion, had taken Mande-St. Etienne, where the high ground offered a better position than Monty, where the 11th Armored had maintained an outpost. Miller wanted all the high ground, beyond the village, but the Germans resisted, and D Company on the right and F on the left could not get to the tree line. The Germans had automatic weapons concealed in the trees. The approach was uphill over barren ground so Miller ordered the two companies to stop and dig in.

Company E set up in reserve in the town, with the command post and the aid station. There wasn't too much left of the buildings. Mande-St. Etienne had been battered heavily by Allied air attack earlier. The few buildings that remained standing were under constant artillery fire from the Germans in the woods above, and snipers were dug in all around the town. One sniper covered the door of the command post with a Schmeisser, others fired into the buildings from three directions. Only the southeast approach was safe. The artillery rounds came in constantly; once an 88 threw two rounds into a room of the command post, which was full of sleeping men. Luckily they were rolled in blankets, so there were no serious casualties, although several men could collect Purple Hearts later, if they got back, and if they remembered the incident.

Lieutenant McRory brought up three 57 mm. guns from the 115th Antitank Battalion. Several times during the afternoon tanks appeared east of town, and the guns fired. McRory's trouble was that he had only 12 rounds per gun, and the battalion was out of communication with Regiment.

Several times Lieutenant Colonel Miller expected the German tanks to roll into town. Each time, McRory's guns stopped them.

Back at Regiment the position of the battalion was not understood yet. Lieutenant Stem, the battalion S-4 (plans officer), was sent up with a pair of two-and-one-half ton trucks with trailers, carrying ammunition and supplies. He was ambushed on the road by the Germans. Both trucks were destroyed, and several of his men were killed. Stem showed up at the command post, his helmet riddled with bullet holes, to report the loss. Someone had to go back and tell Regiment the situation. Lieutenant Michael Garafino, the battalion adjutant, took a patrol and headed toward the regimental command post.

When Garafino explained the problem to Colonel James Coutts, the regimental commander, Coutts decided to come up and have a look. He also sent some tanks that were still in the area to deliver .30 and .50 caliber ammunition. The temporary presence of the tanks and increasing visibility that afternoon caused the German armor to move back.

After Coutts left, the fire resumed. That afternoon two jeep ambulances came into the town, but the fire on the road was so heavy that they waited until after dark to begin evacuating casualties. At least they had plenty of plasma for the aid station.

After dark the most serious casualties were moved out by jeep. Supplies came up from Regiment, and the wiremen laid a telephone wire back from the command post.

In the town, it was dark, cold, and miserable. The enemy was too close, so there were no fires. German artillery harried the town all night, and after midnight the Germans tried to infiltrate. There were not enough men to make a tight defense. The Americans found themselves fighting within 10 yards of their positions with grenades and even knives.

Back at SHAEF, intelligence knew there weren't any Germans out there, and the VIII Corps was ordered to attack. The 17th Airborne and the 87th Division were to attack abreast. Second Battalion of the 513th was to take off and move to the Ourthe river, 10 miles north. Colonel Coutts had given the orders but could give no information about the enemy dispositions or even the terrain. He did not have it.

Second Battalion's first problem was to get up that hill 200 yards north of D Company. E Company would stage that attack, then move up, D and F would come along, and they would hold the top of the hill and await further orders.

On the left, 1st Battalion's B and C Companies would move ahead, with A Company in reserve, and take Flamizoulle.

At 8:00, as it grew light, the weather was foggy and snow was falling on the hillside. The men in Company D could not see the enemy 200 yards away.

First Battalion moved out and had little trouble, as it went along the ravine, separating their sectors from the Bastogne highway. They captured a few prisoners, stragglers. At 8:15 2nd Battalion's E Company moved up through D Company and fought up the hill, the way paved by artillery fire from Regiment. Lieutenant John Deam, company commander, reported at 8:30 that his men were in the enemy foxholes of their first objective.

What no one knew at that moment was that the Germans had strong positions on three sides of the hill crest. Company F found out: The men moved forward into a murderous hail of fire. Only the artillery saved any of them. The platoon commander on the left, Lieutenant Stositch, was hit. Lieutenant Puckett, his assistant, took over and edged his men to the right into the wood. But from the right rear came another murderous hail of fire from dug-in Germans. The platoon was pinned down.

Artillery moved its fire to the right. Several men made it into the woods. Then the fire resumed and the others were pinned down again.

The center platoon never made the forest. The fire dropped them.

Lieutenant Colonel Miller watched the decimation from his command post, only 150 yards away. He sent word to Lieutenant Deam to move his reserve platoon into the forest, flank the Germans, and save F Company.

"Go in, but don't swing to the left."

"Don't worry," said Deam, "I'll start them off myself."

He called Lieutenant Richard Manning, and told him to order bayonets fixed, and the men to move. Lieutenant Deam started off with them to be sure there was no mistake about their objective. He had gone two steps when a rifle bullet killed him.

Manning went on. The Americans used grenades and bayonets. They did not want to take prisoners. When the wood was cleared, 200 Germans were found dead there, and 23 prisoners were sent to the rear.

As they cleared the woods, Manning counted noses. He had lost only three men. But then a grenade exploded, and it was four: Manning lost a leg.

Lieutenant Colonel Miller came up with Company D. The position was secure, and F Company could be pulled in for reorganization.

The right-hand platoon had only 10 men and no officers left. The center platoon had 25 men, and the left platoon, 30.

The battalion moved forward toward the river, still not knowing exactly what force it faced. E and F Companies met opposition in the woods, but not heavy infantry fire. Most of the Germans seemed to be in armored vehicles, moving north of the battalion. It was hard to see in the fog, but F Company knocked out two light tanks with grenades.

To F Company it looked like the war was over, as they went toward the river; the men moved far ahead of the battalion's sector, and a platoon even went in to occupy Flamizoulle, which was in 1st Battalion's territory.

After 2nd Battalion took the hill above Mande-St. Etienne, Lieutenant Colonel Miller lost touch with Regiment again. He was moving fast, and his men, particularly F Company, were moving too fast for him to keep up.

Miller had his first sense of unease when he began to see men from the 1st Battalion moving back. There was no time to stop and quiz them. Soon enough he would know.

First Battalion had moved freely until C and B Companies approached the Bastogne highway near Cochleval. There they ran into German armor in force. The high-velocity fire stopped them completely. They tried to flank the enemy, but the German line extended farther than they could move, and as they tried, 10 German tanks and several self-propelled guns came from the west into the woods and opened fire. They were under frontal and enfilade fire then.

The German tanks from the woods lumbered on until they were within 100 yards of the infantry, and opened fire at point blank range. The men began to run. Major Harry Kies came up from the battalion command post and then went back to send up bazooka ammunition. But within half an hour, the companies were surrounded. A hundred men surrendered.

Only the 3rd Platoon of C Company managed to bring men back. They were lucky; they had not gotten up far enough to be surrounded. Of the two companies' officers, only one was left.

When Colonel Coutts learned of the disaster to 1st Battalion, he ordered a withdrawal, with 3rd Battalion to defend the move. The situation was so desperate that Regimental Headquarters Company was sent up as a rifle company to the left of 3rd Battalion. To meet the German armor, Coutts managed to assemble five 37 mm. guns and a handful of 57 mm. guns behind them. Five medium tanks were ordered up from 11th Armored Division, but en route three of them were knocked out by self-propelled 88s, and the other two withdrew. The Shermans could not stand up to Tiger tanks and 88 mm. guns.

Lieutenant Colonel Miller had been moving so fast in the attack ordered from on high that he did not receive the message sent by runner from Regiment to stop and dig in. It probably would have made no difference at all. For, having decimated 1st Battalion, the Germans were ready to turn their attention to 2nd Battalion, and they did. In the advance, 2nd Battalion had strung out, and now it hit F Company, which consisted of only 25 men. They struggled through the snow and made it to E Company. The platoon that had entered Flamizoulle was overwhelmed. When last seen, the men were fighting against a growing force of Germans.

The enemy kept pushing from Trois-Ponts and Flamierge, and the Americans pulled back to the regimental area. The cost of the day had been high. Second Battalion, for example, had 50 percent loss. When reorganized, F Company had 40 men and D Company had 85 men.

That night all the regiment's ambulances and jeeps were engaged in moving the wounded back, and supplies came up from Division.

On January 5 at 9:45 A.M. the Germans began an armored

drive astride the Bastogne highway, with tanks and self-propelled guns. They came into the areas assigned 1st and 2nd Battalions. These held in spite of several thrusts by tank units. Late in the afternoon Major Irwin Edwards, executive officer of 2nd Battalion, called Colonel Coutts to report six enemy tanks approaching his right flank. He asked for orders.

"Stop the attack," said Coutts.

Second Battalion held again.

January 6 was quiet, but that evening Division ordered the 513th Regiment to attack. The 193rd would be on their right and the 194th on the left. The flank regiments would move out first, so that there would be no German flanking for the front. Second Battalion, so badly mauled, was kept back in reserve. The objective was forest land on the high ridge southwest of Flamierge.

Third Battalion reached its first objective at Vivier du Four in spite of German fire from tanks and 88s. The Germans fought a rear-guard action in the forest, retreating but giving ground slowly. The weather was again cold and foggy, with snow falling.

First Battalion appeared at the objective shortly afterward, and the Americans dug in. At 11:30 six German Mark IV and Mark VI tanks attacked on the road from Mon Nicolay and through the snow-drifted fields. They moved forward to the bald crest of the hill but pivoted back into ditches and farm buildings near the road. The enemy tanks came to the crest of the hill and fired down. The 1st Battalion tried to raise Division artillery, but there was no response. They would have to deal with the tanks themselves.

Fortunately, this time, the 513th had some armored support. Five tanks of the 22nd Tank Battalion of the 11th Armored Division had joined them for the attack. Major Morris Anderson, commander of 3rd Battalion, talked over the situation with Lieutenant John Dixon, the tank commander. It was going to be hard going, Dixon said; visibility was so poor that much of the time the tankers could not see 100 feet. Anderson proposed to load the tanks with as many troopers as they could carry and then rush the hill. He would ride the outside of Dixon's tank.

But as the tanks moved up to load, they ran into a mine field and the tracks were knocked off three of them. The two others moved left, and as they did, an 88 shell knocked out one and wounded three men. The fifth tank sat tight; one tank was of very little use.

Anderson moved out with the infantry. The tanks still had some value: The tankers stuck with them and used them as pill-boxes, firing their guns to support the infantry advance.

The troopers went up the hill as best they could. Machine guns and bazookas drove several German half-tracks off the hill. A bazooka team destroyed one Mark VI on top of the hill.

At noon General Miley came up and reported the 193rd and 194th had fallen behind, and he said the 513th was to dig in and wait. But the battalion commanders asked permission to take their objectives, and it was granted.

The tanks had retreated into Flamierge. Third Battalion went after them, down the hill 1,500 yards into Flamierge. The Americans had no artillery support and no heavy weapons, and they had to move across rolling ground into tank fire, artillery, machine guns, and mortars. The enemy played havoc with the battalion.

Twenty snow capes had been issued to the battalion's officers and key noncoms, but these proved to be identifying marks for snipers. The men abandoned them. The Germans concentrated on men carrying special equipment, but the battalion kept on, and Major Anderson's radio operator carried his damaged set throughout the entire advance, through knee-deep snow.

Colonel Coutts had arranged for an artillery barrage to be laid down on Flamierge. When the 3rd Battalion was 150 yards from the town, shells began falling. Coutts had no direct contact with the battalion; somebody had made a good guess. The barrage lasted ten minutes and gave Anderson time to organize his men. The moment the guns stopped, G Company headed to clear the left side of town, and H, the right side. They went in with M-1s, tommy guns, and BARs, firing from the hip. The enemy pulled back as the Americans came up throwing grenades into the windows of the houses. Two enemy tanks were stopped by bazookas. One was knocked out by a light machine gun when the gunner hit a vital spot, and the tank clanked to a halt. The crew began climbing out, and the Americans mowed them down. Snipers were troublesome, however. Major Anderson saw a hole in a haystack and tossed a grenade into it. He blew out one German sniper.

By 3:15 the town was secured. The cost had been high. In the morning 525 men of 3rd Battalion had set out; in the evening Major Anderson counted 375 men. All but two of the battalion aid men had been hit and left behind at Vivier du Four. Those two, Technician, Fourth Grade, Terrence Kelly and Technician, Fifth Grade, Bohner, were the heroes of the advance on Flamierge; no wounded man was too exposed for them to find and treat.

First and 2nd Battalions had hard going, because both were well below strength and both ran into pockets of trouble. But by 5:00 Colonel Coutts could call General Miley and tell him the regiment was in place. Even Corps sent down its congratulations, just as the men noticed new signs of German activity all across their front.

The Germans had infiltrated around the regiment's positions, and all three battalions needed resupply and, if possible, reinforcement. Communications were out to the rear, so in the evening Lieutenant McLain of the 466th Field Artillery and Private, First Class, Rolland Bragg of Headquarters Company, took a captured German ambulance back to explain. They also took one seriously wounded rifleman on a litter in the ambulance.

On the way they ran into two German stragglers, who surrendered. They put one German between them on the front seat and forced the other to stand on the running board as a shield against enemy fire. The German tried to jump off and run. McLain cut him down with his tommy gun. An enemy machine gun began firing at the ambulance. The German between McLain and Bragg was killed, but neither American was hit. Bragg drove on through. At the command post they stopped for the first time. When they opened up the back they found that German fire had killed the wounded man.

The whole area was spotty with American and German positions, so anyone coming up from the rear had to be careful. That night Lieutenant Colonel Ward Ryon, the regimental executive officer, moved up with Captain Joseph Rawn to visit 3rd Battalion. They reached 2nd Battalion, where they got directions and a patrol to take them on up. Ryon took a compass reading, and then saw fires ahead that must be Flamierge. They headed for the light. As they reached the edge of the town, they were challenged.

"Halt!" shouted a voice. *"Geben Sie——"*

"Very funny," said Colonel Ryon. "This is Colonel Ryon."
Captain Rawn broke in.

"Was wollen Sie?" he demanded.

He was greeted by a torrent of German.

He shouted back, in German, that he had made a mistake and
motioned Colonel Ryon to get out fast. They moved away from
the lights, half expecting to be followed by rifle fire, but behind
was silence. When they returned to 2nd Battalion, they found
they had missed their way and ended up at Flamizoulle, which
was held by the enemy. A scout led them, and in an hour they
were in Flamierge.

Next day, as the enemy movement indicated, was going to be a
rough one. That night Regiment sent up 400 rounds of bazooka
ammunition, and supplies for riflemen and machine gunners and
mortarmen. The battalion asked for antitank guns, but it was early
morning before Ryon was able to move up a platoon of the 602nd
Tank Destroyer Battalion. He located the men and weapons in
burned buildings and then went back to the regimental command
post to discover that the officer in charge of the platoon had
panicked and led his men back. He had returned, even before
Ryon made it back. The officer was sent to the rear, to face
charges, but the forward troops were left without antitank
weapons.

So far, the training of the men of the 17th Division had carried
them through one of the most difficult battles the Americans faced
in the war. But it took combat to sort out the leaders.

That night the Germans tried to infiltrate 3rd Battalion, using
the technique of donning American uniforms, which had been so
successful in the opening days of the Ardennes breakthrough. The
Americans captured two of them. One had wire cutters in his
pocket.

At the battalion command post Major Anderson began to
interrogate the men.

At first the Germans gave name, rank, and serial number and
then were silent. *"Nicht verstehen"* was their answer to questions.
The Americans, recalling the murder of men of the Seventh Army
in the breakthrough by Germans in American uniform, were not
gentle. The Germans were cuffed. Anderson reminded them that
the uniforms they wore established their identity as spies. He

threatened to shoot them—after he was through with them. A circle of grim faces backed him up. One of the prisoners broke. In colloquial English he said he was not a spy but had put on the uniform so he could desert. His regiment had bales of American uniforms.

He was a spy, said Anderson, and he would be shot unless he talked.

The German then gave the locations of enemy infantry and armored units. In the morning, he said, the Germans were attacking in this sector, particularly to take Flamierge.

Anderson wanted to shoot the prisoners right there, but he sensed that if the Germans took American prisoners in the fight to come, it might go hard for them, so he sent the Germans, in their American uniforms, back to Regiment under guard with the recommendation that they shoot them there. He also called for artillery fire on the coordinates indicated by the German prisoners. Unfortunately that message got lost.

The German attack began at 6:00 A.M. when 20 tanks and several platoons of infantry moved in on Flamierge from the north, while 6 tanks and 6 self-propelled 88s moved across the fields between 2nd and 3rd Battalions. Had the tank destroyers remained, they would have had a field day. As it was, the men had only small arms and the 57 mm. guns. The range was so great that the visibility was limited, and Anderson told them to hold fire.

One 57 mm. gun was hit by an artillery round, and another froze up. The gunners should have been able to clear it in a few minutes, but they panicked and took refuge in a nearby house. Lieutenant Colonel Miller found them and ordered them back to their gun. They refused to go. He threatened them with his pistol, but they were too frightened; he might have shot them and they still would not move. This same crew had fought valiantly in the last engagement. But Lieutenant McRory had been given company responsibility and a sergeant had taken over.

This cowardice in the face of the enemy became an important factor in the battle of the 513th that day. There were no guns to fight the armor.

Second Battalion was hit by tanks coming down the Bastogne highway. The Americans had the advantage of terrain, and the advance cost the German infantry heavily, but they came on. Soon the enemy had overrun the perimeter and the fighting was going on in the forest. The tanks came up, knocking down trees "like match sticks," as one trooper put it. But the battalion held. The men knocked out 5 tanks, with bazookas and mortars, but 14 tanks still came on. Then from the west came another half-dozen, with infantrymen equipped with flamethrowers.

Against these, the battalion was fighting with rifles. The bazooka ammunition was exhausted and they had no more grenades. The artillery had never made contact, so there would be no support fire. Miller pulled his men back. They were supposed to fall back on Company F and reorganize. But reorganize what? The men returned without ammunition. They had their weapons but could not fire them. They moved to the rear, where, finally, ammunition was handed to them as they came by the supply dump at the road junction of the Flamizoulle and Bastogne roads. The infantrymen continued to withdraw back to the forest from which they had started two days earlier.

Lieutenant Edgar Thommasino, the battalion intelligence officer, and the 81 mm. mortar platoon, and 25 troopers stayed at the junction to fight a rear-guard action. They remained until all the ammunition in the dump was expended and then moved back to the forest.

When the battalion was reorganized there, Miller found he had 100 men and officers left. Ninety percent of them had no ammunition, and the others only a few rounds. The 2nd Battalion had not suffered from cowardice, but from attack by a superior force of enemy, heavily armed, and from a distinct lack of support by any sort of antitank guns.

Major Anderson's 3rd Battalion faced the same sort of attack. Early in the morning the wire to the rear went out, and from that time on the battalion was out of touch with Regiment. German tanks and infantry surged toward them, but the riflemen drove back the infantry, and the bazooka teams in their foxholes kept the tanks out of the perimeter. The tanks tried to spot bazooka teams and then fired directly into their foxholes.

When 2nd Battalion withdrew in Flamierge, 3rd Battalion faced a renewed and redoubled attack. Kelly and Bohner were still the only aid men in town. They tried to reach the wounded, but the Germans paid no attention to the red crosses on their sleeves and drove them back time and again.

The Germans again tried trickery. Some infantrymen wearing

American helmets came up, trying to lure the troopers into fire. The troopers watched for these infantrymen and sniped at them particularly. Eventually they either shot them all or caught them—the ruse ended.

At 2:00 that afternoon the men got in touch with Regiment by radio. They had finally put the radio up on a window ledge of one of the buildings to get sufficient volume. At last, they could hope for some artillery help. As the artillery began to adjust, three rounds hit the building, knocked out the radio, wounded the radio operator and sergeant, and killed three civilians who were in the command post talking to Major Anderson. Anderson was lightly wounded.

Private, First Class, Corley Wright volunteered to take the telephone line back to the rear. Anderson said he couldn't do it— the line ran through the fields and the German tanks were out there. Wright said he could try and he went on, crawling under fire. He was wounded three times but reported back that he was going on. Anderson ordered him to return to the command post. Wright made his way back then. They were cut off.

The German tanks continued firing. At dark they withdrew, except for two that sat at one end of the town's main street. All night long the darkness was punctured by flashes from mortars, artillery, and the tanks, but the battalion held.

By nightfall, Colonel Coutts was in communication with 2nd Battalion, which had withdrawn into the forest between Millomont and Nivier du Pape. Colonel Miller gave him the bad news about his casualties. Coutts knew that 3rd Battalion was cut off at Flamierge and assumed its condition was equally woeful. He reported to Division that the regiment was too weak to hold off a strong enemy attack. General Miley ordered the 507th up behind the 513th and told Coutts to withdraw 3rd Battalion from Flamierge.

Since Coutts was out of communication with 3rd Battalion, he sent out two patrols. One got to the buildings short of town and found them occupied by Germans. They headed back and told the other patrol that the Germans had the town; the battalion was gone.

Coutts did not believe this and prepared to send another patrol. Just then, Captain McGuire, of the 3rd Battalion, came into the command post to announce that the battalion was holding. Anderson had the radio operating but did not want to use it steadily, because every time they opened transmission, the Germans began firing on the position. Regiment, said McGuire, should open up at 9:00 P.M. for five minutes, and then every thirty minutes for five minutes. Corporal Gridley, the radio operator at the regimental command post, finally made contact an hour after midnight. He and Coutts knew the Germans must be listening in.

"Do you have an M209 Code Converter?"

"All codes and machines have been lost."

"All right," said Corporal Gridley. "Now listen carefully. My favorite song has always been 'When the Cowboy Herds His Dogies Back to the Old Corral.' "

"Got it," said Battalion.

"Stray dogies move fast," said Gridley.

"Got it," said Battalion.

They were to break into small groups to make their way back.

"A wheel always stays with crippled dogies," said Gridley.

Major Anderson, who was lying on a snow-covered straw pile listening to the exchange, knew what that meant. They were to leave an officer to arrange the surrender of the wounded. He realized for the first time that he was being ordered to evacuate. It was the worst moment of his life. He wanted support, not withdrawal. But orders were orders. He prepared to move out.

He ordered the men out in groups of 8 and 10, each with an officer or a noncom. They had no password, so they invented one: "Phoenix," with the countersign "City." Any paratrooper would know that honky-tonk town just outside Fort Benning.

The walking wounded moved out with the others, but the seriously wounded were left with Lieutenant Charles A. Lewis, who had been hit in the head and foot. Medics Kelly and Bohner also elected to stay with their charges.

Before they left, the men of the battalion booby-trapped all the houses except the aid post. Then they began to evacuate Flamierge; almost all of the men left reluctantly.

Major Anderson was the last to leave, and it was nearly dawn before he got away. As his party moved out, the Germans began to shell the town.

They drew back to Regiment, and Anderson took stock. Third Battalion had lost more than half its men.

The Americans gathered strength with resupply. On January

10 the 513th moved to Senonchamps. On the eleventh they fought again. On the thirteenth, 3rd Battalion was back in Flamierge. It had been an expensive fight. On January 2 the 513th went into action with 144 officers and 2,290 men. On January 15 the regimental strength was 81 officers and 1,036 men. The loss meant the regiment was down to 30 percent of its effective fighting strength, but the Germans were stopped and the drive could go on.

The decimation of the two battalions of the 507th brought orders that the division was to go on the defensive and hold its line, for even higher headquarters agreed that it was hard to fight tanks and flamethrowers with "our bare hands," as General Miley put it.

In the next few days the troops patrolled their sector, as the 101st was ordered to take Noville. On January 13 the division began to move, as the Germans pulled back. The troopers moved fast and reached the third day's objective at Wigny-Bertogne, on the morning of the second day. By January 14 the division had secured the river line and was in contact with British forces on the far side. The rest of this campaign was spent mopping up by-passed units, and braving the tricky defenses of the Germans, who had mined and booby-trapped the woods behind them.

"There are mines under every tree," said General Miley. "We haven't been able to move without having an engineer sweep in front of us."

For this he credited the devilish ingenuity of General Remmer of the German Remmer Group—"the prize son of a bitch of this war."

The 17th Airborne had indeed received its baptism of fire. On Christmas Day 832 officers and 12,711 men of the division had assembled in France. Twenty-four days later the division strength was 654 officers and 9,689 men; the Battle of the Bulge had taken 178 officers and 2,022 men.

Even SHAEF had come to the conclusion that there had been Germans out there.

With the success of the Allied drive against the Japanese in New Guinea the way was opened for an attack on the Philippines. The American Joint Chiefs of Staff agreed that this would be a

MacArthur show, although the Central Pacific command of Admiral Nimitz had the ships and the equipment. Nimitz would simply have to lend MacArthur what he needed, and then support the attack with the new fast carrier task force that had taken air superiority away from the Japanese. During the late summer months the buildup began in the Southwest Pacific. The target would be the island of Leyte, midway along the Philippine archipelago. A number of airfields there would make it possible for the Americans to maintain air superiority over all the islands, once they were captured. The Japanese were stronger in Luzon, the northern island, and Mindanao, the southern island, was vast and primitive. With Leyte taken, the Philippines would be cut in half, and the Dutch East Indies—Java and Sumatra—and other southern islands still held by the Japanese, would be cut off and the Japanese there could wither on the vine.

The American forces moved that fall against the Palau Islands, which gave them an airfield within striking distance of the Philippines, and against the Caroline Islands, which gave them a major fleet anchorage at Ulithi. All was ready then, for the assembly of the troops and ships to invade the Philippines. The paratroops were to participate, but not primarily as paratroops. They would go along as infantry, but be prepared for aerial operations if these seemed to be indicated.

Paratroops at Leyte

After weeks of jump school and life in the "Fuzzie-Wuzzie" land of New Guinea, the 187th was committed to the battle of Leyte, in the Philippines. As with so much else in the Pacific war, the paratroopers had operated on a do-and-make-do basis, and 88 percent of the men, including glidermen, had qualified for a jump in combat. As they got ready for takeoff, they learned the mission: The 187th was to relieve the 7th Infantry Division on Bito Beach. There was not to be a jump at all, but they were to destroy all the Japanese in the sector. General Yamashita had promised that the Imperial soldiers would fight "decisive battles" on Leyte and would push the Americans into the sea.

There was a good deal of confusion in the beginning, and the 187th Glider Infantry was assigned to guard communications. The 674th and 675th Parachute Field Artillery Battalions were separated from their weapons and assigned to guard the Air Force headquarters in the area. It had the sound of a dull, routine assignment. But early on the morning of November 29, 1944, three Japanese transport planes came roaring in low over the beaches. Nobody paid much attention; they looked much like the C-47s that had been coming by all day long, and although it was still dark, they might be the regular courier planes coming up from the south. Then one of them crash-landed on the San Pablo airstrip, and when the ground crews hurried up, they saw the rising sun insignia. All the occupants of this plane were killed on impact. They were airborne troops, apparently pathfinders for an airborne unit.

The word had barely gotten out, when the second Japanese plane was found, crashed near the command post of the 20th Armored Group. Two dead Japanese were found in that plane. But where were the others? Out in the jungle, apparently, preparing for action. The third pathfinder plane also crashed, and its occupants were killed. So the Japanese airborne attack on the beaches, which had been half anticipated, never came off.

The men of the 187th did jump at Leyte, or some of them did. On December 4 troops of the 457th Parachute Field Artillery and of B Company of the 187th went into action at Manawar Mountain. For the 187th it wasn't a big operation; no scores of men streamed from C-47s, but a handful of men jumped from L-4 liaison planes. So the Americans secured the mountain, and Burauen Heights, where the 2nd Battalion of the 187th was in position, and they held Bito Beach. The Japanese were preparing a combined air and land assault to take the three airfields in the area, and on the evening of December 6, just about at dusk, along came a string of Betty bombers, escorted by fighters, to soften up the area. Their bombs were not well aimed; most dropped in the jungle west of San Pablo airstrip. Then two flights of Japanese transports came in over the airstrip at 700 feet, and the Japanese paratroopers jumped. These were troops of the Katori Shimpei force.

The Japanese suffered a bit of confusion in the drop. Some of the parachute quick-release harnesses released troops 400 feet above the ground. Some who hit the ground milled around and let the Americans have time to recover; many of these Japanese became casualties before they could begin to fight. But enough of them were left to do their job: set fire to aircraft, destroy the fuel and ammunition dumps, and smash the camp. The only American troops in camp were the Headquarters Signal Company, the 127th Engineers Detachment, and Headquarters Battery of Division Artillery. The Japanese were holed up all around the strip when Colonel Hosak and men of the 674th arrived on December 7. They pushed the Japanese back from the airstrip so that a handful of L-4s that had been concealed could take off; then they dug in. Next day Colonel Hildebrand and the 1st Battalion came up and cleared the area.

Other Japanese of the 16th Division were obeying orders to fight and die. They attacked the 44th Station Hospital, and men of the 187th under Lieutenant Hurster drove them off. Other troops of the 187th cleared the other airfields. The Japanese 16th Division remnant had moved back up into the mountains and sent forays of troops down to attack the Americans. They held a pair of parallel ridges, with their strongest concentration on the rear ridge (known as Purple Heart Hill, as time went on). The 187th made a frontal assault, and then, finding no way up, went around end to attack Purple Heart Hill from the rear. They were marching on Christmas Day. On the twenty-sixth they arrived in position and opened up with mortars and machine guns that night. Next morning the soldiers went up the hill, in a bloody fight. When it was over they held their position, and they counted 238 more or less whole bodies, plus fragments of so many others that they could not count them. But that was the end of the action. They had wiped out the Japanese remnants who threatened the airfields and cut the supply line to the beach. On January 15, 1945, the 187th had come back down to Bito Beach, which was now regarded as a safe area for rest and recuperation.

The Japanese kept throwing reinforcements into Leyte, by destroyer, submarine, junk, and sampan. Still, the war went slowly because of these reinforcements. It was a case of fighting for nearly every foot of ground again, as the Japanese had shown in the island warfare of Guadalcanal. The Americans had earlier captured the Marianas Islands, and in November 1944 B-29 Superfortresses began bombing Japan regularly. This bombing of the homeland signaled the great change in the war to all Japanese. For the first time Japan at home was on the defensive. It also strengthened the determination of the Japanese soldiers and sailors and airmen to fight so hard in the Philippines that the Americans would be forced to end the war, leaving Japan alone. If that was a forlorn hope, it was the only hope the Japanese still had, particularly after the Battle of Leyte Gulf virtually destroyed the remains of the Japanese Imperial Navy.

On January 9, 1945 General MacArthur felt that the Leyte campaign was well enough in hand that he could take the next step, invasion of Luzon and capture of Manila. The Americans landed at Lingayen Gulf on Luzon. They attacked Manila on February 5 and it was captured on February 23. But again, the Japanese fought desperately everywhere, and each position had to be won by military force.

Back to Corregidor

The 11th Airborne Division was sent to the Pacific and operated in the beginning on Leyte Island more as a regular infantry division than an airborne unit. But even then there were unmistakable airborne characteristics. Much of the supply of the division in the Leyte mountains was carried out by airdrop. The division surgeon organized two "parachute hospitals." The medics and doctors jumped into action and for six weeks operated in territory that was inaccessible by anything but liaison plane and four-wheel-drive vehicles.

The 11th Airborne was a different sort of outfit in one way: Parachute troops and the glider troops were both parachute qualified. Thus anyone, so to speak, could do anything, and the division could make utmost use of the materials on hand.

On January 31, as their fellow airborne troopers were fighting along the edges of Germany, troops of the 11th Airborne dropped near Tagaytay on Luzon Island. There was a mix-up and one supply parachute was dropped prematurely, whereupon most of the paratroops of the 511th Parachute Infantry followed out the doors of their C-47s. When they hit the ground they found themselves six miles northeast of the drop zone. When the jumpmasters of the second flight came over and saw the parachutes on the ground, they also jumped in the wrong place. Luckily the enemy was on the run, and the troopers organized and soon made contact with the 188th Glider Infantry. Next day the two units were moving along the highway toward Manila.

The 503rd Parachute Infantry was involved in the Leyte operations and landed by ship at Taragona, then moved inland to fight as infantry. But there was virtually no infantry contact in their area, and in February 1945 the regiment was sent to Mindoro, where they occupied San Jose after some fighting. On February 16 the 2nd and 3rd Battalions jumped on Corregidor Island, which one paratrooper called "the worst jumpfield in history." Company E of the 2nd Battalion suffered 10 casualties from small-arms and knee mortar fire, and 21 men were injured on landing in the bad terrain.

The Japanese were dug in there, in trenches, foxholes, and pillboxes. On the second day D Company took one pillbox, with six casualties. That day the company killed 60 Japanese defenders. Two days later, the Japanese made a suicide attack on the company command post. They came swarming up from caves along the shore and through the ravines, to the high ground above the command post. Half the men on the perimeter were overwhelmed and killed, and the enemy closed in on the command post. It was located on Wheeler Point in an old plotting room that had a lovely view of the ocean on three sides—and no point of observation overlooking the land. There was no way anyone could see what was going on except by leaving the command post, and D Company was even cut off from support by the .30 caliber machine guns that were set up in an old coastal gun position. The post was moved, as soon as the initial attack was over, to a spot in the ravine 50 yards from the western end of the drill field. It was not nearly so scenic, but it was considerably safer. Even in the move, the company command was harried by Japanese stubbornness. A Japanese soldier crawled out from under one of the abandoned parachutes on the field and opened fire. One man was wounded.

At the end of the day Company D counted 113 men killed in action and 12 wounded. They killed 150 Japanese in the banzai charge.

Next day, men of Company D went to clean out the Japanese in the ravine and also clear the caves on the waterline, so that there would be no more banzai charges. They were preceded by a barrage laid down by the artillery and mortars.

The men started down the ravine that morning at 8:30. They found four Japanese hiding under a culvert and killed them. They came to a pillbox farther down the trail and flushed two more of the enemy. They destroyed six antiaircraft guns and then came to a cave that seemed much larger than the others. One squad approached from one side, and another circled around and came to the other side. The Japanese fired at the attackers, and Private Brady was killed, and Lieutenant Buchanan and a medic named Bowers were wounded. They discovered that this was a tunnel system. With grenades and rifle fire they killed the 26 Japanese inside and blew up the entrance holes, sealing off any others who might be alive in there.

For the next few days the paratroopers continued to rout out a few Japanese. Most of them were hidden in caves, particularly around Banzai Point, as they called the area. On February 24 the company moved in to clear the area below the big-gun position. The Japanese came out and then retreated to their caves. Private, First Class, McGarey was killed, and Privates Drew and Keller were wounded. They were taken to the beach and evacuated by landing craft to a hospital. When the company reached the point, the men turned back, and came under fire from Japanese in caves on the hillside who had brought a light machine gun to the mouth of a cave. Unfortunately the company had put itself in the position of an amphibious attack force, down on the beach, and the Japanese had planned for just such a fight. They had laid out overlapping fields of fire. The company began to take casualties. Riflemen Holt and Combes were killed, and Pucket was mortally wounded. Finckler, Rabe, Jenkins, and Richard were hit. The company called for help, and landing craft came in to pick them up. They had killed 20 Japanese that day, but the enemy was still up there. During the next week, the battalion cleared them out—it had to be done and the way made safe for General MacArthur's symbolic return to Corregidor on March 2.

After Manila fell, the 11th Airborne also moved to clear out pockets of resistance. The 511th Parachute Infantry and the 188th Para-Glider Regimental Combat Team went to Los Banos to free civilian prisoners in the camp there. They dropped on February 23, after making arrangements with the Filipino guerrillas to mark the drop zone for them. In the action they killed 240 Japanese guards, freed the prisoners, and lost two men killed and three wounded.

The 503rd moved to Pulu Pandan, on Negros Island, and to

the Patog river area, where they fought again as regular infantry, clearing out pockets of Japanese and chasing stragglers. They worked with the 40th Infantry Division against an estimated total of 12,000 Japanese air corps and ground troops on the island. The casualties came in ones and twos, but the Japanese fought as they headed into the hills. The Japanese were tough, even if hopelessly outnumbered and surrounded. On April 20 Lieutenant Watkins of D Company led an attack on a ridge in the Mulaga river country, starting at 11:15. There was no resistance—that is, they could not see any Japanese. But they were under heavy mortar fire all the time, and when Lieutenant Preston moved on the hill on the right fifteen minutes later, the platoon came under accurate fire. Platoon Sergeant Rabe was killed by a knee mortar shell. Lieutenant Preston was wounded. Private Ladig was so close to an exploding round that he suffered concussion, and the platoon was forced to withdraw.

Lieutenant Nickle, the company commander, took over the attack and led Lieutenant Marams and his platoon to the hill. It seemed easy—no resistance this time. But when the hill was secured, the enemy began a concentrated barrage with knee mortars, plus machine-gun and rifle fire from the front and both flanks. A mortar shell killed Lieutenant Nickle. Technician, Fourth Grade, Upchurch's leg was blown off, and he bled to death. Private, First Class, McLaughlin was wounded by the same round. A few minutes later Private, First Class, Huerter was wounded by shrapnel and Lieutenant David, commander of the machine gun platoon, was killed by a sniper.

With Manila secured and General MacArthur noisily operating his public relations machine there, not much was heard about the "mopping up" operations in the interior, but they were as deadly as any other aspect of the Pacific war.

This day, after Lieutenant David was killed, his body lay exposed on the forward slope and Privates, First Class, Schupp and Fischer tried to go out and get it. Both were wounded. Private Lapidas was shot in the neck. (He died two days later.) The Japanese were dug in and determined, and the platoon was pinned down. At 2:00 that afternoon the 2nd Platoon joined the 1st, and Sergeant Minor led a squad to secure the ridge. Lieutenant Collins took command of the company and brought up 3rd

Platoon to strengthen the position. Fire continued all day from the Japanese. At 5:00 a platoon from E Company came to assist them, but it was pinned down alongside the others by mortar and grenade fire. That night the Japanese tried to infiltrate and attack a machine-gun position. The Americans were alert and drove them off. One Japanese body was recovered.

Just before dawn a party of Japanese, including a machine-gun squad, attacked D Company frontally and entered one of the forward trenches. Sergeant Circo and Corporal Bokencamp were killed before the Japanese were driven out. Again, only one Japanese body was recovered.

Small-arms fire continued all day, with neither side able to move much. At 1:30 P.M. Sergeant Cleres was killed by a sniper while observing mortar fire.

Battalion needed that position and ordered an attack by D Company next morning. It began badly at 5:30 with a short round from an E Company 60 mm. mortar landing in the midst of the machine-gun platoon, killing Privates, First Class, Alexander and Hendricks, and wounding Sergeant Pittenger and Private Jackson. Fifteen minutes later 3rd Platoon moved out, with a light machine gun, to attack the ridge to the left, where much of the mortar fire originated. The attack was supported by .50 caliber machine guns, 81 mm. mortars, and 60 mm. mortars. Riflemen of D and E Companies gave small-arms support. The Japanese responded with mortar fire against 3rd Platoon, but obviously they were keeping their heads down, for the fire was inaccurate and there were no casualties.

At 6:00 A.M. the 1st Platoon moved to the ridge in front, and the 2nd Platoon joined the 3rd Platoon attack. The position was soon taken, but the Japanese fell back and resumed their knee mortar fire. Sergeant Stowe and Private, First Class, Seims were wounded, but it was obvious that the enemy was not given time to set up.

At 1:30 F Company sent word that two Japanese had been spotted on the opposite slope of D Company's ridge. Five men from the 2nd Platoon went down to investigate. They found the Japanese in a cave and attacked with grenades. They killed the two Japanese soldiers and then headed up the road to see where the enemy had gone. He had not gone far: Fifty yards up the road the patrol was smashed with mortar and rifle fire. Private Drew, the patrol leader, was killed, and the rest had to fall back. Later in the day Sergeant Minor led four men out to recover Drew's body.

That was the way it went; the Japanese contested every foot of ground, even though they were outnumbered and their supply lines were destroyed. The fighting of the 503rd was an indication of what was going to happen when the Americans hit Okinawa. Almost every night the Japanese counterattacked or tried to infiltrate. Their mortar fire and sniper fire were particularly troublesome and accounted for the most casualties, particularly among specialists and officers.

On the night of April 26 a banzai charge resulted in the killing of at least 19 enemy troops. In the daytime the Americans demolished one cave after another. They began setting booby traps at night for the banzai chargers, and the traps proved effective. But in daylight it was slugging warfare all the way. An attack on April 18 cost the company 10 casualties, and the 1st and 3rd Platoons had to be combined until enough replacements could come up from the rear. Replacing paratroopers was not easy; their use as ordinary infantry was a costly way to wage a war.

But it continued that way. In May the battalion moved south, and the difficulties of the enemy became apparent, although his will to fight never faltered. The Japanese stripped bodies of everything valuable; on May 8 Sergeant Nagy led a patrol that discovered several recently abandoned Japanese positions and large quantities of U.S. .30 caliber ammunition. On May 22, when the Japanese evacuated the area, the Americans found the defense had consisted of 24 pillboxes in three supporting lines, surrounded by slopes too steep to climb and fight on at the same time. It had taken a month to clear the Japanese out, and when they left it was to withdraw to another prepared position.

By June 11 the paratroopers were in Bago village. In July they were fighting stragglers, for the most part. On July 14, when Lieutenant Ward and D Company led a platoon across the Nimagaan river, they wounded a Japanese and then came upon him on the other side. He committed suicide with a grenade. They found that he was a naval petty officer, fighting to the last. On that same patrol, Private Michael was shot by a sniper and wounded in the foot. So even though the war was drawing to an end, it was still war for the men of the 503rd. They continued to patrol and kill Japanese in the Nimagayan river area through July, sustaining no casualties themselves now that the enemy were so few and so disorganized. On the day the first atomic bomb dropped on Hiroshima, the 1st Platoon was engaged in a firefight with a small number of Japanese. Afterward, no casualties were found. On August 11 a patrol saw one Japanese, who escaped in the forest, near the Himtican river. The patrols were out every day, but no enemy were seen. The battalion was so far out front that supply had to be carried out by Piper Cubs. On August 15 peace was declared, and all patrols were called in. And on August 16 the 503rd went into garrison, having fought the war to the very last minute.

The Battle of the Bulge turned out to be a decisive Allied victory for the simple reason that in this desperate attempt the German armies had used up all their reserve fuel. Further, as the Americans took the offensive, the German armored vehicles were destroyed, and these, too, represented the German reserves. The Germans did manage to hold open the gap in the Allied line until all their troops had gotten safely back inside Germany, but they had "shot their wad." The drive against Bastogne represented the last German offensive.

In the north General Montgomery finally managed to get moving. In the south the Americans and Canadians moved ahead and by March 1945, they had reached the Rhine's west bank and held it from Dusseldorf to the Dutch border. The Americans crossed the Rhine over a bridge they saved at Remagen. Patton crossed the Rhine further south. The Allies were advancing all along the front at the rate of 40 miles a day.

Across
the Rhine

In the spring of 1945 the 17th Airborne Division was assigned to Field Marshal Montgomery's army, as that general prepared one of his elaborate attacks—this one to cross the Rhine river in the north. The Americans had already crossed in the south, but that was not part of the master plan, and was not to interfere with Montgomery's operation. The British 30 Corps was to cross the Rhine southwest of Rees. The British 6th Airborne Division and the 17th Airborne were to drop behind enemy lines, and 30 Corps was to link up with them.

The airborne men had learned one thing from Montgomery in the months of joint British-American operations: Always keep liaison men with other commands, so Division would know what was happening all up and down the line. On this occasion, G-3—operations—had officers with the British Commando brigade, the 15th Scottish division, and the 6th Airborne; and they all had radio communication with Division.

From 12 fields in northern France and Belgium the division came in 903 airplanes and 897 gliders. The British were also using 699 planes and 429 gliders for the 6th Airborne, and the result was that some of the 17th Airborne men (the 513th Parachute Infantry) had to be carried in C-46 aircraft instead of the usual C-47s. One characteristic of the C-46 was its deeper belly, useful for heavy cargo. But another was the placement of its wing tanks. If a tank was punctured, the fuel ran down along the fuselage, and a tracer would set fire to the whole aircraft.

On the drop, 72 C-46s were used, and 22 were lost to ground fire. Of these, 14 began to burn the moment they were hit, and the parachutists were in danger from that point on. Most of them got out of the flaming planes, but two C-46s came down burning in the 507th's drop zone: Nobody got out of those two. At the end of the operation General Ridgway issued orders that never again were his men to fly in C-46s for airdrop.

Colonel Edson Raff was still jumping and fighting, still commander of the 507th Parachute Infantry Regiment, and he and his men dropped that day.

Their planes—all C-47s—took off from Chartres at 7:20 A.M. on March 24. The flight was uneventful until they reached the Rhine. It should have been: The Eighth Air Force had 1,253 fighters patrolling east of the Rhine and the British had 900 fighters over the target area. The Germans put up only 100 fighters all over northern Germany that day.

But when the transports and gliders crossed the Rhine, the moment they reached the east bank—Germany proper—the flak began to come up. The 507th was in the lead element, and its drop zone was near Pluren. The 1st Battalion, however, dropped near Diersfordt Castle, and Colonel Raff was the first man to jump. Like the others he carried ammunition for a half-day's combat. The moment he and his men hit the ground and released, they were ready to go into action. They even carried radios as they went down, so no time would be lost in searching for equipment.

The battalion set out for the west. The men captured an artillery battery of 150s—and found these were horse drawn. So far had the German weapons deteriorated.

There was something wrong—Raff knew it when he tried to orient himself. His map was useless: They had been dropped outside the zone. But the 1st Battalion soon moved against the high ground that was really an objective of the 513th and captured it. Then Major Smith, the commander, was ordered to seize Diersfordt Castle, even though that was 3rd Battalion's objective. In spite of the confusion caused by the drop, the men moved quickly. By noon the situation was well enough under control that Colonel Raff could put most of 1st Battalion into the woods nearby as regimental reserve.

Company A was withheld and sent to the castle. Near the castle the Americans were stopped by small-arms fire from the edge of the woods, and the 2nd Platoon assaulted the position.

They killed 9 Germans and took 15 prisoners. They captured an 81 mm. mortar. The 3rd Platoon moved along the woods and entered the castle from the east. Two tanks stood inside the grounds. They wrecked one with bazooka fire and captured 10 prisoners.

The 3rd Battalion dropped too far to the east and ran into heavy German ground fire at the drop zone. Eight men from Company I were killed before they could disengage from their parachutes. Staff Sergeant Smith of H Company went after the German position near him and captured 35 Germans and three machine guns. That stopped the firing.

By 11:00 P.M. 90 percent of the battalion was assembled in the woods and made contact with 2nd Battalion. Third Battalion's objective was the high ground and Diersfordt castle. On the way, H Company destroyed three Mark IV tanks west of the castle, and G Company and H Company cleared the ridge above.

In the assault on the castle, H Company laid down fire while G Company tried to move in from the north. But at the moat around the castle, the Germans had set up guns and company G could not advance farther. Captain Alley, commander of G Company, was wounded. Lieutenant Keehen, his executive officer, took over and called for artillery fire on the castle. With A Company of 1st Battalion coming in from the other side, G Company moved in, and at 6:00 the castle was in American hands and the Stars and Stripes was run up the flagpole on the tower.

The paratroopers captured 300 prisoners here, including an artillery colonel and 21 other officers.

The regiment's objective was to seize and hold the high ground around the castle so that the Germans could not come up to harry the Allied forces crossing the Rhine. In two hours the 464th Field Artillery Battalion had set up 10 guns in support of the 507th. At Division, they said the operation was going very well, so well that General Miley gave the 507th additional duties; and on the night of D day General Ridgway, commander of the XVIIIth Airborne Corps, ordered them to make contact with the British working up from Wessel. Patrols were sent out, and did make contact, but not before an American lieutenant was shot by mistake by a British soldier. Even at this late date, there were still difficulties in combined operations.

On D + 1 the 507th began moving east. But the area around

Wessel was not secure. A company of 2nd Battalion was sent to clear the south, and one from 1st Battalion to the southeast sector of troublesome antiaircraft and machine-gun installations. The rest of the battalion attacked eastward and by midnight had advanced five miles.

On D + 2 the 507th was to move up to the southern part of the Autobahn and make contact with the 513th and 194th ReCompany C of the 1st Battalion sent a platoon to clear a bridge, which would maintain contact with the 30th Division on the south. The Germans were in strength here. The platoon captured 29 prisoners after a fight, but the Germans blew the bridge. The U.S. engineers, however, were well enough organized to bring up and install a Bailey bridge.

A platoon from Company B of the 1st Battalion moved across the Autobahn, and as it did, the Germans cut loose with two machine guns. The platoon was pinned down, then, until artillery and mortar fire quieted the Germans, and the men could be pulled back. When the barrage had done its work, they moved forward again.

The going was hard, and the regiment took casualties, but moved steadily. The regiment took Drevenack, and then Peddenburg, one battalion moving up, and then the next going through to the second objective. Occasionally they encountered a German 105 mm. gun or an 88, but the American and British tanks pushed them back, and the artillery moved up behind. At Scharmbeck they met stiff enemy resistance from tanks and guns. They had been moving along the Autobahn, tanks and vehicles on the road and troopers on foot on either side, clearing out buildings a thousand yards on both sides.

On the morning of the 27th, 2nd Battalion moved out, with F Company riding tanks from the 771st Tank Destroyer Battalion. Outside Peddenburg they encountered heavy resistance in the woods alongside the road. One tank hit a mine and was disabled. Two of the crew were hurt, but none of the men riding was injured. Another tank hit another mine as they fanned out from the road to quell the opposition. Two tanks on the right were hit by 88 shells. No troopers were hurt here, either, although one of those shells penetrated a tank and exploded the ammunition inside, killing the whole crew.

The battalion moved up and captured 50 prisoners, most of them in Company F's sector, while the other two companies met almost no resistance.

On March 27 they reached Dorsten. On the twenty-eighth they pushed on for Wuffen. The Germans retreated ahead of them, blowing up ammunition and supply dumps as they went.

Wuffen is surrounded by marsh and water, with canals leading into the city. Major Smith took Company B of 1st Battalion around to the south, and the British armor moved in from the north, and they captured the town with very little resistance. There they questioned a German staff sergeant who had been left behind to destroy three 88s because the Germans had no means of towing them out. There had been seven 88s in the town; three of them had been taken out by horses, one by a motor vehicle. The Germans had left just minutes before the Americans arrived, so the sergeant had not had time to destroy his three guns.

The 507th moved to Haltern and stopped to take up a position defending the corps line of communication and to reorganize after six days of battle. On April 2 the regiment took Münster, and, from that point on, the German retreat became a rout. Prisoners came in by the hundreds. The 507th slogged on. In a matter of weeks they would meet the Russians, and the war would end.

In this Rhine operation the 513th Parachute Infantry had a much rougher time than the 507th. Many of the 513th troopers had welcomed a change to C-46 aircraft, because, they said, a larger number of troopers could jump faster through the double doors of the larger aircraft. But in action they learned quickly enough that the C-46 was a potential death trap. On D day the 3rd Battalion had emplaned at Achiet, France, in 21 C-46s. For some flights, all went well. But in one C-46 a trooper got stuck in the door, when several drop bundles jammed. The men wanted the pilot to make another pass, but the flak had scared him and he would not; so 13 men from this plane did not jump. In the aircraft carrying Headquarters Company, two men were stuck when more bundles jammed, and one man in the wide doorway was hit by flak. By the time he was moved, it was too late for the rest of the company to jump.

There were also casualties among the jumpers on the way down. Captain Arthur Young, the medical officer, saw one parachute floating down with no man in it. Somehow he must have pulled the release in midair. Young saw another man plummet down when his parachute failed to open.

By this time the quick-release gear was standard equipment for parachute troopers, but some of the troopers had trouble with it. Lieutenant Rollie Cantley of Company H said he had to cut three men out of their leg straps after they hit the ground. With hard falls and other difficulties, plus enemy fire, the 3rd Battalion suffered 100 casualties in this jump—which included the troopers aboard three of those C-46s that crashed.

In this drop, when the troopers came down, they were for the first time in truly enemy country. The civilians could not be expected to shower them with wine and kisses, but to shoot at them. Lieutenant Mark McAllister, battalion communications officer, landed on a barn roof and saw three troopers shot by small-arms fire as they tried to get out of their harnesses. Master Sergeant Louis Levasseur was hung up in a tree, and a German rifleman shot him as he hung there. By the time the battalion began to assemble, the horror stories were circulating: One man said he saw a civilian woman come up and stab a sergeant as he struggled on the ground to free himself from his harness.

Third Battalion's bad landing outside the drop zone created problems. Major Morris Anderson, the executive officer, began yelling the moment he got down and at the end of an hour had rounded up 300 men. Lieutenant Colonel Edward F. Kent, the battalion commander, gathered 150 men around him.

Both groups headed toward their assigned targets. Anderson's group had to fight its way through farms where all the buildings were occupied by German infantry. Colonel Kent headed for the Issel Canal east of the drop zone. He was able to orient himself by the steeple of the church in the town of Hamminkeln. Colonel Kent then took the men to the bank of the Issel. They dug in there and waited for the artillery to lay fire across the canal. The battalion remained there on the bank during the nights of March 24 and 25; on March 26 the men waded through three feet deep water to cross the canal.

Because of the faulty drop the battalion had not been able to recover all its ammunition and guns: G Company had three of nine machine guns, Company I had six of nine, H had three of nine, and Headquarters Company had two of eight. After crossing the canal and running into Germans holed up in the farms beyond, they found the British glider landing field and cleaned the gliders out of guns and ammunition left behind by hurrying troops.

Early on the morning of the twenty-sixth Colonel Coutts, the 513th regimental commander, ordered an attack through the strong German positions to reach the Autobahn. The 3rd Battalion moved at 9:00 and by 9:15 had captured 200 prisoners. The slackening of resistance was noticeable; many Germans came in to surrender. Not all, though. Some of the Germans fought as fiercely here as they had in the days when the Third Reich ruled Europe.

On March 27 the men of 3rd Battalion rode tanks of the Coldstream Guards toward Dorsten. As there was virtually no opposition, they reached Dorsten by 1:00 P.M., to find that it had already been cleared out by 2nd Battalion. Third Battalion moved through and took the lead. That afternoon Lieutenant Kahn of G Company saw a column of enemy moving back, on a road parallel to their own. He called it to the attention of the tank commander, who ordered the guns of the 50 tanks turned on the enemy. That barrage broke up the German column, but it also brought an artillery barrage down on the British-American column, which forced the column to halt at the edge of Lippramsdorf. Colonel Kent sent two platoons of G Company ahead. The right platoon captured two 88s, which put an end to the artillery fire against the tanks.

German soldiers retreated steadily, blowing up installations as they went along. More seemed ready to surrender, but late that day, as the column reached Haltern, it encountered two enemy strong points armed with *Panzerfausts,* which opened fire on the tanks. Luckily darkness was falling, and there were no hits.

Lieutenant Kahn led his men along through the town; they advanced on both sides of the tanks. In the darkness they heard signal whistles, but no one fired on them. They moved to the center of the town and parked the tanks alongside the cathedral. Company G covered the square in front of the cathedral. Company H moved on to capture the bridges on the other side of town. The paratrooopers reached the first bridge, and Lieutenant Robert Hammerquist and Lieutenant Charles Martin jumped off the tanks they were riding and cut the demolition wires. At the next, the troopers were not so lucky. As the tanks came up, the Germans blew the bridges in their faces.

The battalion encountered trouble as the men moved out at 3:30 on the morning of March 29. They flushed a truckload of German soldiers, who leaped into the ditch alongside the road and sniped at the column, then slid off into the fields. The tank column encountered a Panther tank and knocked it out. A *Panzerfaust* wrecked the lead British tank, and it was apparent they had encountered an antitank defense unit. Six tanks sped around ahead of the column and pinned a German mechanized unit between the battalions and the tank guns.

The battalion kept on, pushing to Buldern. They took the town at noon on March 29, or thought they had taken it. They spent the rest of the day fighting for it, street by street. Then they were on to Appelhulsen and Albachten, and then to Münster. There, after the city was taken, the 3rd Battalion moved into the barracks of the Hermann Goering Parachute Armored Division west of the city. There was a certain grim satisfaction for some of the troopers; they had come almost full circle since the day that the 82nd Airborne had faced that Hermann Goering division in Sicily.

Anyone who wished to understand the treatment of American blacks by the parachute forces would have to study the racism of the American military, which represented the essential racist policies of the U.S. government and the majority of the American people. Blacks had always been considered to be inferior. Only at one time, during and after the Civil War, were blacks encouraged to join the American (Union) fighting forces as soldiers. Partly, this was a matter of necessity; the Union needed cannon fodder. Partly, it was a gesture of defiance against the Confederacy, whose racial policies had been the excuse if not the reason for the war. After the war, blacks had a short heyday in which they held Congressional office and controlled several southern states. But by 1877 all that was ready for reversal, and in a political compromise that gave Rutherford B. Hayes the Presidency, the Democrats were given back political control of the south, and racism became a vital American policy.

By the time that World War II began, a few blacks had managed to worm their way into the mainstream of the American military. These token figures did not number more than two or three dozen. The U.S. Army and Navy continued to segregate black enlisted men. The Navy policy was to use blacks as servants; most of the stewards aboard the U.S. warships were blacks or members of other minorities. The Army policy was to organize the blacks into labor units, which were sent to do the manual work in construction of bases and other facilities.

For example, the Ledo road, which was built to connect Assam province of India to Yunnan province of China and thus replace the old Burma road that ran from Rangoon northward, was built largely by black American soldiers on the Assam and Burma side, and Chinese coolies on the other side.

When the paratroop concept caught on in the United States army doctrine, some blacks asked to join the force. The request created consternation in Washington; already in 1941 the civil-rights movement was beginning to shake out of its cocoon. The Army came up with a typical Army solution: Blacks could become paratroopers, but they would be organized in all-black regiments, battalions, and companies. The rationale was that the blacks would feel more comfortable when not surrounded by a sea of white faces. Some blacks responded, of course, because the paratroops quickly became the darlings of the Army and those highly polished high brown boots were symbols of prestige. But many blacks muttered "another Jim Crow deal" and what might have been a burning enthusiasm turned to ashes. The story of the blacks in the American services in World War II is very much the story of the 555th Parachute Infantry Regiment.

The Poor Old 555th

The civil-rights pressures that were building in the United States before and during World War II did not fail to affect the armed services. The policy had been rigid: Blacks were used as service troops and organized into "Jim Crow" units. There were a few exceptions, but very few; and unfortunately, when the question of black paratroopers came up and the high command was pushed into okaying the idea, the 555th Parachute Infantry Battalion was organized with all-black personnel. The deed was done on November 25, 1944 at Camp Mackall, North Carolina.

From the outset the unit was in trouble. A few blacks had been trained as paratroopers, but there were not enough black officers to go around. The blacks simply had not been given proper exposure for a long enough period to become military specialists and officers. It all looked good on paper, unless one looked carefully. Then the truth appeared: The 555th was a public relations unit and could hardly be anything else.

Its roots had been with the 555th Parachute Infantry Company, which (the records showed) was organized at Fort Benning on December 30, 1943. It consisted of *one* officer, Lieutenant James Porter, and *one* enlisted man. By the fall of 1944, when the company was redesignated as the 555th Parachute Infantry Battalion, it consisted of 7 officers and 165 enlisted men. And when the officers tried to bring their unit up to battalion strength, they found they had a real problem.

In the beginning, the commanding officer did all the usual things written in the book: He submitted to higher headquarters (the Airborne Center itself) a requisition for troops. He needed about 200 men capable of qualifying as jump troops. The request was duly processed and produced virtually no results. So, Porter asked for permission to send officers and men out through the army camps, to recruit volunteers. This sensible plan was rejected out of hand by the top brass, who obviously had no feeling for the black troops or their attitudes toward the military organization. Instead, the Pentagon sent a circular through the Army Ground Forces, saying that applications for parachute training would be accepted. What the 555th had wanted to do was sell young men on the idea that they would be going into a crack outfit—they would be trained and then assigned to that outfit. But that was not the Army way.

After the Army had begun to get a few volunteers from the black labor battalions and other black units, the Pentagon sent down an order to Camp Mackall. The 555th Battalion was to detail one officer and 17 enlisted men to the parachute school at Fort Benning to help train blacks and take over their care and feeding. So they went off to Benning just before Christmas. When they got there they found 200 volunteers, but in a week or so the number was down to about 100, because about half of the men could not meet the physical requirements. Another 10 percent were washed out for educational and other failures. That first company cadre came limping back to Camp Mackall with about 80 men, and another group set off at the end of the month. But the situation was unchanged; it was apparent that no care was taken in selection of men who might apply for jump training; obviously the commanders of various units were using this device to get rid of the worst "foulups" and yardbirds in their organizations.

So it went on. The rejection rate on this second batch of volunteers was so high that even the parachute training school became concerned. The commander of the 555th complained to Airborne Center that they could never get a unit going at this rate. Airborne Center processed the complaint and asked for a list of rejectees by name, rank, serial number, former organization, and medical reasons for rejection. All Porter had done was make himself some more work.

With another handful of men, the second company cadre came back in February, and a third company cadre was sent off to Fort Benning. Four months went by; the war in Europe ended, and volunteers dropped off. By June there were one or two men coming to Fort Benning to be looked over with an eye to becoming paratroopers.

Back at Camp Mackall, Captain Porter never did get going on a proper training program. There simply were not enough enlisted men. Airborne Command had promised that when they got up to 80 percent of strength, they would get the airplanes and the equipment for proper training. They never reached 80 percent; for a short time they hit two-thirds, but that was the best that could be done under the sort of recruitment used by the Army. The training time was used to qualify jumpers and instruct men in the use of their weapons. They also gave jumping demonstrations, but as a battalion the 555th never really existed.

In March, when the going was still rough on the European Western front, the battalion had orders to put together one really good reinforced company that would go into combat. Porter skeletonized the battalion and gave Captain Edwin H. Wills, his operations officer, command of the new unit. There were high hopes as real training began, and Wills brought the men up to snuff. He had eight weeks in which to do it, and at the end of the first four weeks everything was going well. Then "higher command" reversed itself; the reinforced company was sent back into the battalion, and the 555th was given a "security mission," which meant it would be sent off to the American far west.

The Japanese, trying anything at all to stop the American advances in the Pacific, had hit upon the idea of setting such tremendous fires in the western forests of the United States that the Americans would have to stop fighting and put out the fires. From that point, according to this bit of Imperial strategy, it would be a short distance to a negotiated peace that would leave Japan alone to rebuild her shattered empire. So several Japanese submarines were duly loaded with balloons carrying firebombs, and when they reached the American west coast they surfaced and released them. In April 1945 the bombs landed and started some forest fires in Oregon and Washington. The U.S. Forest Service went into a flap and called for help. Someone in the Army remembered the poor, mistreated 555th and decided to give them this "emergency" mission. They called it The Fire-Fly Project. It wasn't combat, but at least it was action, the first, and only, the 555th would see.

The battalion was shipped to Pendleton Field, in the heart of the dry upland and forest country of eastern Oregon. For administration, the 555th was under the Ninth Service Command at Fort Douglas, which meant that for all practical purposes Captain Porter and his men were alone.

The battalion was shipped to Pendleton Field, in the heart of the dry upland and forest country of eastern Oregon. For admin-Porter had to do what he could to pull things together for men who had only what they could carry with them. He began a physical training program and started map-reading exercises. The troops were going to have to jump with shovels and other fire-fighting equipment and put out the Japanese firebomb fires. How they were going to train was another matter; Pendleton Army Air Base did not have any firing ranges, or parade grounds, or any of the facilities that were needed to work a large unit of men.

It took the Forest Service several weeks to get used to the idea, and then Forest Service officers came to teach the troops their techniques of putting out fires. Of course everything was different—the service's equipment, even the maps, were nothing like those used by the Army. When the men were not going to lectures, they marched, for if Captain Porter had no training facilities, he still had to train and bring the men into good physical condition for jumping. They marched everywhere with full field equipment; they marched outside the base to a field where they could march. They marched along the asphalt highway to the hills, and they marched back again. Sometimes they ran, without full field equipment. Then they marched again. On some days the marches were 4 or 5 miles. On some days they marched 25 miles, in the boiling sun. One day they marched 9 miles in two hours with full field equipment. Another day the men marched 25 miles in eight hours with the same equipment.

On July 7 a detachment was shipped down to Chico Army Air Field in northern California. The forest fires had begun in the Klamath National Forest. And from that time on, the 555th had work to do. There were 17 forest fires that summer in Klamath, Trinity, and Mendocino National Forests, and the new "smoke jumpers" did their job. In September a bad fire in Mendocino forest called on 65 paratroopers, and in October 75 men jumped into Trinity National Forest. All were from the Chico detachment.

Up north the battalion was just as busy. There were three big fires in Montana, in the Meadow Lake, Bitter Root, and Cabinet National Forests. There were four major fires in Idaho, three of them in the Salmon National Forest. Washington and Oregon, the prime targets of the wily Japanese, were hit with a dozen fires, not all of them caused by balloon bombs. As always, there were fires caused by spontaneous combustion, or by careless campers. The worst was a blaze in the Chelan National Forest on July 18, which took 104 men to extinguish. A week later the war was over, but the fires kept going, and it was late October before the 555th and the Chico detachment flew back to Camp Mackall.

After the war, the Army's historical service began putting together the unit accounts of the fighting in Europe and in the Pacific; and in due course, Captain Porter received a form to be filled out, offering all sorts of opportunities to speak of unit derring-do. But Captain Porter had a sad little report to make: In that summer of 1945 the 555th had furnished a total of 1,255 men on 36 occasions to put out forest fires. One man had been lost in the whole of the actions, to a fire. A few men had suffered fractures and lesser injuries. That was the war record of the 555th. No campaigns, no battles, nothing to put down under item "h": Commanding Officer in Important Engagements. Nobody had distinguished himself in combat. At Pendleton they had gotten up at 5:45 and eaten breakfast at 6:30. They had policed the barracks and their areas in the mornings and had eaten dinner at 11:30. They had marched or learned map reading in the afternoons and eaten supper at 4:30. They had marched to their meals. They had marched in the morning at 8:00 to 50 minutes of physical training. Sometimes they had a 30-minute run. At 9:00 they had 30 minutes of dismounted drill.

At 1:00 the 555th had suffered through 30-minute lectures on military discipline, customs of the service, and military courtesy— whatever had seemed to be lacking at the moment. At 2:00 they had gone out for two hours of organized athletics at the battalion gymnasium or on the surrounding field. They had risen at odd hours, sometimes 1:00 or 3:00 A.M., to rush to the parachute maintenance shed, ready for jumping. Captain Porter called these fire alerts. These alerts might also interrupt a physical training session or a lecture on military courtesy. He had mixed them up on purpose. They had come back to Camp Mackall a highly disciplined, spit-and-polish outfit of fighting men. Their only problem was that nobody had ever given them a chance to fight. The closest they ever came was a tactical problem on July 25, 1945, when they made a simulated attack on the Zillah airstrip on the edge of the Rattlesnake Hills.

The 555th did not have much more strictly military history. It was such a crack outfit, however, and Captain Porter had his men in such fine physical condition, that it became one of the Army's finer marching units. Detachments went to New York to march in Army Week parades, to Charlotte, North Carolina, for a civic celebration, and to Montgomery, Alabama, for the Armistice Day Parade of 1947.

That was the year the 555th went out of existence. Early in January 1947 the 555th had been attached to the 82nd Airborne Division at Fort Bragg. A few months later it moved over to join the 504th Parachute Infantry Regiment. Then, the men were taken to join the 505th, and on December 9, 1947, the 555th was no more. The Army's policy had changed; there would be no more racially segregated units. The men of the 555th were transferred to the 3rd Battalion of the 505th Airborne Infantry Regiment. Only one digit in their unit designation was changed, but it meant a whole new world was opening for the men of the 555th.

By 1945 the paratroop concept had been repeatedly proved to a reluctant military management not once, but on every level from the combat team to the Allied Airborne Army. What followed in the next few years would be incomprehensible, then, unless one took into account the general attitude of the people of the United States. After three and a half years of war, Americans were as sick of it as if they had been fighting as long as the Chinese (14 years). Hardly had the occupations of Germany and Japan begun when American Congressmen began demanding that "the boys be brought home." The demand soon became a chorus, backed by millions of wives, mothers, sweethearts, and employers who wanted to get the industrial show on the road again. In this atmosphere, with Congress demanding severe cuts in the military's expenditures, the generals had no option but to survey their ranks and begin slicing off whole sections. The great war was ended, and so shock troops seemed hardly an essential in the peacekeeping machinery. They were expensive to train, expensive to maintain, and they earned a higher pay for the risk factor than did ordinary infantrymen. Many paratroopers wanted to leave the service, too, and as they left, the ranks thinned out.

In the disbanding of the American military machine in 1946 and 1947 it seemed hardly likely that another war was on the horizon anywhere. Had not the gallant Allies, America, Britain, China, and Russia, defeated all possible enemies of "Democracy?" There, of course, was the rub. What was Democracy? Within two months after the signing of the Japanese peace treaty it became apparent that the vast differences in interpretation between the Western Allies and the Soviets and their adherents would create a new friction immediately. But once begun, the military policy of disbandment was irreversible. What happened next is illustrated very well in the history of the airborne in America.

Korean Offensive

As the European war ended in the spring of 1945, the generals in Washington had to decide what they were going to do with the airborne organization. They had planned an enormous buildup; Japan was to be invaded by a combined air-sea force, and the 11th Airborne was to play a major role. The 101st, 82nd, and 17th were all earmarked for the Pacific.

But when the war in the Pacific ended in the summer, reaction set in. Congress insisted on cutbacks. The conservatives of the military had never liked the "trick outfits," and their view had not changed a great deal. In October the word came to General Gavin, then head of the American occupying forces in Berlin, that the 82nd Airborne was to be shipped home and disbanded. The XVIII Airborne Corps was deactivated at Camp Campbell, Kentucky, but the 82nd was saved.

The generals decided that the airborne was a thing of the past. Airborne troops would be used for special assignments but otherwise kept as part of the regular infantry force. In 1948 the 82nd Airborne was redesignated a regular army infantry division.

The 11th Airborne Division, which had been training for the invasion of Japan after the end of the Luzon campaign in June 1945, had been rushed to Okinawa and then to the Tokyo area, along with the 27th Infantry Division, to undertake the military occupation of Japan. In Japan the paratroopers got a new name—*rakkasan*—which in Japanese means literally "falling down umbrella."

From the years of occupation the 187th Glider Infantry, which had attained parachute competence, also took the name Rakkasan. The 187th had fought in the Philippines campaign, but stories of its exploits were buried beneath the tales of more glamorous organizations, fighting in more glamorous territory, and accompanied by many war correspondents. The 187th was to have its day.

The airborne concept got new life in June 1950, when the North Koreans marched into South Korea.

Had the United States forces been fully alert and prepared for the North Korean invasion that summer, paratroops might well have stopped the drive against Seoul. Certainly nothing the Americans then had in Korea could have done so; even in 1946 Lieutenant General John R. Hodge, commander of the XXIV Corps that occupied South Korea, warned Washington that he could not hold any line at all against an attack. If anyone wanted to defend South Korea, the power would have to come from Japan. After 1946 the military situation changed for the worse as Americans went home. And when the North Koreans marched, they very quickly drove through Seoul and down toward Pusan on the southern tip of the peninsula.

The political aspect of the Korean War soon changed it into an East-West confrontation, with the Americans operating as an arm of the United Nations, aided by small contingents from various other countries. The airborne forces had deteriorated badly in the years after World War II, but the abandonment of airborne organization in America proper resulted in the strengthening of the 187th. Many veterans of the 82nd Airborne and the 101st Airborne reenlisted to join that organization.

At the outbreak of the Korean War, the 187th Airborne Infantry Regiment as it was then known, was redesignated the 187th Airborne Regimental Combat Team, under Colonel Frank S. Bowen.

There were many changes in the airborne concept. The 8081st Quartermaster Airborne Air Supply and Packaging Company was created at Fort Campbell, Kentucky, with personnel from the old 11th and 82nd, and the Quartermaster Corps. They would handle the problems of supply. Another unit was established, the 187th Quartermaster Parachute Maintenance Detachment. On September 1 the forward elements of these groups were on their way to Tokyo. The 187th would have its own supply group, but the quartermasters would do much more. In one year they would make 150 airdrops, using 118,000 cargo chutes and supplying United Nations forces—airborne and others—with 14,000 tons of food, weapons, and equipment.

The 187th's first experience in Korea came on September 24, 1950, after General Douglas MacArthur began the drive back north with landings at Inchon. The 1st Battalion was assigned to make an airdrop at the airfield. Parachutes were issued and the battalion rigged for airdrop and loaded with monorail bundles for paradrop. But when the C-119s ran into antiaircraft fire off the coast of Korea, they were turned out to sea and changed direction. At about mid-morning, they landed at Kimpo. The marines had gotten there first and supposedly cleared the airfield. In the plane of Sergeant J. H. Alexander of Company A, the men thought the field was clear, and they got ready to deplane. The C-119 came to a stop, and the last man on the left side opened the door. He was promptly killed by a sniper bullet between the eyes. The others got down and unloaded in a hurry, taking all the cover they could find. It was a hurried job because the planes were landing and taking off all the time, and the pilots had orders to get off the field.

Company A soon assembled and marched five miles south to Suwon. But they had no trucks with them, so they carried gear. "I carried ten bandoliers of M-1 ammunition, five grenades, two boxes of M-6 ammunition, and my field gear," said Sergeant Alexander. "Some march."

They bivouacked at Suwon for the night. A North Korean sniper kept hurrying the men, so the platoon leader rousted Sergeant Alexander, Sergeant Pulber, and Corporal Munture and told them to find the sniper and get rid of him. They listened for a bit to get the direction of the fire and then moved out along the road. About 350 yards from the bivouac area, they located the sniper in a covered hole in the bank. From the field above, Alexander moved up till he spotted the entrance to the hole, which was covered with cornstalks. He moved close to it and shouted to Corporal Munture, who had a BAR. The corporal fired several rounds into the hole, and out fell a dead North Korean. From his hand clattered a Russian rifle with a fixed bayonet.

The 187th was given the task of clearing the Kimpo peninsula between the Han river and the sea. The enemy force was said to consist of 3,000 men, most of them from units that had been broken up by the American advance. But they still had plenty of weapons and were dangerous.

The 187th moved out, L Company in the van. At noon on September 27 the company had rolled into a village and was halfway out the other side when an ambush was sprung from both sides of the road. The fight lasted four hours; then L Company withdrew in the face of superior enemy strength (estimated at 400). The company lost three men: Sergeant, First Class, Fred Bailey, Sergeant Kenneth E. Stevenson, and Private, First Class, Clark M. Bradford. But other troops were moving through the peninsula, Sergeant Alexander's A Company among them. Any of the old hands from World War II would have recognized the North Korean tactics. They had adapted the Japanese trick of playing dead, and some of them had the same tenacity of the Japanese to fight to the bitter end. At one village, Alexander's company was chasing a company-sized force that seemed to be fleeing. But suddenly on their flank a machine gun began firing. They flushed the gunners, but then the resistance stiffened, and eventually they had to call for naval gunfire to drive the enemy out of its position. It was that sort of fighting all the way, routing the enemy out of cornfields, holes in the sides of the road, and caves in the hills. But it was done; and at the end of it the 187th Airborne Regimental Combat Team had cleaned up the Kimpo peninsula, killing or capturing all but 10 percent of the estimated 3,000 enemy who had been there in the beginning.

What the troops were waiting for, however, was an airdrop. They were not quite certain when it would materialize. The first practice drop was conducted on the sand flats of the Han river. From this point on the 187th would never want for publicity, because a handful of correspondents came from *Life, Stars and Stripes, Agence France Presse,* and the American newspapers and news services to write about the glamorous paratroops.

Plans were made to use paratroops in several of the operations in October. But the ground forces were moving so rapidly north that the plans were scrapped, one after the other. By the time the operation could be airborne, the foot soldiers had taken the objectives, so the first two October plans were knocked out. But in October came one apparent opportunity that only paratroops could exploit. The North Koreans were beginning to stop and hold as the Americans came closer to Pyongyang, their capital city. General Bowen, commander of the 187th, was told that the North Koreans were about to send a trainload of officials and American prisoners of war out of Pyongyang to the Sukchon–Sunchon area, and here the 187th was to intercept and capture the train, at the same time sealing off the North Korean escape route from Pyong-yang.

The drop zone for the 3rd Battalion was just outside Sukchon in an area of rice paddies, where three mountains protected the road eastward. Third Battalion was to block off the road and railroad. Second Battalion's mission was to take the town of Sun-chon and capture the train.

For several days before the operation the troopers were briefed with maps and intelligence reports. At 7:00 P.M. on Octo-ber 18 pilots and jumpmasters were given a final briefing at Kimpo air base. But a drizzling rain had started that day, and the weather grew worse. It seemed that the drop was going to be postponed, until at 2:30 A.M. on October 20 reveille sounded and the men fell out in the rain. The train carrying North Korean officials and prisoners had already left Pyongyang. Bad weather or good, if the paratroopers did not drop soon, it would be too late. At 10:30 the men were at Kimpo air base, chuting up.

Times had changed since the days of World War II, when the C-47s had been the backbone of the airborne operations. The new C-119s carried two "sticks" of 23 men each, and 19 bundles; 15 of them moved along monorails in the aircraft and 4 were placed near the door.

Each of the paratroopers of the 187th carried a reserve para-chute, pack, water, rations, ammunition, a .45 caliber pistol, and a carbine or M-1 rifle. Some had an extra container, filled with ammunition.

Colonel Bowen led the way in the first C-119. At noon they began taking off, 73 planes of the 314th Troop Carrier Wing and 40 C-47s from the 21st. As they moved over the Han river, Colonel Bowen stood in the doorway of his lead plane, looking for landmarks.

There was very little antiaircraft fire or enemy fighter activity anywhere en route, and none when they neared the drop zones at

1:30 P.M. Below them the men could see American fighter planes working over the area. The 20-minute warning light went on. At 1:50 the green light flashed, and men began moving. Colonel Bowen yelled "Go!" and jumped.

Someone yelled "Geronimo!"—a relic from World War II. Then all the men were out, and they and the equipment chutes were drifting to the ground, 1,470 paratroopers and 74 tons of equipment.

At 600 feet the men began loosening their harnesses, unsnapping reserve chutes, checking the release forks. There were some injuries in the drop, but not many—most of the men jumped into flat, dry rice paddies. When they hit the ground, they were greeted by a scattering of rifle fire from the north end of the drop zone.

First Battalion landed at 2:05 and caught the enemy by surprise; troopers hurrying to check the houses around the paddies found a number of North Korean soldiers who had slipped civilian clothes over their uniforms.

The 1st Battalion's mission was to clear Sukchon and hold the high ground to the north. Intelligence said there were 1,800 North Korean soldiers in and around the town. The North Koreans delayed the movement for about 45 minutes at Songnoni-Ni before they were forced back. Here Sergeant Marcuso and his squad took 15 prisoners and then used them as porters to move the engineers' equipment up on handcarts. By 5:00 the command post of the regimental combat team was established and dug in at Chany-Ni.

Lieutenant Coleman's platoon spotted a burning air force fighter and the pilot who had managed to bring it down in a crash landing, in a rice paddy, and save himself. The pilot dragged himself from the wrecked plane and began to crawl across the paddy. He came under fire from North Koreans as he tried to reach cover. He stopped crawling and lay still. The North Koreans stopped shooting. The Americans tried to keep the Koreans away by laying down fire, but they could not reach the pilot. The contest continued for an hour. The North Koreans moved. The Americans forced them back. The Americans moved; the North Koreans laid down heavy fire. Finally at dusk the North Koreans sent out a patrol. They killed the pilot and then retreated into the

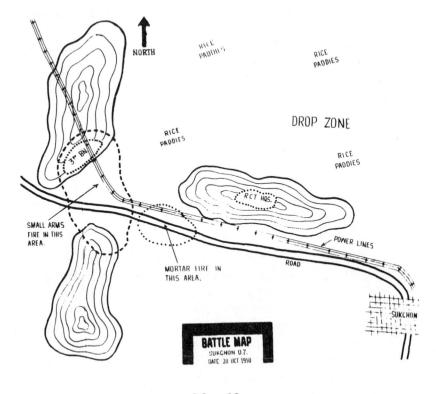

NORTH

RICE PADDIES

RICE PADDIES

DROP ZONE

RICE PADDIES

RICE PADDIES

3ᴰ BN

RCT HQS.

SMALL ARMS
FIRE IN THIS
AREA.

POWER LINES

ROAD

MORTAR FIRE IN
THIS AREA.

SUKCHON

BATTLE MAP
SUKCHON D.Z.
DATE 20 OCT 1950

Map 10

hills. The platoon chased the enemy but lost them. On return they encountered rifle fire and flushed three Koreans. Two tried to escape and were shot down; the paratroopers were not feeling gentle after the fighter-pilot killing. There was no use keeping the third North Korean; he was just a nuisance, so they shot him, too, and went on.

Sunchon was taken without much trouble by the 2nd Battalion. But at the Kimchon river bridge at Sinhung-Ni, which the engineers were to prepare for demolition, the battalion came under such heavy fire it was stalled. Matters were not helped much by the Republic of Korea 6th Regiment, which kept firing on the Americans until recognition and contact were established later in the day.

Near the end of the day, Colonel Bowen could report back that all the initial objectives of the combat team had been achieved that day, with relatively small losses, many of them sustained in the drop itself.

At 7:00 A.M. on the twenty-first the 1st and 3rd Battalions continued the attack but found little resistance. The regimental team had dropped across a North Korean fixed defense line. They did find a quantity of enemy military stores, but few enemy troops. But as they moved into the mountains, the North Korean resistance grew stronger. The enemy here was equipped with tanks and artillery, and American artillery had to be brought up to train on the hills.

The enemy proved very tough on D+1, when I Company moved against Opari. The company took the town, but it was attacked by a North Korean battalion armed with 120 mm. mortars and 40 mm. guns, and two Rakkasan platoons were overrun. When the remainder withdrew, 90 men were found to be missing. I Company was very nearly wiped out. Private, First Class, Richard G. Wilson tried desperately to save a wounded soldier and was killed. (He was the first of the 187th to earn the Congressional Medal of Honor.) But the North Koreans failed to exploit their advantage and drew back from the town. By this time the United Nations forces were closing the trap around the Koreans. It was complete when Company K made contact with an element of the British 27th Brigade at Yongyu.

One objective of the Rakkasans had not been achieved. The bad weather on D day had delayed them, and they had missed the Pyongyang train.

On the twenty-first, near Myonguch'am, a Patrol from F Company discovered what had happened to at least some of the prisoners of war from that train. They had, indeed, been moved out of Pyongyang on the morning of the drop but not out on the way north. The paratroopers came across a pile of bodies—75 American prisoners shot by their captors. They also found 18 wounded survivors of the massacre. The men told the Rakkasans that the shooting had been done at 10:00 A.M. on October 20, two hours after the mission should have arrived if the weather had not delayed it.

In the south the North Koreans were moving up, driven by X Corps into the trap. The North Koreans must either break through the Rakkasans or they were lost.

At 2:00 A.M. on October 22, trying to break through, they attacked the 1st Battalion ammunition dump in the drop zone. All day long the zone had been replenished by airdrop under the Koreans' observation. In the darkness a reinforced platoon of North Koreans came in with submachine guns and rifles and tried to destroy the supplies. They were driven off with heavy losses.

On the high ground east of Yongyu, Company K was attacked by an enemy force of two battalions; and a Korean patrol infiltrated the company command post and wounded the executive officer. They tried deception, too. A column of singing Koreans approached on the road toward Company L, and when the Americans fired on them, they shouted that they were ROK (Republic of Korea) soldiers. The paratroopers held their fire to let the "friendlies" identify themselves. But when the others brought up a Russian truck, there was no more question. The Rakkasans knocked it out with a recoilless rifle. The respite had been a North Korean ploy to give them time to bring up a heavy gun, but each time they placed it, the Rakkasans knocked out the crew. Having had time to set up fields of fire along the road, the paratroopers delivered a withering barrage on every concentration that developed. A platoon of North Koreans tried to rush across the open paddies to the road. None of them made it back. The light machine guns and Sergeant Martin's .50 caliber machine gun did the job.

The enemy had the immense advantage of numbers. If bodies could win wars, they would have crushed L Company and Headquarters Company of the battalion. Late in the morning a group of 350 Koreans charged on the L Company positions, but the company held. Then 450 Koreans came charging at Headquarters Company. The Americans had the advantage of terrain and weapons. Master Sergeant Ryals headed the defense at the base of the slope. When three gunners were knocked off the .50 caliber machine gun, he took it over himself. He brought a 3.5-inch bazooka

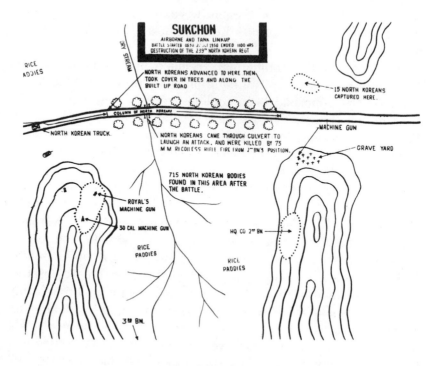

SUKCHON
AIRBORNE AND TANK LINKUP
BATTLE STARTED 0550 2/ OCT 1950 ENDED 1100 HRS
DESTRUCTION OF THE 239ᵗʰ NORTH KOREAN REGT

RICE
PADDIES

DRY STREAM

NORTH KOREANS ADVANCED TO HERE THEN
TOOK COVER IN TREES AND ALONG THE
BUILT UP ROAD

15 NORTH KOREANS
CAPTURED HERE.

COLUMN OF NORTH KOREANS

NORTH KOREAN TRUCK.

MACHINE GUN

NORTH KOREANS CAME THROUGH CULVERT TO
LAUNCH AN ATTACK, AND WERE KILLED BY 75
M M RECOILESS RIFLE FIRE FROM 2ⁿᵈ BN'S POSITION.

GRAVE YARD

715 NORTH KOREAN BODIES
FOUND IN THIS AREA AFTER
THE BATTLE.

ROYAL'S
MACHINE GUN

50 CAL MACHINE GUN

HQ CO 2ᵈ BN

RICE
PADDIES

RICE
PADDIES

3ᵈ BN.

MAP 11

up to the draw through which the North Koreans tried to rush the
position. The gunner let the draw fill with running men, and then
fired a single round, which blew them back out the other end.
Those Koreans that the bazooka did not get, the .50 caliber
machine gun knocked down the slope.

An armored element from the British 27th Brigade came up
the road, driving the enemy troops, and the tanks and the soldiers

pursued them west. They disappeared at about 11:00 A.M., and the Rakkasans began counting corpses. They counted 713 North Korean dead in front of the positions of the two companies. Because of those American prisoners of war, they took only 18 prisoners.

Altogether, 3rd Battalion had engaged 2,500 men of the 239th North Korean Regiment and had totally destroyed the unit, killing 805 and taking 681 prisoners.

On October 9, 1950, General MacArthur, the commander of American armies that were fighting under the banner of the United Nations, sent his troops across the 38th parallel and to the Yalu river, which was regarded as an essential point by the Chinese. On the other side of the Yalu was the Liaotung peninsula of Manchuria, where an enormous concentration of industry had been built by the Japanese and rejuvenated by the Chinese. Had General MacArthur promised that the United Nations forces would never cross the Yalu and never interfere with Communist China's territory, all might have been different. But such a statement from General MacArthur would have been most unlikely, and probably not even binding, given the American attitude of the time. The key was in the American use of words: Communist China was Mainland China. Free China was Formosa. The symbolism colored all that America did, and it caused the Americans to back a very definite threat to Communist China. There was talk in Washington that MacArthur ought to drive all the way to Peking. (Some said Vladivostok.) Such comment and the generally victorious and militaristic attitude of the Americans caused Mao Tse-tung to order his troops mobilized as the Americans threatened Manchuria.

Too late, some Americans remembered that this war had been started by a North Korean invasion of South Korea, and the reason had evaporated with the occupation of Pyongyang, the North Korean capital. Certainly it had ended completely when the Americans neared the Manchurian border, and if the Americans had peaceful intentions toward China (which nobody believed), they ought to have been revealed by November 20. Such intentions were not forthcoming; at least there was no enunciation of them. So on November 26 Red China entered North Korea and the war became, as they say in Washington," an entirely different ball game."

The Drop
at Munsan-Ni

After the People's Republic of China entered the war and General MacArthur's drive was stopped, in the spring of 1951, the authorities in Washington realized that the Korean War was going to involve a sustained effort—and that, as matters stood, the military establishment was not prepared to deliver it.

The drop at Sukchon had shown the usefulness of the airborne in this war. The XVIII Airborne Corps was brought back to life at Fort Bragg, and the rebuilding program began. In Korea, after fighting as ground infantry during the stormy days of the American withdrawal in the north, the 187th went into camp at the airstrip near Taegu. In February two Ranger Companies, the 2nd and 4th, were attached to the Rakkasans, and a training program was begun to teach them and quartermaster troops jump techniques.

Two training jumps were staged, and of 4,000 men, only one was killed in dropping, an indication of the improvement in technique and equipment.

General Ridgway had become commander of the U.S. Eighth Army and his appointment gave the paratroopers the feeling that at last they had a high command that understood their operations and potential. The chance to show these again came in mid-March.

The Chinese Communist Third Army was located near the 38th parallel, where it was a constant threat to United Nations forces. Intelligence reported the Chinese were building up for a new offensive. Supported by North Korean troops, they had established positions near Munsan-Ni. Several columns had recently crossed the Injin river.

The 187th was assigned to a pincers movement designed to destroy the enemy at the Injin river crossing. The troopers would drop behind the North Korean 19th Division as a column of U.S. tanks moved up to link with the combat team.

The Rakkasans boarded their planes at 10:00 A.M. on March 23, carrying light machine guns strapped to their bodies. Many riflemen carried two cases of ammunition strapped to pack boards that were slung over the packs at their knees. One section of troopers carried two 75 mm. recoilless rifles, four light machine guns, half a dozen rocket launchers, and ammunition for all weapons. One sergeant equipped himself with one rifle, a pack board with ammunition, a 3.5 rocket launcher, five bandoliers of M-1 ammunition, a combat packet, and a T-7 parachute assembly. "I must have weighed 300 pounds," he said.

As the aircraft crossed the North Korean coast, the paratroopers could see the enemy dug in around the drop zone, which was ringed by farmhouses. The pathfinders had landed and put up the white T, augmented by colored smoke signals, to direct individual units. L Company, for example, was to take a hill in the southwest corner of the drop zone and open the way for the Ranger companies to seize Munsan-Ni. The company dropped. Having established their positions (one man dug his machine gun in at the same hole he had occupied in December during the retreat), they went to the edge of the town and erected a little sign for the Rangers:

"Welcome to Munsan-Ni, Courtesy of Company L."

On the flight, the plane of the leader of 1st Battalion developed engine trouble and fell out of formation. The flight continued; but without the leading jumpmaster, all the paratroopers ended up dropping in the wrong place and found themselves in an area occupied by strong communist forces, who had them under fire even before they hit the ground. First Battalion took many casualties in that initial hour of battle, and so did 2nd Battalion. After 1st Battalion got organized, the men marched all night to reach 2nd Battalion, which had run into the main elements of enemy power. But, as hoped, the airdrop had been a strategic surprise to the enemy. They were trying to spring their own trap, pretending to withdraw, then bring in the UN ground forces north and envelop them. The airdrop had put a crimp in that enemy plan, and the Chinese found they were the ones surrounded; but

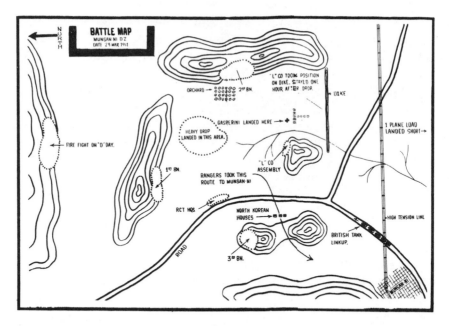

MAP 12

they had greater strength in the area than the Americans had expected to find. The Chinese had dug in heavy artillery, heavy mortars, heavy machine guns, and plenty of small arms and grenades.

The UN forces linkup was made at Munsan-Ni. At 2:50 P.M. on March 23, the armored force coming up the road was reported only 15 miles south of the town. Patrols from the 187th reached the force at 6:55.

On the second day regimental artillery Battery B went into the hills east of the drop zone to support the attack led by 2nd Battalion. The artillery was cut off there from the infantry by the Chinese, but the artillerymen dug in and alternated as gunners and riflemen, driving off several enemy attacks. They were resupplied by air, and not only held but gave effective support to paratroopers advancing east and north of Uijongbu. But the enemy artillery was powerful enough to hold the Americans back and the enemy began to slip northward, out of the trap.

That day, the tanks having linked up, the task was to catch the retreating enemy. It would mean a 26-mile chase.

Troopers climbed aboard the tank and began to move. It was raining hard, and the roads soon became little rivers. The paratroopers were soaked, and a dry cigarette became the most valuable commodity in the regiment. The tanks would carry the paratroopers up for a few miles, drop them, and go back for more men, while the troopers then slogged on through the rain and mud. In that fashion the whole regiment was hurried forward in forced march. By morning on March 25 the paratroopers reached the enemy. The Chinese and Koreans opened fire with heavy mortars, which did considerable damage to jeeps and other vehicles. They had dug in on the ridges above Paron-Ni. They would have to be driven out of each position.

The 3rd Battalion came under concentrated mortar fire that caused many casualties that day. The 2nd Battalion cleaned out the ridges. Next morning the 3rd Battalion took over and moved to its final objective, a hill called Hill 228. The enemy had been building defenses there for a long time—a system of deep bunkers, well defended. Some trenches were 15 feet deep. The enemy troops also seemed to have an unlimited supply of small-arms ammunition and grenades. The troopers took the hill the hard way, in hand-to-hand fighting, with trench knife, M-1, and grenade. Finally it was done.

That was the end of airdrops for the airborne troops in Korea. The quartermaster corps and the troop carrier commands kept on with air supply by drop in the difficult terrain. The Korean War was marked by rapid development of the airdrop technique, which was an important method of resupplying all forces. The ROK army, in fact, was so impressed with airdrop that its units put out drop symbols whether they needed supplies or not; and finally the quartermasters set up a system of signals of the day, to confuse the ROKs.

In the east in May, the Chinese launched a major attack on the U.S. X Corps and the ROK III Corps. The ROKs began to collapse, and the U.S. 2nd Division was outflanked. The 187th and the 3rd Division were brought up to seal up the holes. They arrived just before the enemy closed the trap. The trap was reversed, and before the action was over the communists had taken 105,000 casualties. This was not an airborne operation, but it was supported by airdrop, managed by the 8081st Quartermasters. That unit continued to supply the forces on the ground. It had put up 1,953 drop missions already. Seven 8081st men had been forced to make emergency parachute jumps, and four were missing in action. The 8081st continued to supply the troops through the active fighting, and toward the end began teaching the men of the 187th the techniques of heavy supply dropping, in the Iron Triangle and at Heartbreak Ridge. By the middle of 1952 the 8081st knew the war had wound down; the quartermasters were preparing cargo shipments of books and magazines instead of ammunition.

The Korean war ended in an uneasy stalemate which created a lasting tension across the 38th parallel. In the end, all that had been accomplished was to repel the North Korean invasion below that parallel. This had been accomplished in October 1950, with 10 percent of the effort and casualties that the United Nations forces suffered during the entire war. There was a lesson in Korea, relating to the difficulties of an army that had to transport its troops and matériel across a wide ocean; but that lesson seemed to have been forgotten almost immediately. The Korean War wound down in 1953. By that time the French were deeply mired in Indochina, where they wanted to restore the old colonial system, or a facsimile of it. The Americans were generally sympathetic to that cause for no other apparent reason than that North Vietnam had been pushed into the hands of the communist bloc when rejected by the United States in 1945. The French suffered a dreadful war of attrition in Indochina and eventually troubles at home caused them to withdraw their troops. For "reasons" that are not reasonably explicable, except that the Republican administration in power in Washington reacted with Pavlovian precision to the word "communist," the United States began to take France's place as backer of the puppet government the French had installed in Saigon. That government became more or less independent but remained in the hands of the well-to-do who had been friends of the French in colonial days. The miring of America was gradual. President Eisenhower began it. President Kennedy furthered it. President Johnson made it inevitable that we should be involved in a full-scale war that was never declared or called a war, and in a manner that made certain we could do nothing but take casualties and waste money. The bombing of North Vietnam was forbidden. So was invasion of North Vietnam. Altogether it was a political war; from the military point of view, a disaster from the beginning, and one that could not end satisfactorily.

The sort of war it was, too, did not indicate the use of paratroops under most conditions. It was a hit-and-run war. There was no point in sending a paratroop unit to capture bridges, because the Viet Cong and the North Vietnam troops never stayed still long enough to be surrounded or cut off. Thus, to meet new conditions, it was necessary to develop new techniques of warfare, involving new sorts of airborne weapons.

The New
Airborne—Airmobile

The Korean War brought many changes in airborne techniques, some of them developed in the field, many in testing back in the United States. One change. was to improve paratroopers' parachutes.

During World War II Colonel Raff's discovery of the German quick-release device in North Africa had finally brought about adoption of the T-7 as the standard parachute for troopers during that war. When used in jumping from a C-47, the T-7 was satisfactory enough.

But in Korea, the C-119's higher speed made the T-7 almost obsolete. It was dangerous to jump in that chute at high speeds. Between June 1951 and June 1952 the investigators discovered that at least 10 jump fatalities could be attributed directly to the T-7. It developed trouble when jumped at over 115 miles per hour.

The quartermaster researchers then developed the T-10, which gave its wearer less shock at 150 mph than the T-7 did at 115. The T-10 oscillated less in landing, and the rate of descent was slower (which could be both an asset and a liability, depending on whether the wearer was under fire as he came down). The T-10 was adopted, but it was 1953 before it came into use.

At the same time came another vital change. In Korea's hill country the army had found helicopters immensely useful for evacuation of the wounded and in movement of personnel. In August 1952 the army formed 12 helicopter battalions, which was the first major move in a new concept of "airmobility." It was furthered by observation of the French use of helicopters in the

Algerian war and the British use of them in Malaysia. General Gavin, who had become G-3 of the army, supported enthusiastically the idea of a new "cavalry"—an airborne cavalry. Out of this came the change of the Airborne Command into the Airborne-Army Aviation Department. General John T. Tolson was put in charge of the new operation and sent to Fort Benning to work out a tactical program for the use of helicopters. The result was the establishment of the army's own tactical air force, and by 1960 the army had 5,000 aircraft of various sorts in its commands.

Dominating all of them were the helicopters, from the light liaison craft that replaced the fixed-wing observation planes to the gunships that mounted enormous firepower.

All this while the United States was becoming more deeply involved in the French war to keep Ho Chi Minh's Viet Cong from taking over the old Indochina colony. As the French faltered, the American presence grew: The alternative posed to Presidents Eisenhower, Kennedy, and Johnson was to withdraw and let the North and South fight it out with full knowledge that the tougher and more resilient Viet Cong would defeat the Republic of Vietnam.

The American buildup soon involved helicopters. In 1961 they began arriving in some force. In 1962 the 93rd Transportation Company flew into DaNang air base from the helicopter carrier *Card* in the South China Sea.

In America the Hawze Board recommended an entirely new approach to airborne warfare—the establishment of airmobile divisions. Soon the U.S. Marines, with their own helicopter units, came in to the old French base at Soc Trang in the Mekong delta. In their way, helicopters were nearly to wipe out the old differences between airborne and regular infantry units. They replaced the old glider infantry concept; only the paratroopers would retain their particular status. The army became totally air conscious for the first time, with the development of this airmobile concept. Harry Kinnard, late of the 101st Airborne, was now a major general and commander of the 1st Cavalry Division, the first airmobile division of the army.

The month of July in 1965 marked as great a change in American concepts of airborne warfare as had the establishment of the first parachute infantry regiment in World War II. It was the month in which the 1st Cavalry (Airmobile) was born, and on August 25 its lead elements arrived in Vietnam to establish the world's largest helipad. Already the 173rd Airborne Brigade had come to Vietnam from Okinawa to secure the bases at Bien Hoa and Vung Tau, and the 173rd men were learning the airmobile concept of helicopter operations. On June 28 the 173rd's first two battalions had their baptism of airmobile operations, going deep into the interior of War Zone D to destroy Viet Cong supply caches. Three weeks later the 173rd had been involved in search and destroy operations in the Song Dong Nai river area.

The summer of 1965 marked a basic change in the war in Vietnam. Until that time U.S. troops had been involved in hit-and-run operations against Viet Cong irregulars. Then, in October, North Vietnamese army regiments began to appear in the south to challenge American forces. The 7th Cavalry's 1st Battalion encountered troops of General Chu Huy Man's Western Highlands Field Front Headquarters near Ia Drang.

Soon the number of airmobile units was growing in mushroom fashion, and since airborne units were already conditioned to similar methods, they were prime candidates for the new training. The 101st Airborne Division's 1st Brigade arrived in Vietnam on July 28 from Fort Campbell, Kentucky, and began to train in airmobile tactics.

In October 1965 North Vietnamese troops attacked the Special Forces camp at Plei Me. They were driven off and retreated. The 1st Cavalry's General Kinnard was in charge of the operations. He decided to send the 3rd Brigade after them. This unit, called the Garry Owen Brigade, was a mixed unit consisting of the 1st and 2nd Battalions of the 7th Cavalry. For this operation Colonel Thomas W. Brown, brigade commander, was also given the 2nd Battalion of the 5th Cavalry.

The North Vietnamese unit sent to Plei Me was the 33rd Army Regiment. It had lost nearly 900 men killed, 100 missing, and 500 wounded in that attempt. But General Chu Huy Man decided that what was left of the regiment would again be involved in another attempt to destroy the camp. The 33rd began reorganizing in the valley between the Ia Drang river and a prominent peak of the Chu Pong range called Hill 542. So decimated was the unit that it was re-formed into a reinforced battalion. General Chu also assigned the 32nd North Vietnamese Regiment, which

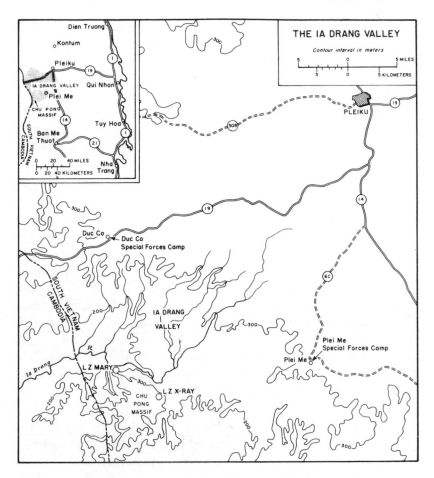

MAP 13

had suffered far fewer losses in the last battle, and the newly arrived 66th North Vietnamese Regiment.

On the afternoon of November 13 Colonel Brown met Lieutenant Colonel Harold Moore of 1st Battalion at a command post south of Plei Me. Brown told Moore to set up an airmobile assault into the Ia Drang valley north of the Chu Pong peak early next morning. For two days the troops would conduct a "search and destroy" mission.

The brigade was supposed to have 24 helicopters available each day, but in fact it had only 16. Gun support would be provided by the 21st Artillery, which had one 105 mm. howitzer within range and would move in another by airlift. Colonel Moore would land all his troops in one landing zone, since they might have to fight immediately on setting down.

First Battalion's 20 available officers had nearly all been with the unit since the infant days of air assault training at Fort Benning, but the situation of the enlisted force was much less comforting. The battalion had suffered heavily from malaria and the failure of the conscript army in the malaise over the Vietnam war that was creeping over America. A third of the enlisted strength of the table of organization was missing due to disease and because men quit the service as their draft period ended. But these were facts the new army had to live with, and Colonel Moore had adjusted himself to them. Previous operations had been managed; a commander used more units than usual; that was the solution.

On the morning of the fourteenth, Moore chose Company B to land first. That company was not in the best of shape, for its men had been on duty the night before, guarding the brigade command post. A local Viet Cong group had attacked, killing 7 men and wounding 23. The others had been up all night. Captain John D. Herren, company commander, was worried about their physical condition, particularly their alertness.

A reconnaissance party, organized to look over the ground, boarded two UH-ID Huey helicopters and, escorted by two UH-1B gunships, set off for the target area at 6:30 A.M. By 8:15 the reconnaissance mission was back at Plei Me, which would be the point of departure for the troops. The mission had settled the matter of landing place. Colonel Moore wanted the largest possible landing zone, to accommodate many helicopters. Three zones had been tentatively outlined. One had been shown to be impossible because of tall trees that did not appear on contour maps; the colonel wavered between the other two, X-Ray and Victor, both of which could accommodate 10 big helicopters at a time. That meant Moore could put down at least a platoon and a half at the beginning. This was important: Airmobile warfare had many of the characteristics of the old airborne, but in Vietnam the troopers had to be prepared for ambush on the moment of impact.

To take a last precaution against such ambush, Colonel Moore sent a helicopter from the 9th Cavalry on reconnaissance, to fly

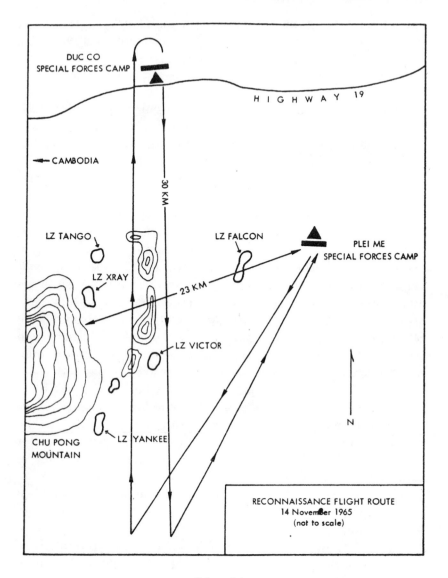

DUC CO
SPECIAL FORCES CAMP

HIGHWAY 19

CAMBODIA

30 KM

LZ TANGO

LZ FALCON

PLEI ME
SPECIAL FORCES CAMP

LZ XRAY

23 KM

LZ VICTOR

N

CHU PONG
MOUNTAIN

LZ YANKEE

RECONNAISSANCE FLIGHT ROUTE
14 November 1965
(not to scale)

MAP 14

low over the Ia Drang valley and check for signs of enemy activity at both possible landing zones. The ship was gone only 40 minutes; on return the pilots reported they had seen several trails, presumably enemy, but had drawn no fire. One of the two landing zones, Victor, had proved to have many high tree stumps sticking up. At the other, X-Ray, they had seen communications wire along a trail, indicating enemy presence. So the primary landing site was to be X-Ray, an open landing zone, with the enemy nearby.

Intelligence reports had placed three enemy units in the X-Ray vicinity. By this time, after repeated visits by helicopters, the North Vietnamese would be thoroughly alert. To confuse the enemy Moore ordered the artillery to put diversionary fire on both rejected landing sites. Then the artillery was to turn to X-Ray and fire for 20 minutes on the surrounding area.

Company B was to land first and secure the landing area. Then Companies A, C, and D would come in. Companies A and B would attack northeast. Company C would move west. Each rifle company would bring one 81 mm. mortar, and Company D would bring three. Each rifleman would have to carry 300 rounds of M-16 ammunition, and each grenadier would have three dozen shells for his 40 mm. grenade launcher. Machine-gun crews would bring 800 rounds for each 7.62 gun and every man would have two fragmentation grenades. The platoon would also carry 66 mm. mortars, smoke grenades, C rations, and water.

At 10:17 that same morning the artillery began firing. At 10:30 the first helicopters lifted off in a flurry of red dust. Soon 16 Hueys were in the area, traveling in platoons of four. Ahead of them the gunships moved over X-Ray field, each working over an area for 30 seconds with rockets, then standing by with half its ammunition still on call for the troops. Ahead of the troopships were gunships of the 229th, which sprayed the area with fire. Then down came the helicopters, the door gunners firing into the trees and elephant grass, just in case.

Colonel Moore took the men of B Company out into the trees, snap-firing at the points where enemy soldiers might be. But there were no soldiers. The other helicopters began to come down and deposit loads of men.

The North Vietnamese had spotted the landings, as expected. The 66th and 33rd Regiments were sent to search and destroy the Americans at the landing zone. By noon they were preparing to assault from positions at the base of the hills.

Lieutenant Alan Deveny of B Company captured an enemy soldier only 50 meters from the zone. He turned out to be a deserter who had been living on bananas for five days. He told them the North Vietnamese had three battalions on Chu Pong mountain.

Captain Herren's Company C was to move to the foot of Chu Pong and it headed that way. A mile from the landing zone, Lieutenant Deveny's 1st Platoon met the enemy first, when a North Vietnamese platoon attacked on his flanks and pinned his men down. Lieutenant Henry Herrick went to help with his platoon, encountered a squad of North Vietnamese, and flushed them off the trail. But the enemy were experts at this sort of warfare. Herrick met more Vietnamese troops, attacked, and was in turn attacked on the right flank by a fusillade of fire that killed a grenadier. His 3rd Platoon was soon pinned down. Staff Sergeant Clyde Savage rescued the grenadier's M79, and the platoon managed to dig in and form a perimeter. They lost one M60 machine gun, all four gunners killed, and the Vietnamese turned the gun on Herrick's men. The company was surrounded.

Captain Herren realized that his company was up against a large force; at least two companies. He was in touch with Colonel Moore by radio. As he turned from the radio, he saw a North Vietnamese soldier, 15 meters away, aiming a rifle at him. Herren fired a burst from his M-16, ducked for cover, and threw a grenade.

Back at the landing zone Colonel Moore was bringing in his other troops. The enemy now began mortaring the landing zone. But up above were the air resources, and Colonel Moore called for air strikes, artillery and aerial rocket fire on the lower fringes of Chu Pong and down to the landing zone. In a few minutes Pleiku-based aircraft were blasting the target area, but with such a blanket fire that the results were unknown.

Company A and Company C were sent to join the fight. The Vietnamese continued to try to flank the Americans, and Company A ran into a strong force. Lieutenant Robert E. Taft was killed and so was one of his squad leaders.

By this time the fifth airlift was coming in, with elements of Company D and some from Company C. The enemy had moved many men into the landing zone perimeter and the helicopters were greeted by small-arms fire as they came down. One pilot and a door gunner were wounded.

Captain Louis LeFebvre, Company D commander, was getting ready to leave the helicopter when he was creased by a bullet. Another killed his radio operator. He grabbed the radio, ran for cover, and four men followed him. Outside, he radioed the other helicopters not to come in. He brought up men from his antitank platoon, and soon was joined by Captain Herren, who returned, scouting for North Vietnamese. The enemy closed in around them. LeFebvre was badly wounded in the right arm by a fusillade of fire. His mortar platoon leader, Lieutenant Raul Requera-Taboada, was hit in the leg. The North Vietnamese had moved in in many platoon units, trying to surround the individual American platoons and annihilate them. Company C managed to dig in well enough to withstand a strong attack by a reinforced Vietnamese company, and by 3:00 the enemy attempts to overrun the landing zone had failed, although the Americans had taken a number of casualties.

The Vietnamese put up strong ground fire. An A-IE Skyraider was hit, flamed, and crashed two kilometers northeast of the landing zone, killing the pilot. When enemy troops started for the plane, gunships destroyed it with rockets.

Shortly after 3:00 Colonel Brown had to make some changes in his estimates, Colonel Moore said he faced at least 500 Vietnamese and needed help. Colonel Brown secured permission to send in elements of the 2nd Battalion. Some were sent to landing zone Victor, three kilometers away, and some would move in by foot. They would attempt in the next 24 hours to outflank and ambush the North Vietnamese. Three loads of troops of Company C of the 2nd Battalion were soon out of their helicopters at the X-Ray landing zone, but the enemy fire was so heavy two copters were disabled. The crews were evacuated, and the troops guarded the helicopters.

By mid-afternoon the battalion surgeon had arrived with four aid men, and they established an aid station near Moore's command post. By 4:00 wounded men were being evacuated.

Lieutenant Herrick was still cut off in a dry creek bed, protected only by artillery and mortar fire from the surrounded Vietnamese. The enemy was laying in small-arms fire so close to the ground that most of the men could not dig in. But they were taking a heavy toll of the Vietnamese with their M-16s. Sergeant Savage alone killed a dozen. But Lieutenant Herrick was hit by a bullet that went diagonally through his entire body, from left hip to right shoulder. After he died, Staff Sergeant Carl Palmer took over, but then he too was killed. The sergeant of the second squad took over, but was soon killed. Sergeant Savage, leader of the third squad, took command of the cut-off force. He radioed for artillery fire and got it around the perimeter within 20 meters of the Americans. It stopped the enemy, but the position was still precarious. Of the 27 men who had set out, 8 had been killed and 12 wounded.

The soldiers of Company A and Company B were sent on an assault to relieve the trapped men and flank the enemy. Lieutenant Wayne Johnson was hit and badly wounded. The enemy was very hard to find, concealed in the elephant grass, their brownish-yellow khaki uniforms blending into the ground colors. Some were in trees, some in the tops and sides of the anthills that bumped up all around the area.

Lieutenant Marm pushed his platoon to an anthill occupied by enemy soldiers. He exposed himself deliberately to draw fire and then fired an M72 antitank round at the mound. He inflicted some casualties but the fire continued. He motioned to one of his men to move up and throw a grenade. The man misunderstood the gesture and threw from his position. The grenade fell short. Marm dashed across the ground, picked up the grenade and hurled it into the position. Then he jumped up on the mound and finished off the Vietnamese soldiers with his M16. Just after that, Marm took a bullet in the face and had to be evacuated. (He won the Congressional Medal of Honor for his exploit.)

Captain Nadal of 1st Battalion's Company A counted his casualties. He had lost all his platoon leaders and his artillery observer. Four men were killed within six feet of him, and there seemed little chance of moving out to do anything useful before dark. At 5:00 he asked Colonel Moore for permission to pull back, and he received it. That request convinced Colonel Moore that he should move all his troops back to X-Ray zone and hold till morning. The battle had not turned out at all as had been expected. It was a moot question just then as to who was searching and destroying whom. All came back except the cut-off platoon in the dry riverbed.

At 5:05 the troops of 2nd Battalion began to land and strengthened the perimeter. The other troops were brought back with considerable difficulty, and either dug in or found shelter that suited the officers in command of the companies. By 7:00 the night perimeter was organized. Just before dark, a helicopter resupply mission came in with ammunition, water, medical supplies, and rations. As night fell, Colonel Moore made the rounds of the units, talking to the men. Morale was high even though the casualties were high, too.

That night, enemy forces harried and probed the perimeter, but each time artillery was called up and stopped them. Two howitzer batteries in the landing zone fired 4,000 rounds that night into the draws and fingers of the ridges of Chu Pong. The North Vietnamese and the Viet Cong were out there moving, but their advance was hindered by the fire.

Still out beyond the perimeter was Sergeant Savage's command. The enemy came at him several times, but each time he was able to call up artillery fire to keep them off.

At brigade headquarters Colonel Brown called on General Kinnard for another battalion, and Kinnard sent the 1st Battalion of the 5th Cavalry to help extricate the Americans.

In the morning the Vietnamese were moving forward, on hands and knees, as the Americans sent squads out to probe ahead of the perimeter. Two reconnaissance units were hit hard and took several casualties. The Vietnamese began moving up. Captain Robert Edwards of Company C saw 20 Vietnamese 200 meters off, moving up. He called on Colonel Moore for artillery fire and then began firing his M-16 at the enemy. He also asked Battalion to commit the reserve against what he expected to be the major enemy attack. Colonel Moore refused. He did not believe this was the main attack. So Edwards had to go it alone. The enemy came in great numbers in spite of heavy artillery fire and tactical air strikes. The North Vietnamese soldiers fell by the dozens, but others took their places and by sheer number pushed to the foxhole line.

Suddenly two enemy soldiers appeared 40 meters away. Edwards stood up and tossed a grenade, and then fell with a bullet in the back. Still conscious, he asked for reinforcement. This time Moore was convinced and sent a platoon from Company A, but C Company was now pinned down by automatic weapon fire. Lieu-

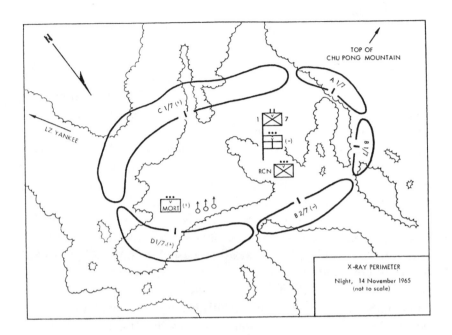

MAP 15

tenant John Arrington, the company executive officer, came up to talk to Edwards. He was shot in the chest. Lieutenant Franklin, commander of 3rd Platoon, came up. He was wounded seriously. The enemy now renewed the attack and also came from the flank. Company A's relieving platoon was hit and came under heavy fire as it reached the Company C perimeter.

The enemy was all around. Anyone who moved toward the Company C sector drew fire. One rifleman covered 50 meters of ground and in that advance shot 15 North Vietnamese with his M-16.

The fighting continued for two hours. An F-105 jet arrived and dropped two tanks of napalm *inside* the perimeter, burning some of the men and blowing up M-16 ammunition stacked there. The colonel called off the air strike. But by 9:00 the North Vietnamese were slowing down. By 10:00 the attacks stopped. Colonel Tully's 2nd Battalion of the 5th Cavalry was coming up by foot from landing zone Victor. Now the Americans had the Vietnamese sandwiched.

Colonel Moore sent out a relief force to find and rescue Sergeant Savage's cut-off platoon. As the men moved out on a broad front, they ran over scores of enemy bodies, weapons, and equipment and saw bloody trails where the wounded had been taken away. But not all those dead were Vietnamese. The 7th Cavalry had lost the equivalent of a rifle platoon. Some Americans lay among the Vietnamese dead. One rifleman was found with his hands clutched around the throat of a dead Vietnamese. Another American was found in a foxhole, surrounded by five enemy dead.

The relief force reached Sergeant Savage, and his men were saved. Savage had done a remarkable job; after he took command the Americans did not have another casualty, and they still had plenty of ammunition.

The fight seemed to be over, but as Captain Bennett, the commander of Company A of the 5th Cavalry, was walking on the perimeter near the landing zone, he was shot in the chest by a sniper. They did not find the sniper who fired the last shot. That night the Vietnamese carried on harassing activity, and then a major attack was launched at 4:22 A.M. It failed, largely due to the effectiveness of the artillery, firing phosphorus shells and high explosives. Enemy soldiers managed to get to within five meters of the foxhole line, but not inside. Two more attacks came before dawn, but by daybreak the enemy attack had ended.

Colonel Moore directed the men to spray the areas in front of their positions with fire. They did, and flushed a Vietnamese platoon. They also found many enemy soldiers in trees and shot them down. They conducted a number of sweeps around the area and killed several dozen more North Vietnamese. By this time, all Americans were accounted for, wounded, dead, or fighting.

Later in the day the Americans policed the area, preparing to move out, back to Camp Holloway. They took out with them 57 Kalashnikov AK47 assault rifles, 54 Simonov SKS semiautomatic carbines with bayonets, 17 Degtyarev automatic rifles, 4 Maxim heavy machine guns, 5 rocket launchers, 2 81 mm. mortars, and various other enemy equipment. They destroyed all the rest, hundreds of grenades, weapons, and tools.

American casualties were 79 killed, 121 wounded, and none missing. The figures given for the enemy were 634 dead, 581 estimated dead, and 6 prisoners. Those figures would not be acceptable to an increasingly skeptical press, but it was apparent that the North Vietnamese had not accomplished their aim. The attack on Plei Me Special Forces camp was obviated, and the Vietnamese had taken serious punishment. In terms of war, the Ia Drang fight showed all the frustrations and lack of satisfaction of the struggle. The Americans had "won," but they were airlifted out, and once they were gone the territory was just as much the enemy's as it had been before.

The Airborne in Action

The parachute concept did not have much application in Vietnam. Airborne operations of the classic style were most effective when vertical envelopment could cut off an enemy force and deny him territory that the Americans wished to hold. So much of the Vietnam war was nonterritorial in nature that the use of parachutists was not indicated. Parachute drops were made by the hundreds by special forces, on special missions, but this was a different matter. The use of paratroopers as they had been employed in World War II and Korea never did occupy a vital role in the war.

In November 1966, the 2nd Battalion of the 502nd Infantry was involved in a typical Vietnam battle at Phong Cao. Times had changed for this old paratrooper unit; the battalion was one of three battalions assigned to the 1st Brigade, 101st Airborne Division. It was operating with a local Civilian Irregular Defense Group, and was taken into battle in four helicopter landing zones northwest of the town. The commander was Lieutenant Colonel Frank Dietrich, who had served with the 504th Parachute Infantry from North Africa to the Rhine. There were many old paratroopers in the unit, but nearly all else had changed.

That day the strike force was trailing the 5th Battalion of the 95th North Vietnamese Regiment. The problem was to catch them before they slipped away from the hill on which they were camped. The solution was to put platoons down in a checkerboard pattern and surround the enemy. A recondo platoon (reconnaissance platoon reinforced to 50 men) found the enemy on November 8 in a company-sized base camp. Companies A and B and C prepared to close the trap around the North Vietnamese the next morning. At 10:00 the recondo platoon set out, and soon one section engaged an enemy platoon. The fight began to develop. Lieutenant Alden Holborn came up with Company B's 2nd Platoon. Lieutenant John Marshok brought 3rd Platoon around behind the enemy, and other units moved up. Colonel Dietrich called for a helicopter and at noon was in the air. Below, he saw the various units lay out cloth panels and ignite smoke grenades to show the troop disposition. Following the firelight below, Colonel Dietrich was able to direct his troops almost as if he were playing chess on a board. His next step was to pull them back and call for an air strike on the enemy. At 2:40 P.M. two fighters came in, but their bombs sprayed the American positions, so the strike was canceled. The army would use its own air force—the helicopter gunships. They made the strike, and a battery of 155 mm. howitzers was called into action. After an hour the infantry moved forward again and occupied the position held by the enemy. The encirclement of the area was complete. Next morning the strike force tightened the noose. A helicopter came down with a loudspeaker, and a Vietnamese voice told the 5th Battalion to give up, that it was all over. But two hours of broadcast did no good. By dark the Vietnamese were encircled atop a hill, but they still did not surrender.

On the eleventh the psychological warfare teams were out again, and they persuaded a number of North Vietnamese to give up. But a handful continued the fight until they were killed or escaped in the battle. It was impossible to know the extent of the Vietnamese dead and wounded because they almost always dragged the bodies away with them as they went. But the blood trails indicated heavy casualties, and the Americans had 36 prisoners. The cost had been 5 Americans killed and 15 wounded in the three-day battle; but, once again, the territory still belonged to the enemy.

The one major parachute landing operation of the war occurred in February 1967. At 9:00 on the morning of February 22, Brigadier General John R. Deane, Jr., led the 2nd Battalion of the 503rd Parachute Infantry out the door of one of the new C-130 aircraft, successor to the C-119 as the major drop plane. The men dropped north of Tay Ninh City in this first jump since the Korean War.

General Deane's unit was operating as part of the 173rd Airborne Brigade, which was involved in Vietnam along with the 101st Airborne Division. The 101st was now an airmobile division delivered by helicopters and was not available for the parachute operation.

The decision to use paratroopers in this different sort of war was an experiment. The Americans were projecting Operation Junction City, which was designed to smother enemy bases north of Tay Ninh City. If it was to be successful, the move would require fast action by a large body of troops to surround the area. The use of paratroopers might make it possible to put a large force on the ground quickly and have helicopters left to follow up with what was now called a heliborne assault. The paratroopers, by dropping from C-130s, would free 60 Huey helicopters and 6 Chinooks for use by the 1st Infantry Division and the artillery.

The paratroopers' drop zone was to be the farthest afield of all landing positions. They were carried by 13 C-130s, and their equipment came in another 8 C-130s.

The battalion dropped from 1,000 feet. Twenty minutes later all the units were in their proper places around the drop zone, and company commanders reported that of the 780 troopers who dropped, only 11 were slightly hurt. The new parachute harness and new techniques had cut sharply into the accident rate.

The 2nd Battalion had no trouble at all in the beginning. Within an hour the 1st Battalion of the 503rd began to arrive by helicopter, and that afternoon the 4th Battalion came in by heliborne assault in two nearby landing zones.

There were some difficulties about mixing parachutists and helicopter operations. In the old days the gliders came down and stayed, and if they skidded over a handful of parachutes, it made no difference. But the helicopters tended to tangle up in the fabric and lines.

The 173rd continued in this assault until the middle of May. The experiment was supported for the rest of the operation by helicopter supply. In the fighting, the troops "tamed" what the French had called War Zone C, which had been a Viet Cong stronghold for years. The enemy lost 2,700 dead, 800 tons of rice, and large amounts of ammunition and medical supplies. But the parachute operation was not repeated, largely because the nature of the Vietnam war made it less useful than helicopter assault. There had been no real need to use parachute troops at all. Had the Americans decided to cut off the forces in South Vietnam by invading the north and undertaken a drive where a pincers movement would have been effective, the airborne might have been used profitably. But the Americans were forced by politics to assume a defensive posture in the war; they stayed out of North Vietnam, and thus parachute operations turned out to be little more than a stunt.

As in the Battle of the Bulge, however, airborne troops fought valiantly and effectively in Vietnam, although in the new capacity as heliborne.

But what had happened in Vietnam by 1969 was a realignment of thinking. The 101st Airborne Division came to the war in 1966 as airmobile and went into action in a night assault by helicopter near Tuy Hoa. By 1969 the 101st was titled an "airmobile" division and was experimenting with such new concepts as the radar raid, which involved rapid movement by helicopter of divisional 105 mm. howitzers, the firing on enemy positions, and movement to another position, again by helicopter.

The 173rd fought at Dak To and helped create disaster for the 1st North Vietnamese Army Division there. In September 1968 the 101st was involved in another new sort of warfare in its combined operations with the 1st ARVN Division (Army of the Republic of Vietnam) in Thua Thien province. The 2nd Brigade of the division and the 1st Battalion of the 501st Infantry struck at Vinh Loc Island, 15 miles east of Hue. They swept the island, along with ARVN troops, and once the operation was over, two enemy companies, reinforced with hamlet guerrillas, simply ceased to operate. Lieutenant Colonel Jim Hunt's 1st Battalion of the 501st carried out a similar operation with an ARVN battalion at Phu Bai east of Hue, and the result of that combined operation was establishment of control by government units.

(The 82nd Airborne was experimenting with helicopter concepts back at Fort Bragg during this period, and had been since the earliest tests of the 11th Air Assault Division, which finally became the 1st Cavalry. The 82nd was chosen to undertake the pacification of Santo Domingo in 1965, when the Dominican Republic erupted in a revolution that was frowned upon by the Johnson administration. The 1st Brigade served for a whole year in the Dominican Republic and did not return to Fort Bragg until the summer of 1966.)

In Vietnam in the early hours of January 31, 1968, the enemy launched a major offensive. It came during the Tet religious holidays, and no one was prepared for it. The 82nd Airborne's 3rd Brigade was airlifted from Fort Bragg to rush to Vietnam and reinforce the 101st in the defense. The brigade went into combat in the Hue-Phu Bai area; and then, when the enemy were overcome, it was moved south to help with security in the Saigon area. The brigade went back to Fort Bragg to join the division in December 1969, after 22 months in Vietnam. Other troops could be used for security. The paratroopers had a different mission, one that had not proved really germane to the sort of operations carried out in the American involvement in Southeast Asia.

The New Air Concept

With the emergence of airmobility as a basic military doctrine, the concept of airborne operations changed considerably. The army decided in the 1960s that it could maintain only one airborne division of parachute troops, and the 82nd Airborne was selected. That did not mean the 82nd stood still while the 101st became airmobile and other airmobile divisions were formed. The 82nd Airborne began to make full use of helicopter techniques for landing and resupply, but the concept of a striking force of parachutists, who could come in swiftly, very nearly silently, and cut off and confuse the enemy remained sound doctrine. There was still a need for parachute troops in the American military concept. So the 82nd developed as a division of shock troops, always on the alert, prepared for any sort of operation in the world, whether it be a brushfire war in the Middle East or Asia, or the quelling of riots in Washington. In other words, the division was to be prepared to go anywhere in the world on no notice at all, fight on its arrival on the ground, and survive until it could be reinforced.

The 82nd of the 1970s was a far cry from the old division of World War II. It had more striking power than the combined 82nd and 101st Airborne divisions had had during that war. The airborne concept of the 1970s included tanks, powerful antitank weapons, including guided missiles, and heavy artillery. It would be hard for a modern paratrooper to conceive of the combat conditions of General Ridgway's force at Normandy, where the men fought almost entirely with rifles, grenades, and bazookas when most of their antitank guns and 75 mm. pack howitzers were lost in the swamps. And it would be equally hard to recall that then the only antitank weapon developed by the American forces to face the Tiger tank was the old 37 mm. gun. It had been like shooting elephants with a .22 caliber rifle.

In the 82nd's sector at Fort Bragg someone would always be ready, around the clock, to go anywhere at all and fight on arrival. The new division was not developed in company teams, and battalion and brigade forces. The initial ready company, the division ready force, and the division ready brigade can begin to move within 18 hours or less after notification of crisis.

The 1978 division ready brigade, for example, consisted of 3,500 men. If they had moved into action they would have had available the 155 mm. howitzers, with rocket-assisted projectiles, and cannon-launched guided missiles.

The days of the C-47 are long gone, and so are those of the C-46 and C-119. Specimen aircraft sit up on the hill behind the 82nd Airborne's museum at Fort Bragg for the admiration of children and the delectation of old soldiers who come back to reminisce about the days in Normandy or the Bulge, or the jungles of Vietnam. The new jump craft, the C-141, would be recognizable, but just barely, to the old hands.

The training level of the 82nd has remained spartan. At least twice a year the troops must undergo live fire exercises, which include day and night attack and defense operations, air assaults, and antiarmor exercises. The helicopters come into play, particularly helicopter gunships to support the airborne.

Every year each battalion conducts an off-post training exercise in some different environment; it might be the Alaskan tundra or the Mojave desert.

The readiness quotient is measured every month. The division conducts a no-notice emergency specifically to test the ability of a unit to get away effectively in less than 18 hours, stay out for three days, and come back fit. In the field, much of the training is conducted at night, on the principle that in a war the enemy will strike more often at night than in the daytime. And the troopers prepare for anything. For five hours at a time on maneuver they wear protective masks while carrying on all their normal duties.

To match this concept, the Army and the Air Force researchers created new technology. In the World War II days, "training" meant learning how to board an air craft, how to jump without getting killed, how to disengage from a troublesome chute, and how to get into action. Those first paratroopers wore washbasin helmets and puttees and carried the Springfield 1903 rifle. Their most effective special weapon was the bazooka, whose shaped charge was about as comparable to today's charges as the arrowhead to the M-16 bullet.

The new MC1-1B steerable parachute made the paratrooper far less vulnerable to ground fire and unfavorable wind and terrain. The trooper could steer his chute, make 360 degree turns, and control his landing. New delivery systems extended the airborne division's airhead and area of viability. The container system and pallets developed by the Quartermaster Corps meant that all classes of supplies could be airdropped into unprepared areas. The big X-130 aircraft and the C-141s could carry anything the paratroops might need, and a paratroop unit could subsist indefinitely in the field, with resupply and reinforcement by air. No longer must the paratroop unit link with armor to survive, for tanks and other vehicles could be brought in by air. The Sheridan armored reconnaissance vehicle, 105 mm. howitzers, Vulcan air defense guns, bulldozers, and all sorts of heavy equipment could come in by air. Ammunition and ground and aviation fuel could be delivered without loss or destruction.

One important change was the adverse weather aerial delivery system. It involved navigation by C-130 aircraft, which could fly anywhere, anytime, day or night. Weather—with the exception of high winds—had also been eliminated as a decisive factor in the timing of a parachute drop. The earlier pathfinder concept had been developed to insure accurate airdrops, but it had one grave disadvantage: It tipped the hand of the attackers. That system was abandoned with the adoption of the adverse weather system. No longer would any drop be compromised by telling the enemy where it would come; and for airdrop purposes the worst weather conditions could be the best, for they would enhance the surprise element, which had always been a major factor in the success of paratroop operations.

The two old bugaboos of the paratrooper, aircraft and tanks, were made much less dangerous by the 20 mm. Vulcan weapons batteries, each battery mounting the 12 Vulcans assigned to each brigade. Each Vulcan could fire 3,000 rounds a minute and could be moved by jeep. The weapon proved extremely effective against strafing aircraft.

The light antitank weapon made a major change in that concept. A single trooper could carry five LAWs or one antitank mine in a kit bag. A new medium-weight antitank weapon, the Dragon, was also jumped by individual troopers, and there were 30 of these in each battalion. Every battalion also was equipped with 18 TOW systems for long-range antitank warfare and this heavy weapon could be broken into five parts and jumped individually, or dropped ready-assembled. Lasers, television guidance systems, and many other new weapons totally changed the old ways. The 82nd used helicopters too, light observation copters to control the movement of weapons against enemy concentrations.

So with 54 Sheridans and their 152 mm. missile/gun systems, plus all these other weapons—supported by 33 Cobra helicopter gunships, F-4 phantom jet fighters delivering 2,000-pound bombs where indicated, a refined M-21 sniper system that employed the M-14 rifle with a ranging telescope, and the new breed of paratroopers trained to use these highly technical weapons—the airborne had found a new role for itself.

In the 1970s another change came to the 82nd, it enlisted its first women paratroopers starting in 1978 with five parachute-qualified women soldiers. The women, like the men, must be totally qualified—no special considerations were given them, except allowance for certain physical differences. As in the beginning, all paratroopers were equal, and all were ready to go into action within 18 hours of notification. There may not be many airborne soldiers in the U.S. Army today but the 82nd is the vanguard.

Notes and Bibliography

Many people in the American armed forces have contributed to the writing of this book. Captain Robert J. Aman, of the 82nd Airborne Division at Fort Bragg, spent considerable time instructing me in the division's history, operations, and capabilities. David Schoem, chief of the support division of the Office of Air Force History of the U.S. Air Force, guided me to some materials. So did Colonel William F. Strobridge of the Historical Services Division of the Department of the Army. Henry B. Davis, Jr., director of the Quartermaster Museum at Fort Lee, Virginia, was most helpful and lent me *Supply by Sky,* by William H. Peifer, a history of the quartermaster airborne development, published by the Department of the Army. Colonel Donald C. Shuffstall, of the Army Public Affairs office at Fort Benning, steered me to materials. Thomas M. Fairfall, curator of the 82nd Airborne's Museum at Fort Bragg, made available many documents. Lieutenant Kevin Hart, post historian at Fort Campbell, steered me to materials about the 101st Airborne Division. Harvey W. Keene, public affairs officer at the army's Natick Research and Development Command, was helpful. So was Lieutenant Colonel Ron David, public affairs officer of the XVIII Airborne Corps. I am also indebted to archivists at the U.S. National Archives, Washington; the Federal Records Center, Suitland, Maryland; and the Imperial War Museum, London, for their assistance.

Most of the tales of unit and individual activity of airborne troops came from army records, especially after-action reports by various units and interviews conducted by army historians following major engagements. I also used James A. Huston's *Out of the*

Blue (Lafayette, Ind.: Purdue University Press, 1972), as a basic guide to paratrooper activity in World War II. James Mrazek's *The Glider War,* Robert Hale, London, 1975, was useful, and so was Milton Dank's *The Glider Gang* (New York: J.B. Lippincott, 1977), General M. B. Ridgway's memoirs, *Soldier* (New York: Harper & Row, 1956), and so were James M. Gavin's *Airborne Warfare* (Infantry Journal Press, 1947), and *On To Berlin* (New York: Viking Press, 1978). The story of the fight at Ia Drang comes from *Seven Firefights in Vietnam,* by John Albright, *et al.,* published by the Office of the Chief of Military History, 1970. Some of the material about the 101st Airborne Division in World War II is from *Rendezvous with Destiny: The Story of the 101st,* by Leonard Rapport and Arthur Northwood, Jr. (Infantry Journal Press, 1948). I used Lewis Brereton's *Diaries* (New York: William Morrow, 1946), and Arch E. Roberts's *Rakkasan! 187th Airborne Regimental Combat Team* (Nashville, 1956). John J. Tolson's *Airmobility, 1961-71,* of the army's Vietnam Studies, 1973, and John H. Hay Jr.'s *Tactical and Material Innovations,* of the same series, 1974, were helpful about the Vietnam period. Much of the material about the present 82nd Airborne is from my interviews with divisional officers and a speech delivered in 1978 by Major General Roscoe Robinson, Jr., commander of the 82nd.

Index